Software Tools
in Pascal

Software Tools
in Pascal

Brian W. Kernighan

Bell Laboratories
Murray Hill, New Jersey

P. J. Plauger

Whitesmiths, Ltd.
New York, New York

▲
▼▲

ADDISON-WESLEY PUBLISHING COMPANY
Reading, Massachusetts
Menlo Park, California · London · Amsterdam · Don Mills, Ontario · Sydney

This book was set in Times Roman and Courier by the authors, using a Mergenthaler Lino-tron 202 phototypesetter driven by a PDP-11/70 running the Unix operating system.

Unix is a trademark of Bell Laboratories. DEC, PDP and VAX are trademarks of Digital Equipment Corporation.

ISBN 0-201-10342-7
HIJ-DO-89876

PREFACE

This book teaches how to write good programs that make good tools, by presenting a comprehensive set, each of which provides lessons in design and implementation. The programs are not artificial, nor are they toys. Instead, they are tools that have proved valuable in the production of other programs. We use most of them every working day, and they account for much of our computer usage. The programs are complete, not just algorithms and outlines, and they work: all have been tested directly from the text, which is in machine-readable form. They are readable: all are presented in standard Pascal. They are documented, so they can be used. Most important, the programs are designed to work well with people and with each other, and are thus *perceived* as tools.

The book is pragmatic. We teach top-down design by walking through designs. We demonstrate structured programming with structured programs. We discuss efficiency and reliability in terms of actual tests carried out. We illustrate documentation by presenting it for each program. We treat portability by writing in a language that is widely available, and by isolating unavoidable system dependencies in a handful of small, carefully specified routines that can be readily built for a particular operating environment. All of the programs presented here have been run without change on at least three different machines and several different Pascal compilers and interpreters. The code is available in machine-readable form as a supplement to the text.

The principles of good programming are presented not as abstract sermons but as concrete lessons in the context of actual working programs. For example, there is no chapter on "efficiency." Instead, throughout the book there are observations on efficiency as it relates to the particular program being developed. Similarly there is no chapter on "top-down design," nor on "structured programming," nor on "testing and debugging." Instead, all of these disciplines are employed as appropriate in every program shown.

The book is suitable for a "software engineering" course or for a second course in programming — more so, we feel, than the traditional dose of "compilers, assemblers and loaders," for the programs presented here are more of the size and nature that will be encountered by most programmers. It is also

suitable as a supplementary text in any programming course; the only prere-
quisite is programming experience in a high-level language. Professional programmers will find it a guide to good programming techniques and a source of
proven, useful programs. Numerous exercises are provided to test comprehension and to extend the concepts and the programs presented in the text.

Software Tools was originally published in 1976 with the programs written in
Ratfor, a language based on Fortran. Ratfor was implemented as a preprocessor; it provided Fortran with modern control flow statements like `if-else` and
`while`, and some cosmetic improvements like symbolic constants and free-form
input. The approach and the tools have proved sufficiently useful that many
copies of them have been distributed, and there is a large, active user group.

Pascal is now the dominant teaching language for computer science courses,
and is becoming widely used outside of universities as well. We feel that the
lessons about the design and implementation of tools from the original book
carry over intact to Pascal. Thus *Software Tools in Pascal* has a great deal of
overlap with the Ratfor original. The same programs are present, except that
there is no preprocessor chapter, since Pascal provides most of the sensible control flow and cosmetic improvements that Ratfor adds to Fortran. On those systems where Pascal needs augmentation, tools such as the macro and file inclusion processors serve as language preprocessors.

The programs here are not just transliterations into Pascal, however. Almost
every program has been improved in some way. Pascal lets us do some things
much better than is possible in Fortran. Recursion in particular is a boon.
Quicksort and regular expression closure are much simpler when done recursively instead of with a stack or linked list; expression evaluation has been
added to the macro processor.

Pascal data types are generally more suitable for the clear expression of algorithms. Records let us deal with a group of related variables as a unit.
Subranges and enumerated types make it easier to constrain the set of legal
values for variables, so that errors are detected sooner and the code is easier to
read. And eight-character variable names are a lot less contorted than six.

Regrettably, though, standard Pascal is far from an ideal language; in many
ways it is less suitable for writing large programs than Fortran is. Since there is
no standard way to specify separate compilation, the growth of libraries to
extend the language is stunted. Since the size of an array is part of its type in
standard Pascal, it is hard to write general-purpose routines that process arrays
of different sizes. The lack of own variables and initialization forces variables
to have global scope where Fortran would make them local to a single routine.
Finally, the operating system interface provided by Pascal is just as unsuitable as
Fortran's, but the language makes it harder to escape to one's own.

There are versions of Pascal that deal with each of these problems, with
some success, but each such extension is non-standard and rarely portable. Our
code adheres to the standard; it will work everywhere. The price we pay is
increased compilation time, sometimes involving the use of one or more

preprocessing steps; larger load modules, to provide an extended environment in the absence of libraries; and slower execution time, because we have consistently traded efficiency for portability. Each of these areas is readily amenable to improvement, however, by tuning the system interface to each local environment.

Building on the work of others is the only way to make substantial progress in any field. Yet programmers reinvent programs for each new application instead of using what already exists. We hope that *Software Tools in Pascal* will instill a feeling for how to design and write good programs that can be widely used, how to use existing tools, and how to improve a given environment with maximum effect for minimum effort.

We are grateful to many friends for careful reading, perceptive criticism, and continuous cheerful support. Ron Hardin, John Linderman, Doug McIlroy, Rob Pike and Dennis Ritchie all spent many hours reading the manuscript and exercising the programs, and made invaluable suggestions on how to improve both. We deeply appreciate their efforts. Our thanks also to Al Aho, Doug Comer, Al Feuer, John Gannon, Peter Grogono, Dave Hanson, Debbie Scherrer, and Chris Van Wyk for helpful comments at various stages. Bill Joy and Andy Tanenbaum provided us with rock-solid Pascal compilers; Bill Joy also made it possible for us to time our programs. Chuck Howerton provided the impetus that got us started in the first place.

Finally, it is a pleasure to acknowledge our debt to the Unix operating system, developed at Bell Labs by Ken Thompson and Dennis Ritchie. We wrote the text, tested the programs, and typeset the manuscript, all within Unix. Many of the tools we describe are based on Unix models. Most important, the ideas and philosophy are based on our experience as Unix users. Of all the operating systems we have used, Unix is the only one that has been a positive help in getting a job done instead of an obstacle to be overcome. The worldwide acceptance of Unix indicates that we are not the only ones who feel this way.

Brian W. Kernighan

P. J. Plauger

CONTENTS

All of the programs described in this book are available in machine-readable form from Addison-Wesley.

INTRODUCTION

We are going to discuss two things in this book — how to write programs that make good tools, and how to program well in the process.

What do we mean by a *tool*? Suppose you have a 5000-line Pascal program and you need to find all references to the variable `time`, to make sure it can safely be changed from type `integer` to type `real`. How would you do it?

One possibility is to get a listing and mark it up with a red pencil. But it doesn't take much imagination to see what's wrong with red-penciling a hundred pages of computer paper. It's mindless and boring busy-work, with lots of opportunities for error. And even after you've found all instances of `time`, you still can't do much, because the red marks aren't machine readable.

Another approach is to write a simple program to find lines containing the identifier `time`. This is an improvement, for such a program is faster and more accurate than doing the job by hand. The trouble is that the program is so specialized that it will be used once by its author, then tucked away and forgotten. No one else will benefit from the effort that went into writing it, and something very much like it will have to be reinvented for each new application.

Finding `time`'s in a Pascal program is a special case of a general problem, finding patterns in text. Whoever wanted references to `time` today will want references to some other variable tomorrow, `readln` and `writeln` calls the day after, and next week an entirely different pattern in some unrelated text. Red penciling never ends. The way to cope with the general problem is to provide a general purpose pattern finder that will look for a specified pattern and print all the lines where it occurs. Then anyone can say

    find *pattern*

and the job is done. `find` is a *tool:* it uses the machine; it solves a general problem, not a special case; and it's so easy to use that people will use it instead of building their own.

Far too many programmers are red pencillers. Some are literal red pencillers who do things by hand that should be done by machine. Others are figurative red pencillers whose use of the machine is so clumsy and awkward that it might as well be manual. One purpose of this book is to show how to build *tools* —

1

programs to help people to do things by machine instead of by red pencil, and how to do them well instead of badly. We're going to do this, not by talking in generalities but by writing real, working programs, programs that we know from experience are useful tools. *Every* program in this book has been run and carefully tested, directly from the text itself, which is in machine-readable form. All of them have been run without change on a variety of machines and Pascal compilers.

The second concern of this book is how to write *good* programs. As we proceed, we hope to convey to you principles of: good design, so you write programs that work and are easy to maintain and modify; human engineering, so you can use them conveniently; reliability, so you get the right answers; and efficiency, so you can afford to run them.

We don't think that it is possible to learn to program well by reading platitudes about good programming. Nor is it sufficient to study small examples. Rather than present ideas like structured programming and top-down design as abstract principles, we have tried to distill the important contributions of each and put them into practice in all our code. That way you can see what they mean, how to use them on real problems, and what benefits they are likely to produce.

We also try to show *how* we went about building the programs, rather than just presenting the finished product, or pretending that we arrived at the final result by some mechanical process. For each program we discuss its purpose, how it should be designed to be easy to use, what considerations affect its structure and implementation, and some of the alternatives that exist. We don't claim that these are the best possible programs, or that our way is the only way to design and write them. But even if you would do them differently, studying the development of a coherent set of well-written and useful programs should help you better appreciate the significance of some of these ideas, and ultimately to become a better programmer.

We have quite a few tools to show you. Most of these are programs of manageable size, programs that one person can reasonably write in an hour or a day or a week. Clearly we can't present giant programs like operating systems or major compilers; few of us have the time, training or need to delve inside such creatures anyway. Instead we have concentrated on the kinds of tools you *are* likely to become involved with, programs that help you to make the most effective use of whatever operating system and language you already have. There is an important lesson in this: well chosen and well designed programs of modest size can be used to create a comfortable and effective interface to those that are bigger and less well done.

Whenever possible we will build more complicated programs up from the simpler; whenever possible we will *avoid* building at all, by finding new uses for existing tools, singly or in combinations. Our programs *work together;* their cumulative effect is much greater than you could get from a similar collection of programs that you couldn't easily connect. By the end of the book you will have been introduced to a set of tools that solve many problems you encounter as a programmer.

What sorts of tools? Computing is a broad field, and we can't begin to cover every kind of application. Instead we have concentrated on an activity that is central to programming — *programs that help develop other programs*. They are programs which we use regularly, most of them every day; we used versions of almost all of them while we were writing this book. In fact we chose them because they account for much of the computer usage on the system where we work. Although we can hardly claim that our choices will satisfy all your needs, some should be directly useful to you whatever your interest. Studying those that are not should provide you with ideas and insights about how to design and build quality tools for *your* particular problems. Comparing our designs with related programs on your system may lead you to improvements in both. And learning to think in terms of tools will encourage you to write programs that solve only the unique parts of your problem, then interface to existing programs to do the rest.

Whatever your application, your most important tool is a good programming language. Without this, programs are just too hard to write and understand; you spend more time fighting your language than being productive. One of the problems with writing about programming is choosing a language for the programs. No single language is known to all readers, available on all machines, and easy to read. We must compromise.

Since Pascal is widely available and well supported, we will use it as our base in this book. Pascal is now the main language in university computer science courses. It is available on almost all computers, and is sufficiently standardized that programs can be written to run without change on a wide variety of systems.

Most programmers can quickly achieve at least a reading knowledge of Pascal. If you are used to some other language, you should have no difficulty following our programs, for properly structured programs seem to read the same in most languages. We avoid most idiosyncrasies of Pascal, and hide the unavoidable ones in well-defined modules.

Although we are not writing a Pascal manual, we will try to explain new constructions as they arise. Chapter 1 describes a few simple tools, as a way to introduce our style of Pascal code and our conventions.

A surprising number of programs have one input, one output, and perform a useful transformation on data as it passes through. We call such programs *filters*. Some filters are so simple that you might hardly think of them as tools, yet a careful selection of filters that work together can handle quite complicated processing. Several smaller filters are collected in Chapter 2, including a powerful character transliteration program.

Not all programs are filters. Chapter 3 discusses programs that interact with their environment in more complicated ways, such as file inclusion, comparison and printing, and an archive system for managing sets of files. The major problem in moving programs from one environment to another is precisely this question of how a program communicates with its local operating system. We deal with portability by specifying a small set of primitive operations for accessing the environment. All of our programs are written in terms of these primitives, so operating system dependencies are confined to a handful of procedures and functions. Programs that use them can move to any system where the primitives can be implemented. We have demonstrated this by moving all of the tools in this book, without change, to several distinct Pascal systems on three different computers.

Some filters are large enough to warrant separate chapters. The sorting program of Chapter 4, the pattern finding and replacement programs of Chapter 5, and the macro processor of Chapter 8 all fall into this category. The pattern finder uses most of the code of the transliteration program in Chapter 2 to recognize character classes, which are just one of a larger set of patterns that can be specified. (The pattern finder is capable of a lot more than finding instances of time, by the way.) Although these filters are biased toward program development, the filter concept is valuable in any application. It encourages the view that a program is just a stage in a larger process, and that stages should be simple and easy to connect. It also encourages the view that all files and I/O devices should be interchangeable, so that any program can work with any file or device.

Chapter 6 contains a text editor that is rather more comprehensive than those normally found in time-sharing systems. The editor incorporates most of the code of the pattern finder of Chapter 5, so it recognizes the same class of patterns. When used with some of the other programs presented, it can do jobs that would otherwise require you to write a special program. Even if you are not working in an interactive environment, the editor will prove to be useful.

Chapter 7 contains a text formatter that is a (much smaller) version of the program used to set the type for this book.

Finally, as we have already mentioned, Chapter 8 contains a modest but useful macro processor, which you can use to extend any programming language.

It might appear from this outline that we stress text manipulation too heavily. Yet a large part of what programmers do every day *is* text processing — editing program source, preparing input data, scanning output, writing documentation. These activities are at the heart of programming; as much as possible, they should be mechanized. Program development is the place where tools can have the most impact. And since text processing programs come in all sizes, they display at least as broad a spectrum of programming techniques as language processors or numerical programs.

As you can see, the book is organized in terms of applications rather than different aspects of the programming process. This is not a reference work on algorithms or data structures or Pascal. Nor will you find separate chapters on design, coding, testing, debugging, efficiency, human engineering, documentation, or any of the other popular themes. We are engaged in the business of building tools, and of building them properly. All of these aspects of programming arise, in varying degrees, with *every* program, and can be kept in perspective only by discussing them as we write the programs. In the process, we will try to communicate to you our approach to tool building, so you can go on to design, build, and use tools of your own.

Bibliographic Notes

The programming language Pascal has had considerable impact on computing practice; it is especially suitable for structured programming and for describing data structures. Read *Systematic Programming: An Introduction* (Prentice-Hall, 1973) by N. Wirth, the designer of Pascal. The special issue of *Computing Surveys* on programming (December, 1974) contains several papers well worth reading, including one by Wirth. Pascal has also influenced the design of newer languages, most notably Ada; you might read "An Overview of Ada," by J. G. P. Barnes, *Software Practice and Experience,* November, 1980, or *Programming with Ada* by P. Wegner (Prentice-Hall, 1980).

The Pascal language is defined in *Pascal User Manual and Report (2nd Edition),* by K. Jensen and N. Wirth (Springer-Verlag, 1978), and with more detail and precision in the proposed ISO Standard for Pascal. (See, for example, SIGPLAN Notices, April, 1980.)

One of the most influential proponents of good programming is E. W. Dijkstra. You should read *Structured Programming,* by O.-J. Dahl, E. W. Dijkstra and C. A. R. Hoare (Academic Press, 1972) and Dijkstra's *A Discipline of Programming* (Prentice-Hall, 1976).

An excellent set of essays on programming and on the problems of developing big systems is found in F. P. Brooks' *The Mythical Man-Month* (Addison-Wesley, 1974). The term "egoless programming" was coined by G. M. Weinberg in his delightful book *The Psychology of Computer Programming* (Van Nostrand Reinhold, 1971).

The Elements of Programming Style (2nd Edition), by B. W. Kernighan and P. J. Plauger (McGraw-Hill, 1978), contains an extensive discussion of how to improve computer programs, with numerous examples taken from published Fortran and PL/I code.

The original version of this book is *Software Tools* (Addison-Wesley, 1976). The programs therein are written in Ratfor, a structured dialect of Fortran implemented by a preprocessor. They have proved sufficiently popular that a user group exists, and the tools themselves are used at several thousand sites. See "A Virtual Operating System," by D. E. Hall, D. K. Scherrer and J. S. Sventek, *CACM,* September, 1980. With the major exception of the Ratfor preprocessor itself, all of the tools from the original are presented here.

CHAPTER 1: **GETTING STARTED**

This chapter is an informal introduction to our way of using Pascal, and to some of the ideas and conventions used throughout the book. It also presents a handful of small but useful programs, to make the discussion concrete. We cannot present complete programs without occasionally using concepts before they are explained, so you will have to take some things on faith as we get started or we'll get bogged down explaining our explanations. Bear with us.

1.1 File Copying

The first problem we want to tackle is how a program communicates with its environment. Since many of our programs are concerned with text manipulation, one basic operation is reading characters from some source of input. To do this we will invent a function called `getc`, which reads the *next input character,* and returns that character as its function value; each time it is called, it returns a new character. For now we'll ignore where the characters come from, although you can imagine them originating at an interactive terminal or some secondary storage device like a disk.

We won't discuss what character set we have in mind, except to say that `getc` can return a value, distinguishable from all input character codes, that indicates that the end of the input has been reached. Similarly, the end of a text line is indicated by yet another unique value that is returned by `getc`. We'll also ignore all questions of efficiency, although we're fully aware that reading one character at a time at least sounds expensive. Temporarily we want to sweep as many details as we possibly can under the rug.

Next we invent `putc`, the complement of `getc`. `putc` puts a single character somewhere, such as a terminal, a printer, or a disk; one of its acceptable argument values signals the end of a text line. Again, we won't concern ourselves with the precise details, nor with the efficiency of the operation. The main point is that `getc` and `putc` work together — the characters that `getc` gets can be put somewhere else by `putc`.

If someone has provided these two basic operations, you can do a surprising amount of useful computing without ever knowing anything more about how they're implemented. As the simplest example, if you put the `getc`/`putc` pair

7

inside a loop:

```
while (getc(c) is not at end of input) do
    putc(c)
```

you have a program that copies its input to its output and quits. A simple task, performed by an equally simple program. Certainly, someone ultimately has to worry about the choice of character set, detecting end of line and end of input, efficiency and the like, but most people need *not* be concerned, because getc and putc conceal the details. (If you want to know how they might work, we will show you simple versions in standard Pascal soon, and also explain why we didn't just use read and write.)

Functions like getc and putc are called *primitives* — functions that interface to the "outside world." They call in turn whatever input and output routines must be used with a particular operating system and compiler. To the program that uses them, getc and putc define a standard internal representation for characters and provide an input-output mechanism that can be made uniform across many different computers. If we use primitives, we can design and write programs that will not be overly dependent on the idiosyncrasies of any one operating system. The primitives insulate a program from its operating system environment and ensure that the high level task to be performed is clearly expressed in a small well-defined set of basic operations.

The program shown above is written in "pseudo-code," that is, a language that resembles a real programming language but avoids excessive detail by from time to time resorting to ordinary English. Writing in pseudo-code lets us specify quite a bit of the program before we have worked out all aspects of it. On larger programs, it is valuable to begin with pseudo-code and refine it in stages until it is all executable. You can revise and improve the design at a high level without writing any executable code, yet remain close to a form that can be made executable.

The next step is to write copy in standard Pascal, ready to compile and run.

```
{ copy -- copy input to output }
procedure copy;
var
    c : character;
begin
    while (getc(c) <> ENDFILE) do
        putc(c)
end;
```

Some explanations: First, and most obvious to people who have used Pascal before, is that this is not a complete program — it is just a procedure. So it needs some surrounding context before it can actually do anything for us. We intend to present all of our programs this way, as procedures that fit into a larger context, so we can better focus on the essential ideas. To make copy run, we actually need something like this:

```
{ complete copy -- to show one possible implementation }
program copyprog (input, output);
const
    ENDFILE = -1;
    NEWLINE = 10;    { ASCII value }
type
    character = -1..127;     { ASCII, plus ENDFILE }

{ getc -- get one character from standard input }
function getc (var c : character) : character;
var
    ch : char;
begin
    if (eof) then
        c := ENDFILE
    else if (eoln) then begin
        readln;
        c := NEWLINE
    end
    else begin
        read(ch);
        c := ord(ch)
    end;
    getc := c
end;

{ putc -- put one character on standard output }
procedure putc (c : character);
begin
    if (c = NEWLINE) then
        writeln
    else
        write(chr(c))
end;

{ copy -- copy input to output }
procedure copy;
var
    c : character;
begin
    while (getc(c) <> ENDFILE) do
        putc(c)
end;

begin    { main program }
    copy
end.
```

The context shown here defines all the constants, types, and functions needed by copy. It is presented in standard Pascal to illustrate the behavior of getc and `putc` in terms familiar to Pascal programmers, and to demonstrate that the primitives can be implemented in a fashion that is supported on all Pascal systems. For most implementations, however, some special treatment would be given to `getc` and `putc`, to make them as efficient as possible.

The advantage of wrapping a program in an outer shell is that we can gradually add to the surrounding environment as we make the programs more sophisticated, without having to repeat a lot of description every time we present a new program. The standard context for the programs in the book is much larger than what we showed here. In particular, we put the definitions of functions and procedures like `getc` and `putc`, constants like `ENDFILE`, and types like `character` in the outer block so they are readily available to the whole program. In Chapter 3 and Chapter 8, we will show some programs that help to automate collecting the pieces of a program. The appendix shows the declarations we use. We will assume without further comment that all subsequent programs are wrapped up this way.

Now back to `copy` itself. The first line is just a comment, of course, that says briefly what the procedure does. This kind of comment will occur on every function and procedure in the book. We use { and } to delimit comments; you may have to use (* and *) if your character set does not include braces.

The lines

```
var
    c : character;
```

declare c to be a variable of type `character`. Note that `character` is not the same as the standard type `char`, for it must represent values like `ENDFILE` that must be different from legitimate values of type `char`.

The lines

```
while (getc(c) <> ENDFILE) do
    putc(c)
```

are where all the work of `copy` gets done. The `while` statement specifies a loop; so long as the condition inside parentheses† is true, the body of the loop (in this case, the single statement `putc(c)`) is repeatedly executed. Eventually the condition becomes false, and the loop terminates. `copy` then returns to its caller, and the whole program terminates. The condition being tested in the `while` loop is

```
getc(c) <> ENDFILE
```

The notation `<>` means "not equal to," so the loop continues while the character returned by `getc` is not `ENDFILE`.

---

† Strictly speaking, parentheses aren't needed here, but they are in conditions that involve `and` and `or`. We intend to stick them in everywhere because it's easier than remembering when they're needed and when they're not.

`getc(c)` returns the next character both as its function value *and* in its argument c so the value can be both tested and saved for later use, all in a single statement. This is an unconventional Pascal usage, but perfectly legal. It is so handy that we use it often.

ENDFILE is a *symbolic constant* that stands for a value that is mutually agreed upon by `getc` and the users of `getc` to signal that the end of the input has occurred — that there are no more characters. (It is not a character that is stored on an external medium.) The particular value chosen above is not particularly magical; it may even be different on different machines. The only restriction is that ENDFILE must be distinguishable from any possible character that `getc` might obtain from a file. We will consistently use upper case names for such constants so they will stand out; all variables and functions will be in lower case.

There are a fair number of symbolic constants in our programs; they contribute a great deal to the readability of the code. You can see at a glance what the test

```
while (getc(c) <> ENDFILE) do
```

means, because ENDFILE is more meaningful than some magic number like -1 would be.

In Pascal, the `const` declaration is a convenient way to replace names like ENDFILE by appropriate values as the program is being compiled. Chapter 8 describes a program that will let you define and translate symbolic constants in a more general way, so that you can use them in any context and have the actual defining character strings written into the source code automatically before it is compiled.

Why is `copy` useful? Most operating systems permit you to specify what external files or data sets or physical I/O devices correspond to the internal files you used when you wrote the program. This correspondence is established after the code is compiled, at the time it is actually run. (Those systems that don't support such runtime file specification can be augmented to do so by our standard interface.) That means you can have programs around, ready to run, and decide at the last moment what files or devices to use. It also means you can treat such programs like black boxes, and pretty much forget about their innards. If you have the primitive `getc` read from a "standard input" — like the file `input` normally associated with a Pascal program — and have `putc` write on a "standard output" — like the file `output` — you can connect them to the appropriate files or devices when the program is run. In Chapter 3 we will show a convenient notation for specifying what files to connect.

By the way, the word "file" has different meanings on different computer systems. For now, we will use it colloquially to mean a place where information comes from (via `getc`, for example), or a place where it can be put (perhaps with `putc`). This might be a disk organized as a permanent "file system" or any I/O device.

Our program copies a stream of characters from any such source to any destination. In an environment such as we just described, you can use it to put keystrokes from a terminal onto a file, list a file on a printer, replicate a file — to perform, in short, a host of utility functions.

Although there are other ways of doing many of these things, this method is general and you can build on it. You can improve it, if necessary, in a number of ways, to make it fancier or faster. copy is a basic *tool*. Useful in its own right, it can also serve as a base for constructing other, more elaborate programs. If you stick to the principle of pushing details as far down as possible, by writing in terms of primitives that read from an arbitrary source and write to an arbitrary destination, your new tools will be compatible with previous ones. You will be building a whole set that work together.

One more major item remains to be provided before copy can be called finished — its user documentation. For a program as simple as copy this may seem silly, for one glance at the code reminds us what it does. Few programs are this simple, however, and source code is not always available as a ready reference. So we present a document we call a "manual page:"

```
PROGRAM
    copy     copy input to output
USAGE
    copy
FUNCTION
    copy copies its input to its output unchanged. It is useful for copying from a terminal to a
    file, from file to file, or even from terminal to terminal. It may be used for displaying the
    contents of a file, without interpretation or formatting, by copying from a file to terminal.
EXAMPLE
    To echo lines typed at your terminal:
        copy
        hello there, are you listening?
        hello there, are you listening?
        yes, I am.
        yes, I am.
        <ENDFILE>
```

The manual page is comprehensive but succinct. It suggests some obvious uses and gives a concrete example that potential users can try out, (a) to make sure copy is installed properly and (b) to reinforce their understanding of the document. (In manual pages, we will print user input in the normal program typeface, and program responses in italics.)

The example is not frivolous, by the way. When you encounter a new language, a new operating environment, or just a new way of doing business on a computer, the first hurdle to clear is learning how to run a program. You must master, perhaps: logging on to the computer, creating files with the editor, running the compiler and/or linker, modifying files with the editor, and invoking the program you've finally built! With all these potential problem areas, the last thing you need is a complex program to contribute troubles of its own. Thus, copy is always one of the first programs we bring up in a new environment.

Exercise 1-1. Make the copy program work on your computer. □

Exercise 1-2. Can you think of an even simpler program you might use to establish a beachhead on a new system? □

1.2 Counting Characters

There are times when all you want to know about a file is how many characters it contains, or how many lines, or how many words. If the file resides on permanent storage like a disk, you may be lucky enough to have an operating system that will tell you at least some of these things. If you are not lucky, or if the "file" happens to be on a tape or cassette, for instance, then the easiest thing is to pass the file through a program that counts what you want to know.

If you can't think offhand why anyone would want merely to count the characters in something, don't worry. This is a book on tool building, remember, and tools work best in combination with others. Applications will occur soon enough.

Counting characters is the most basic operation:

```
{ charcount -- count characters in standard input }
procedure charcount;
var
    nc : integer;
    c : character;
begin
    nc := 0;
    while (getc(c) <> ENDFILE) do
        nc := nc + 1;
    putdec(nc, 1);
    putc(NEWLINE)
end;
```

This program is only slightly more complicated than the previous one. It uses type integer for the counting variable nc, which accumulates the number of characters read. To print the number it has computed, charcount calls putdec, which converts a number to a string of characters suitable for printing and outputs it with putc; this way it does not have to know how output is actually performed. We will present putdec in Chapter 2. The second argument in the call to putdec is the minimum field width: the number will be right-aligned in a field at least this wide.

In no case does putdec force the output device, whatever it might be, to end the current line, because we might want to put several numbers on one line with multiple calls to putdec. Thus we have to ask for a new line explicitly, with

```
putc(NEWLINE)
```

NEWLINE is not necessarily one of the values of the Pascal type char, but it does exist in the standard ASCII and EBCDIC character sets. When sent to a terminal it typically causes a carriage return and line feed; when written to a file it might cause an end of record or it might merely be written as just another character in the output stream or file. So for many environments, the local version of putc may well contain special code for handling the argument value NEWLINE. We will use NEWLINE as a standard character internally for signaling end of line, regardless of the source or destination of information, so that our programs can have a uniform way of identifying line boundaries.

You should observe that if the input file contains no characters, the while test fails on the first call to getc, and so charcount produces zero, the right answer. This is an important observation. One of the best things about the while statement is that it tests at the *top* of the loop, before proceeding with the body. Thus if there is nothing to do, nothing is done, even if this means that we never go through the loop body. Too many programs fail to act intelligently when handed input like "no characters." We will write ours so they do reasonable things with extreme cases; one of our basic tools for accomplishing this is the while.

The manual page for charcount is:

PROGRAM
    charcount   count characters in input
USAGE
    charcount
FUNCTION
    charcount counts the characters in its input and writes the total as a single line of text to the output. Since each line of text is internally delimited by a NEWLINE character, the total count is the number of lines plus the number of characters within each line.
EXAMPLE
    charcount
    A single line of input.
    <ENDFILE>
    24

1.3 Counting Lines

Suppose that instead of counting characters, we want to count the number of *lines* in some input. Clearly, this is just a matter of restricting the count to instances of NEWLINE returned by getc:

```
{ linecount -- count lines in standard input }
procedure linecount;
var
    nl : integer;
    c : character;
begin
    nl := 0;
    while (getc(c) <> ENDFILE) do
        if (c = NEWLINE) then
            nl := nl + 1;
    putdec(nl, 1);
    putc(NEWLINE)
end;
```

This time the body of the while is a little bigger — it consists of an if, which in turn controls the assignment statement nl := nl + 1. The indentation shows what code is controlled by what, and unobtrusively but clearly draws attention to the logical structure of the program. Note how the use of a special value for the newline condition permits linecount to be written as a minor variation on the structure of charcount.

The idea that text information is just a string of characters, with arbitrary length lines delimited by explicit NEWLINE characters, seems pretty obvious when you think about how a typewriter or a terminal works. But for all its obviousness, it's still an uncommon concept in many computing systems, where text must often be forced into either fixed length chunks reminiscent of cards or "records" with inconvenient properties.

As we showed in the full expansion of copy earlier, it is not hard to impose this simplified form of input/output on an existing system, doing input and output one character at a time. Each call to getc must test whether end of file has occurred (using the eof built-in function), and if not, whether the end of a line has happened (with eoln). For putc, we use writeln to terminate the line properly. This is not especially efficient, but it is by far the easiest tactic. The versions of getc and putc that we showed with copy work this way; they will serve temporarily in most systems.

Localizing input and output in a pair of functions is better than spreading decisions about ends of lines and files and character sets all over a program. Of course the input might indeed be a stream of characters from a keyboard and the output might indeed be driving a typing mechanism, and all disk files might be maintained in this format, in which case getc and putc become trivial. But whatever the source or sink, we will stick with our interface and *program* in terms of typewriter-like text, performing all necessary translations as early as possible on input and as late as possible on output, to match up with character sets, terminals, line printers, and disk formats. Chapter 2 contains some examples of programs for matching up to special devices. Having a uniform representation for text solves much of the problem of keeping tools uniform.

How should we test `linecount` to make sure it really works? When bugs occur, they usually arise at the "boundaries" or extremes of program operation. These are the "exceptions that prove the rule." Here the boundaries are fairly simple: a file with no lines and a file with one line. If the code handles these cases correctly, and the general case of a file with more than one line, it is probable that it will handle all inputs properly.

So we feed `linecount` an empty file. The `while` test fails the first time and the body is never obeyed. No lines are counted when none are input. Fine.

If we feed `linecount` one line, the `while` is satisfied for every character on the line; the `if` is satisfied when the `NEWLINE` is seen, and the line is counted. Then the test is repeated and the `while` loop exits. Again fine.

A multi-line file. Same behavior as for one line, only now we observe that after each line, the program ends up at the test part of the `while` — the proper place to begin handling the next line or an `ENDFILE`. The program checks out.

This may seem like excruciating detail for such a simple program, but it's not. There are common coding blunders which could have caused any one of those three tests to fail, sometimes even while the other two tests succeed. You should learn to think of boundary tests as you code each piece of a program — try them mentally as you write and then physically on the finished product. In practice, the tests go much quicker than we can talk about them and cost little additional effort. It is effort that is well repaid.

To summarize `linecount` for future use:

```
PROGRAM
    linecount    count lines in input
USAGE
    linecount
FUNCTION
    linecount counts the lines in its input and writes the total as a line of text to the output.
EXAMPLE
        linecount
        A single line of input.
        <ENDFILE>
        1
```

Exercise 1-3. What happens if the last character of input to `linecount` is not a `NEWLINE`? Does the program stay sane? Is its behavior a bug or a natural consequence of our definition of a "line"? □

1.4 Counting Words

The next counting program has applications in text processing — it counts the words in a file. We use it to answer questions like "How many words are there in this book?" (About 95,000, excluding programs.) For our purposes a word is a sequence of any characters except blanks, tabs and newlines. Every time there is a transition from not being in a word to being in a word, that

signals another word to count. The variable `inword` is used to record which
state the program is in at any given time; initially it is "not in a word."

```
{ wordcount -- count words in standard input }
procedure wordcount;
var
    nw : integer;
    c : character;
    inword : boolean;
begin
    nw := 0;
    inword := false;
    while (getc(c) <> ENDFILE) do
        if (c = BLANK) or (c = NEWLINE) or (c = TAB) then
            inword := false
        else if (not inword) then begin
            inword := true;
            nw := nw + 1
        end;
    putdec(nw, 1);
    putc(NEWLINE)
end;
```

`BLANK` and `TAB` are further symbolic constants, which must be set to the internal character codes that `getc` returns for blank and horizontal tab on your
machine. For example, in the ASCII character set, `BLANK` is 32 and `TAB` is 9,
but the purpose of using constants is precisely so that you won't have to know
(or be tempted to use) specific values except in `const` declarations. It also
helps portability if such values occur only in one easy-to-change place.

`inword` is declared `boolean`, i.e., it can take on only the values `true` and
`false`. We have quietly made use of boolean expressions already — they
appear in all `while` and `if` statements — but this is the first time we found the
need to memorize the result of a test by setting a variable. `inword` is `true`
only when the input is "inside" a word.

This example also shows some more control flow statements. First, an `if`
statement may include an `else`, to specify an alternate action if the condition
of the `if` is not met:

```
if condition then
    statement
else
    statement
```

says "if the `condition` is true `then` do the *statement* following the `if`; `else`
(otherwise) do the *statement* following the `else`." One and only one of the two
statements is executed when the `if-then-else` is encountered. Either statement can in fact be quite complicated; in `wordcount` the one after the `else` is
yet another `if`.

Second, we can replace any single statement by a group of statements separated by semicolons and enclosed by `begin` and `end`, a construction called a *compound statement*; the statements within the `begin` and `end` are treated as if they were a single statement. Thus if `inword` is `false` in the code

```
else if (not inword) then begin
    inword := true;
    nw := nw + 1
end;
```

both assignments are done. `begin` and `end` may in principle be nested to arbitrary depth.

We will consistently position `begin` and `end` as shown: `begin` on the line that controls the compound statement, and `end` on a line by itself at the same level of indentation as the keyword that began the construction.

It is truly remarkable how much heated debate can result from such questions as where `begin` and `end` should be placed, and whether keywords should be in upper or lower case. Rather than continue such a debate, suffice it to say that we find our style convenient and readable, but you are free to do as you like in your own code. We do recommend strongly that you be consistent in applying whatever formatting standards you settle on.

Although the code that follows the `while` in `wordcount` is complicated, logically it is just a single `if-then-else` statement, not a compound, so it needs no surrounding `begin` and `end`. You may insert them if they make you feel more comfortable.

The `else if` construction occurs frequently in our programs, often as a longer chain of `if ... else if ... else`, to perform at most one of several alternatives. Chains are made longer by inserting more `else if`'s at the appropriate places. Three rules make such chains easy to read:

(1) Scan down the tests until you find one that is met — the first one encountered selects the case to be performed.

(2) If no test succeeds, the statement associated with the trailing `else` (if any) is performed.

(3) In either situation, execution resumes immediately after the body of the last `else` (or the last `else if` if there is no trailing `else`.)

We strongly favor this form of writing multi-way decisions, instead of arbitrarily nested trees of `if-then-else`'s, because it tends to be less confusing. We keep all the `else if`'s at the same level of indenting, to emphasize that the structure is really a multi-way decision.

Pascal also provides a "`case`" statement for expressing some kinds of multi-way decisions directly. We will use it when it is suitable, but a chain of `else if`'s is often better because it can handle more situations.

How do we test `wordcount`? The place to begin is while the program is being written. The main assurance you have that a program is correct is the intellectual effort you put into getting it right in the first place. We wrote wordcount with an algorithm based on two states — being in a word, and not being in a word. If we make the transitions between states correctly, set up initial conditions properly, and properly count the transitions for each new word, we can have confidence in the program. Testing is still necessary, however, to check that the algorithm is valid and that the program implements it correctly.

For a program of any complexity, you certainly can't test all possible inputs. As we said, programmers have learned from bitter experience that the boundaries of a program are the most fruitful places to examine, for they are where bugs most often appear. Besides, if you can show that a program works properly at its extremes of operation, you have a convincing argument that it works properly everywhere between as well. Thus a small selection of critical tests directed at boundaries is much superior to a shotgun-blast of random ones.

Although it's hard to give a precise definition, intuitively a "boundary" is a data value for which the program is forced to react significantly differently from an adjacent value. For example, the case of "no input at all" is a boundary for most programs. In testing wordcount, if there is no input, the first call of getc returns an ENDFILE, the body of the while loop is never executed, and the wordcount is zero, as expected. The analogous boundary, input but no words, is also worth checking. If the input consists entirely of blanks, tabs and newlines, the first if is always satisfied, so wc is never incremented; again the result is zero, as it should be.

You should also verify that wordcount works when there is a single word of input, regardless of where in the input it appears, and when there are two input words at various places. If all of these cases are correct, you can be fairly confident that the program is right.

One final observation. In testing wordcount it was obvious what output was expected for each input. That is not always so clear in larger programs. Yet it is a fundamental principle of testing that you must know in advance what answer each test case is supposed to produce. If you don't, you're not testing; you're experimenting. So part of the responsibility of writing a program is to prepare a comprehensive set of test inputs, and outputs against which to compare the results of test runs.

The manual page required for wordcount is somewhat more substantial than the earlier ones:

```
PROGRAM
    wordcount    count words in input
USAGE
    wordcount
FUNCTION
    wordcount counts the words in its input and writes the total as a line of text to the output.
    A "word" is a maximal sequence of characters not containing a blank or tab or newline.
EXAMPLE
        wordcount
        A single line of input.
        <ENDFILE>
        5
BUGS
    The definition of "word" is simplistic.
```

We have introduced an interesting new section on this manual page — a declaration of known bugs. It permits us to document a program exactly as it stands the day the manual page is written, without resorting to fictions about how it ought to work, and it gives the user a warning about problems that might otherwise be overlooked.

Naturally, we debug a program as thoroughly as possible before releasing it for public consumption, so conventional coding bugs are rarely documented in this fashion. Instead, we focus on *design* shortcomings, things that could be made better but often aren't worth the bother for a simple program. wordcount is naive about a construct such as "either/or," which most people would count as two words, and about a word hyphenated at the end of a text line, which is universally regarded as one word, except by simplistic programs.

Since wordcount does just what we want in the vast majority of cases, and since it comes quite close to the right answer even on text prepared without regard to its shortcomings, we feel little incentive to make it more complex. Instead, we are content to document it as it is and move on to other things.

Exercise 1-4. Combine the functions of charcount, linecount and wordcount into one program. In what order should the three counts be printed? Is it better to have one program that does three things, or three programs that each do one thing? □

1.5 Removing Tabs

Suppose that you need to print a text file containing horizontal tab characters on a device that cannot interpret tabs. As a first approximation, you might be content with fixed tab stops every four columns, as they are in this book. A tab character is thus replaced by from one to four spaces. Let us write a manual page for a program detab to do this:

```
PROGRAM
    detab     convert tabs to blanks
USAGE
    detab
FUNCTION
    detab copies its input to its output, expanding horizontal tabs to blanks along the way, so
    that the output is visually the same as the input, but contains no tab characters.  Tab stops
    are assumed to be set every four columns (i.e., 1, 5, 9, ...), so that each tab character is
    replaced by from one to four blanks.
EXAMPLE
    Using → as a visible tab:
        detab
        →col 1→2→34→rest
            col 1   2    34    rest
BUGS
    detab is naive about backspaces, vertical motions, and non-printing characters.
```

This time we present the manual page before the program, a useful way to begin any project — it encourages us to focus from the start on how the final product is going to look to the user. This is important. Many programs grow haphazardly as the programmer learns what works or thinks of interesting new capabilities; the result is often a collection of features hard to use and not clearly related to each other. A program with just a few capabilities that are easy to specify is almost always more useful than a powerful program that is hard to invoke.

Another advantage of writing the manual page first is that it gives us a precise specification of the job to be done. Often it is hard to know when to end a programming project, since there is always one more feature dear to someone's heart that might be worth adding. But once the program does what the manual page says, it is hard to argue that the job is not done. Of all the factors (other than native ability) known to influence programmer productivity, the single most important one is the quality of specification given at the outset — the more precise and unambiguous the better.

This manual page even provides in advance for bugs! Put another way, it is a declaration in advance that the programmer need not be too ambitious in dealing with funny characters; a simple program will do.

Not all programs are documented before they are written, of course (we just presented several that weren't). Sometimes exploration is called for before specifications can be safely frozen, and sometimes the goal is sufficiently clear from the outset that there is little fear of going astray. We work both ways, and will continue to present manual pages at various stages of program development.

detab can have the same structure as copy, except that the body of the while loop is more complicated:

```
while (getc(c) <> ENDFILE)
    if (c = TAB)
        print blanks until next tab stop reached
    else
        print c
```

How do we know when the next tab position is reached? One possibility is to build into the main program the knowledge that tabs are set every four columns; then an arithmetic test suffices to decide if the current column is a tab stop. The trouble with such an approach comes when we decide to change the program, perhaps to allow tabs to be set at positions which aren't related by a simple arithmetic formula. If the "every four columns" decision is firmly wired into the program, it will be hard to cut it out.

A more flexible organization is an array of tab stops, initialized for now to every four columns. This will be a lot easier to change; in fact we haven't even said whether the array contains a list of stops or a `true/false` indicator at each column, like a typewriter. Representing the stops in an array, in whatever manner, leads to a program that will readily upgrade for more general applications.

However we do it, it is still worthwhile to write a separate function `tabpos` which tells the main program whether a particular column is a tab stop or not. This way we avoid muddying up the basic logic of the control loop with tab calculations, and conceal the representation of tab stops from the main routine.

It is clear that the program must also keep track of what column it is in, and it must recognize the end of each line of text so it can reset the column counter. The second cut at the tab remover is thus:

```
initialize tab stops
col := 1
while (getc(c) <> ENDFILE)
    if (c = TAB)
        print one or more blanks and update col
            until (tabpos(col, tabstops))
    else if (c = NEWLINE)
        putc(c)
        col := 1
    else
        putc(c)
        col := col + 1
```

This shows an `else if` chain with a trailing `else`, which is there to cover the "anything else" case, that is, neither a `TAB` nor a `NEWLINE`. Notice that in our pseudo-code we tend not to worry about syntactic noise like `then` and `do`, or even `begin` and `end`, preferring instead to let the indentation show the structure.

`tabpos` returns `true` if column `col` is a tab stop, `false` if it is not. In principle, this is an easy task. But wait a moment, and think over our discussion of boundary conditions.   One obvious boundary is the *last* tab stop. What happens if the input contains a tab in a column after the last tab stop?

One solution is to outlaw tabs after some maximum column, but it's folly to write a program that blindly assumes that its input is legal: real users rarely cooperate.   Or detab could abort or produce an error message (or both), but this is hardly desirable in a general-purpose tool.   Why not do something intelligent instead?   A program should produce reasonable output for reasonable input, and there is nothing unreasonable about a lot of tabs.   Let us build detab so that when a tab is encountered after the last tab stop it is converted to a single blank.

Since the loop

```
print one or more blanks and update col
    until (tabpos(col, tabstops))
```

will end only when it lands exactly on a tab stop, we must make sure that this always happens, even when lines extend past the last tab stop setting.   A safe convention is to assume that there are tab stops set in *every* column after the last one set explicitly.   tabpos must provide this feature.

All that remains is to spell out a few details and write tabpos.   We have chosen a representation where each element of an array tabstops contains true if there is a tab stop at that column, false if there is not.   Here is the final version:

```
{ detab -- convert tabs to equivalent number of blanks }
procedure detab;
const
    MAXLINE = 1000; { or whatever }
type
    tabtype = array [1..MAXLINE] of boolean;
var
    c : character;
    col : integer;
    tabstops : tabtype;
#include "tabpos.p"
#include "settabs.p"
begin
    settabs(tabstops);   { set initial tab stops }
    col := 1;
    while (getc(c) <> ENDFILE) do
        if (c = TAB) then
            repeat
                putc(BLANK);
                col := col + 1
            until (tabpos(col, tabstops))
        else if (c = NEWLINE) then begin
            putc(NEWLINE);
            col := 1
        end
        else begin
            putc(c);
            col := col + 1
        end
end;
```

We have introduced another important mechanism that we will be using heavily. "tabpos.p" and "setpos.p" are the names of files in our file system, where by convention Pascal source files have names that end in .p; the convention will likely be different on another system. The lines

```
#include "tabpos.p"
#include "settabs.p"
```

cause the files containing the function or procedure to be copied into the source right at that spot, replacing the #include lines. We will use #include throughout the book to show explicitly what has to go where without cluttering up presentation of the main routine. Chapter 3 and the appendix discuss how to interpret #include commands and construct whole Pascal programs suitable for compilation.

The function tabpos is:

```
{ tabpos -- return true if col is a tab stop }
function tabpos (col : integer; var tabstops : tabtype)
        : boolean;
begin
    if (col > MAXLINE) then
        tabpos := true
    else
        tabpos := tabstops[col]
end;
```

detab uses settabs to set up the tabstops array initially, according to whatever representation is expected by tabpos.

```
{ settabs -- set initial tab stops }
procedure settabs (var tabstops : tabtype);
const
    TABSPACE = 4;    { 4 spaces per tab }
var
    i : integer;
begin
    for i := 1 to MAXLINE do
        tabstops[i] := (i mod TABSPACE = 1)
end;
```

detab introduces two more control structures, which almost completes our set. The repeat-until is a loop that is repeated one or more times until the trailing test is met. This is opposite from the while, which tests at the top whether to loop, before doing anything. The while seems to occur naturally more often, but each form has its uses. In detab, the repeat is necessary to ensure that each input tab causes at least one blank to be output.

The for statement does a simple iteration from a lower limit to an upper, stepping a variable through successive values in between. Like the while, the for can be done zero times.

The mod operator yields the remainder produced by dividing its first operand by its second. In this case, i mod 4 produces the sequence 1, 2, 3, 0, 1, 2, ... as i increases from 1. Thus a 1 is produced every fourth time, and this is used to set the tab stop. This is a standard use for mod. (The parameter tabstops is declared var in settabs so that the changes made in settabs actually affect the array in detab.)

You might notice, by the way, that even though we spoke of "every four," we wrote the code in terms of a constant called TABSPACE that happens to have the value 4. When "four" becomes "three" or "eight" sometime in the future, the const declaration will be easy to find and change. (We changed it a couple of times while writing this chapter!)

It may seem silly to write a two-line function to be called only once, but the purpose of settabs is to conceal a data representation from a routine that does not have to know about it. For a program the size of detab, this is not absolutely necessary, but it is vital to break larger programs into small pieces that communicate only through well-defined interfaces. The less one part of a program knows about how another part operates, the more easily each may be changed.

Most real programs are subjected to a steady flow of changes and improvements over their lifetimes, and many programmers spend most of their time maintaining and modifying existing programs. This is an expensive process, so one of the most important design considerations for a program is that it be easy to change.

The best way we know to achieve this is to write the program so its pieces are as decoupled as possible, so that a change in one does not affect others. We try to push down into separate modules those details which would make the program less general and commit it to some specific mode of operation. `getc` and `putc`, for instance, conceal all details of character set, lines, records, file assignments and end-of-file handling; that is one reason why we use them instead of direct calls to `read` and `write`. Similarly, `detab` is organized so the main routine is not concerned with the representation of tab stops, only with counting columns.

Factoring the job into pieces also lets us concentrate on one aspect of a design at a time. We are more likely to get `detab` right, and make it understandable, by restricting it to counting columns. And we are more likely to get `tabpos` right by dealing only with tab stops and implementing just one function whose specification is easily remembered. The best programs are designed in terms of loosely coupled functions where each one does a simple task.

It is not always clear how to organize a Pascal program so the information is readily available where it is needed without at the same time being excessively visible where it isn't needed. For instance, we chose to make the `tabstops` array a parameter of the calls to `tabpos` and `settabs`; it could just as well have been passed implicitly because it was declared in an enclosing block. We also chose to nest the definitions of `tabpos` and `setpos` within `detab`, although they could have been put in the outer block. In that case, `detab` wouldn't even have to know about the array `tabpos`, so it might be argued that that would be the best representation.

Exercise 1-5. Test `detab`. It must pass all the tests that `copy` must pass (except that tabs are replaced by one to four spaces). In addition, there are several other boundaries involving the tab stops. You might consider testing rows of x's, each with a tab in a different location. What happens if a tab occurs after the last tab stop? □

Exercise 1-6. What does `detab` do if the input contains a backspace character? Modify it so it does the right thing. □

Exercise 1-7. There are obviously several other ways to write `detab`. Implement the following variations and compare them on the basis of size, complexity and ease of subsequent change.

(e) There is no `tabstops` array and no `settabs`; `tabpos` simply computes the right answer and returns it.

(b) The `tabstops` array contains a list of the columns which contain tab stops; the list is terminated by a zero entry.

(c) Each element of the `tabstops` array contains the number of columns to the next tab stop; the last entry is a zero.

(d) Repeat (b) and (c) using an explicit count of tabs stops instead of an end-marker.
□

1.6 Pascal Synopsis

You have already been introduced to most of the control flow parts of Pascal; as the need arises, we will introduce more of the language, particularly things related to data structure.

To assist you, here is a summary of what we've done so far. In the following, a *statement* is any legal Pascal statement, and *condition* is a boolean expression. Any Pascal statement or group of these can be enclosed in `begin` and `end` to make it into a compound statement, which is then equivalent to a single statement, and usable anywhere a single statement can be used. Semicolons separate the statements within such a group.

The `if` statement is

```
if condition then
    statement1
else
    statement2
```

If *condition* is true, do *statement1*, otherwise do *statement2*. The `else` part is optional. As in many languages, the construction

```
if condition1 then
    if condition2 then
        statement1
    else
        statement2
```

is ambiguous — the `else` could be associated with either `if`. `begin-end` can be used to disambiguate this as desired. Otherwise, each `else` goes with the immediately previous un-`elsed` `if`. The example above is indented to agree with the binding rule, but we will always use `begin-end` in such cases, to make our intent perfectly clear.

The `case` statement is sometimes useful for multi-way decisions:

```
case expression of
    case-list1 :  statement1 ;
    case-list2 :  statement2 ;
        . . .
end
```

Each *case-list* is a list of one or more constants. The *expression* is evaluated and matched against the list of cases; the *statement* thus selected is executed.

The `case` statement is seriously handicapped because it is an error if the value of *expression* does not match any of the constants in the *case-list*'s. It is generally necessary to precede a `case` with an `if` that checks this.

The `while` loop is

```
while condition do
    statement
```

Test *condition*. If it is true, do *statement* once, then test again. If *condition* is false, resume with the first statement after the body of the `while`.

The `for` statement

```
for index := expression1 to expression2 do
    statement
```

defines a loop in which *index* goes from *expression1* to *expression2* inclusive, stepping through all successive values in between. *statement* is executed once for each value of *index*. If `downto` is used in place of `to`, the loop counts down instead of up.

The `repeat until` loop tests at the bottom instead of the top:

```
repeat
    statement
until condition
```

The *statement* is done one or more times until *condition* becomes true, at which time the loop is exited.

Pascal also includes a `goto` statement and a `label` declaration. Although these are sometimes useful, we intend not to use them because it is too easy to create unreadable programs when unrestrained branching is allowed. By restricting ourselves to the control flow structures listed above, we get code that is better thought out, more readable, and hence less error-prone. In our experience, readability is the single best criterion of program quality: if a program is easy to read, it is probably a good program. If it is hard to read, it probably isn't good.

Pascal source statements may appear anywhere on a line; they may even bridge multiple lines, provided they are broken only where blanks or tabs may appear. It is important, however, to indent systematically so you can see what statements control what; this is another aspect of making programs readable. We try to be rigorous about this, so that the same form always appears the same way to the reader and so that we can use our tools to analyze program text.

There are several other components of Pascal just as important as control flow, such as program structure, data types, and communication with the operating system. Rather than attempt a summary here, we will introduce these topics more carefully as we come to them in writing specific programs.

One thing to clarify, however, is what we mean by "Pascal." Pascal is not "standard," in the sense that everyone uses exactly the same language. The *Pascal Report*, by Jensen and Wirth, and the International Standards

Organization (ISO) proposed standard for Pascal try to define the language precisely. We intend to stick to these standards, for this is the only way that we can be reasonably certain that our programs will run on all systems.

Pascal in its pure form has a number of defects that make it hard to write programs well. The worst problem, at least from our perspective, is that the size of an array is part of its type, and so it is not possible to write general-purpose functions and procedures that will process arrays of different sizes at different times. We cope with this problem as best we can, but it is a serious impediment. Chapter 2 is the first place where we really have to deal with it.

A second problem is that all variables are discarded on exit from the function or procedure in which they are declared. This means that if some variable is to remember a value from one call of a procedure to the next, that variable must be external to the procedure. Thus variables have much wider scope (that is, are visible to much more of the program) than they would be if Pascal permitted internal variables to retain values from one call to the next. Similarly, the only way to share a variable between two routines is to declare it in some common ancestor.

A related problem is that variables cannot be initialized except by assignment statements. Thus any variable which is to be initialized must be visible to the initializing routine as well as the places where it is used.

Procedures and functions must all be presented to the compiler at once; there is no separate compilation or library mechanism. Furthermore, their definitions must be nested and must occur before their use, which is the antithesis of the way they would be developed and presented in a top-down refinement of a design. We use #include to overcome this defect because it is just another step in compilation, not a change to the language. Since Pascal also requires separation of const, type and var declarations, we sometimes use #include to collect these parts of a program as well.

One remaining major problem area is the interaction of a program with its operating system. Input-output is one of the least well-defined parts of Pascal, and is not well designed either. We deal with input-output and related matters by defining primitives like getc and putc that provide a clean, well-defined set of operating system functions. All our programs use these primitives, which must be implemented somehow on each Pascal system. This is discussed more fully in Chapter 3; some typical implementations appear in the appendix.

Our decision to use standard Pascal rather than some less restricted variant is made to ensure portability. There are many extensions of Pascal, each overcoming some of the problem areas we mentioned above. But the extensions are all different, which destroys any hope of achieving portability. Our programs avoid the extensions, and hence will run almost anywhere.

1.7 Prospectus

What have we done so far? We wrote several elementary but useful tools. We tried to structure them so they will be easy to understand, and easy to change if the need arises. We wrote them in a language that can be run on almost any computer system without change. We wrote them in terms of primitives that conceal the differences among operating systems. And we documented them so that people can quickly learn how to use them.

What we're going to do is repeat that process for a number of tools that we think will be useful, and which should teach various lessons about programming. Most of these programs are bigger than the ones so far, some a lot bigger. Yet the basic approach of careful structuring and isolation of program from system will remain a constant theme. This is the only way to cope with big programs and real systems.

One thing you will notice is that programs often use code written in earlier sections or chapters. This is important. One way to achieve greater software productivity is to build on what has already been done, instead of endlessly reinventing the same things with minor variations. In a book, however, this organization does place a burden on the reader, since everything needed to run a given program isn't all in one place. We have tried to reduce it by carefully chosen names, reminders, back-pointers and an extensive index. Still, it will sometimes be hard to dive into the middle of a chapter and immediately appreciate what the code does.

One of the best ways to learn good programming is to read and think about actual programs, to ask questions like "Why was it done that way?" or "Why not write it like this?" We believe that the amount of code in this book is an asset, not a liability, and we think you will profit from studying it, even if you would write things differently.

Bibliographic Notes

We assume throughout this book that you have a working knowledge of Pascal. If you need to know more, there are a host of Pascal textbooks.

The (almost) official ISO standard for Pascal is given in *A Draft Proposal for Pascal*. It appeared in the April, 1980 issue of SIGPLAN Notices. More articles about Pascal may be found in "A Categorized Pascal Bibliography," D. V. Moffat, SIGPLAN Notices, October, 1980.

Our style of documenting programs with manual pages is based on *The Unix Programmer's Manual*, Bell Laboratories, 1978.

We are going to continue what we began in the previous chapter — writing simple programs that read a standard input and write a standard output. By obvious analogy to electronics (or plumbing) we call such programs *filters,* because they make useful changes to a stream of data passing through. You will find that many tools fall into this category, including most of those in this book.

2.1 Putting Tabs Back

Let us begin by writing the filter `entab`, to complement `detab`. `entab` replaces strings of blanks by equivalent tabs and blanks. Remember what we said earlier about the benefits of having all your files look as much alike as possible? You might use `entab` on files of fixed length records and produce typewriter-like text. That way, you could convert your files to a standard representation, one that has no wasteful imbedded blank strings. As an added payoff, your files are smaller and they all look alike; that makes it easier to write programs that talk and work together.

Another use for `entab` is to prepare output to be sent to a terminal. You might have a program that expects to drive a smart printer. You would like to speed up the printing by tabbing whenever possible. Rather than rewrite a working program, you are better off with a separate program to filter the output just before it is typed. Thus `entab`.

PROGRAM
    `entab`   convert runs of blanks into tabs
USAGE
    `entab`
FUNCTION
    `entab` copies its input to its output, replacing strings of blanks by tabs so that the output is visually the same as the input, but contains fewer characters. Tab stops are assumed to be set every four columns (i.e., 1, 5, 9, ...), so that each sequence of one to four blanks ending on a tab stop is replaced by a tab character.
EXAMPLE
    Using → as a visible tab:

```
    entab
       col 1   2   34   rest
    →col→1→2→34→rest
```

BUGS
    `entab` is naive about backspaces, vertical motions, and non-printing characters.
    `entab` will convert a single blank to a tab if it occurs at a tab stop. Thus `entab` is not an exact inverse of `detab`.

The trick of getting most filters right is to find an orderly way of recognizing the components of the input stream, so that the order can be reflected in the flow of control of the program rather than in a collection of switches and flags. We got away with one flag in `wordcount`, for that was a small program, but anything larger quickly becomes confusing. If we think of the input to `entab` as a repetition of the pattern: zero or more blanks, followed by a non-blank character (or ENDFILE), then this determines the control structure of the program:

```
col := 1
repeat
    while (getc(c) = BLANK) { collect blanks }
        if (at tab stop)
            print a tab
    while (any blanks left over)
        put them out
    { c is now ENDFILE or non-blank }
    if (c <> ENDFILE)
        putc(c)
        if (c = NEWLINE)
            col := 1
        else
            col := col + 1
until (c = ENDFILE)
```

`col` is the current output column. As with `detab` we will ignore non-printing characters, backspace, etc.

An easy way for `entab` to keep track of the blanks is to use another variable `newcol` that moves away from `col` as blanks are encountered. Whenever a tab is output, `col` is made to catch up to `newcol`. Then, when a non-blank character is encountered, if `col` is less than `newcol` there are excess blanks accumulated (not enough to be replaced by a tab) which must be output before the character can be. The design is complete:

```
{ entab -- replace blanks by tabs and blanks }
procedure entab;
const
    MAXLINE = 1000; { or whatever }
type
    tabtype = array [1..MAXLINE] of boolean;
var
    c : character;
    col, newcol : integer;
    tabstops : tabtype;
#include "tabpos.p"
#include "settabs.p"
begin
    settabs(tabstops);
    col := 1;
    repeat
        newcol := col;
        while (getc(c) = BLANK) do begin   { collect blanks }
            newcol := newcol + 1;
            if (tabpos(newcol, tabstops)) then begin
                putc(TAB);
                col := newcol
            end
        end;
        while (col < newcol) do begin
            putc(BLANK);                { output leftover blanks }
            col := col + 1
        end;
        if (c <> ENDFILE) then begin
            putc(c);
            if (c = NEWLINE) then
                col := 1
            else
                col := col + 1
        end
    until (c = ENDFILE)
end;
```

Again the program is organized so the representation of tab stops is hidden from the main routine; `tabpos` and `settabs` are the same routines used by `detab` in Chapter 1.

Exercise 2-1. Walk through `entab` with a file having two characters, one character, none. Try it with lines containing zero to ten blanks, followed by an x. Try zero to ten blanks followed by end of file. Under what circumstance will a file be restored to its original form after being filtered by `detab` and `entab` in turn? Can you think of any uses for such an operation? □

Exercise 2-2. What happens if `entab` reads a tab character? Make the simplest addition you can think of to the code to handle tabs in the input. What does `entab` do with text containing backspaces? How would you rewrite the code so that it maps an arbitrary string of spaces, backspaces and tabs into the minimum number required to give the same appearance? □

2.2 Overstrikes

You can overstrike characters on a typewriter by backspacing over what is already typed. This is how you underline words, for one thing; it is also a way to build additional characters from existing ones. If you send your output to a line printer, however, the result may be a hash, because a typical printer doesn't know what to do with backspace characters.

Many printers do, however, provide for overstriking entire lines. The Fortran convention for controlling this function (often co-opted into other languages, including some versions of Pascal) is to provide an extra *carriage control* character at the beginning of each line: a blank means "space before printing," and a plus sign (+) means "do not space before printing," i.e., overstrike what has gone before.

The filter `overstrike` looks for backspaces in text and generates a sequence of print lines with carriage control codes to reproduce the effect of the backspaces. If we adopt a viewpoint similar to that for `entab`, that the input is an alternation of zero or more backspaces and non-backspace characters, the resulting code is very similar. If a string of one or more backspaces is encountered, the program ends the current line and inserts the appropriate number of spaces in the overstrike line.

This is not the only way to do it, of course, but it is one of the least complicated. Nasty behavior occurs if the text to be printed contains words underlined one letter at a time. Each sequence of *character, backspace, underline* causes a whole new line to be generated, which can be quite slow. So a better way would be to have two or more line buffers to build the overstrike images as they are needed. But that is harder to code and get right. It is often better to get on with something that does most of the job well enough, then improve and add things as they prove to be worthwhile.

`overstrike` is useful even for text that contains no backspaces, for it converts the typewriter text produced by most of the programs in this book into lines with carriage controls, suitable for driving a line printer. It can serve as a final filter whenever printer output is desired, again encouraging you to keep as much as possible to a standard internal form for text for other programs.

`BACKSPACE` is another constant, like `TAB`, which we use to make a nongraphic visible.

```
{ overstrike -- convert backspaces into multiple lines }
procedure overstrike;
const
    SKIP = BLANK;
    NOSKIP = PLUS;
var
    c : character;
    col, newcol, i : integer;
begin
    col := 1;
    repeat
        newcol := col;
        while (getc(c) = BACKSPACE) do  { eat backspaces }
            newcol := max(newcol-1, 1);
        if (newcol < col) then begin
            putc(NEWLINE);  { start overstrike line }
            putc(NOSKIP);
            for i := 1 to newcol-1 do
                putc(BLANK);
            col := newcol
        end
        else if (col = 1) and (c <> ENDFILE) then
            putc(SKIP); { normal line }
        { else middle of line }
        if (c <> ENDFILE) then begin
            putc(c);                        { normal character }
            if (c = NEWLINE) then
                col := 1
            else
                col := col + 1
        end
    until (c = ENDFILE)
end;
```

The function max finds the maximum of its integer arguments:

```
{ max -- compute maximum of two integers }
function max (x, y : integer) : integer;
begin
    if (x > y) then
        max := x
    else
        max := y
end;
```

This function is used often enough that we will include it in the standard environment for our programs.

We used the constants NOSKIP and SKIP instead of PLUS and BLANK in the body of overstrike because the former describe the function to be performed, and the latter are not universal. Besides, it is important to avoid confusion between a blank being put out to cause a line skip and one used to fill a line. The purpose of symbolic constants is to retain mnemonic information as much as possible.

We need no trailing `else` in the `else if` sequence in this example, since the third alternative (in the middle of a line) requires no action. But we stuck in a comment to make clear what the implied alternative is. We often terminate an `else if` chain with an `else`, if only as a comment to spell out all the possible cases.

PROGRAM
    `overstrike`   replace overstrikes by multiple lines
USAGE
    `overstrike`
FUNCTION
    `overstrike` copies its input to its output, replacing lines containing backspaces by multiple lines that overstrike to print the same as the input, but contain no backspaces. It is assumed that the output is to be printed on a device that takes the first character of each line as a carriage control; a blank carriage control causes normal space before print, while a plus sign '+' suppresses space before print and hence causes the remainder of the line to overstrike the previous line.
EXAMPLE
    Using ← as a visible backspace:
        `overstrike`
        `abc←←←___`
          abc
        `+___`
BUGS
    `overstrike` is naive about vertical motions and non-printing characters. It produces one overstruck line for each sequence of backspaces.

Exercise 2-3. What are a half-dozen test inputs that exercise critical boundaries of `overstrike`? Why did we write

        `newcol := max(newcol-1, 1)`

instead of

        `newcol := newcol-1`

Give a test input and sample outputs that show the difference between the two cases. Our version of `overstrike` simulates the behavior of a terminal where backspaces are ignored once the left margin is reached. Rewrite the code to keep track of where characters should appear but print only those characters that occur in or after column one. □

Exercise 2-4. As we said earlier, if backspaces come one at a time instead of in long runs (for example, if each letter in a word is individually backspaced and underlined), `overstrike` is inefficient, in that it puts out a fresh line for each one. Modify it to put out fewer lines. □

Exercise 2-5. Another standard carriage control is a 1, which causes the next line to be printed at the top of the next page. Modify `overstrike` to look for a special FORMFEED character (ordinal value 12 in ASCII) and map each occurrence into a page

eject. You might also consider adapting `overstrike` to look for long runs of empty lines and replace them by ejects when possible, since this is often faster on line printers.
□

Exercise 2-6. Still another convention for carriage control is to use the ASCII carriage return character `RETURN` (ordinal value 13) at the *end* of a line to be overstruck, instead of the normal `NEWLINE` which causes a linespace. Alter `overstrike` to deal with this convention instead. □

Exercise 2-7. `overstrike` in series with `detab` provides a general terminal-to-printer conversion. Would it be worth combining them into a single program? Can you think of any other functions worth adding? □

2.3 Text Compression

Tabs and backspaces can be viewed as a shorthand; certainly typewriter-encoded files tend to be shorter than card images or printer lines. But they are a very special form of shorthand. What we are going to consider next is a scheme suitable for compressing and expanding any text that has runs of repeated characters. The repeated characters are not necessarily blanks; they can be anything.

We emphasize that this is not the ultimate compression scheme. A file can have redundancy that does not appear as repetitions of adjacent characters — consider a dictionary, for instance. But card images and print lines tend to have long strings of blanks, and computer output in general is often repetitious. So our naive approach should have a reasonable payoff for many of the things we have to deal with.

Certainly a file with no repetitions will end up no shorter after "compression"; in fact it might get slightly longer. All compression methods depend on having some knowledge of the structure of their input — otherwise there would be no redundant information to squeeze out. And so with every method you can always find a special case that gets worse when compressed. A file containing random characters is a good test case, since on the average it has nothing to squeeze.

One measure of the *robustness* of a compression scheme is how bad it gets when it gets bad. We don't want things to blow up in our faces when a file is ill-suited, but we don't mind if the result gets slightly longer; that is inevitable and is thus only a little bit bad. Keep these thoughts in mind as we build the program. We will come back to them later.

The scheme we use is to look continuously for a run of any character. If we get one, we want to output something that says, "This is a run of *this* character, and it is *so* long." Between runs, we simply output characters.

The important thing, as always, is to find a way of looking at the input data that makes it easy to lay out the program. The main problem is that the output is one unit delayed from the input — we can't tell if a run has started without looking at the next character of input. Our first cut is:

```
    lastc := getc(lastc)      { start with one character }
    n := 1
    while (getc(nextc) <> ENDFILE)
        if (nextc = lastc)
            n := n + 1
        else if (n > 1)
            print encoding of n lastc's
            n := 1
        else
            putc(lastc)
        lastc := nextc
put out any characters left over
```

We still have to fill in some details. The main one is the actual representation of a run. Several possibilities come to mind. Most obvious, perhaps, is to expropriate some infrequently-used character, say ~, as an "escape" or "warning" character, and then say that the sequence

    ~ *count character*

stands for *count* repetitions of *character*. We can even arrange to set a threshold THRESH such that a run of less than THRESH characters is not encoded but just copied. A natural value for THRESH is four, of course, since the representation of a run takes three characters.

The character ~ has to be carefully treated when it appears as itself in the input. Easiest is to encode it as a run of length 1, which costs two extra characters.

There is a second, more fundamental concern — how to represent counts as characters. So far we have avoided saying much about the internal or external representations of characters. So long as all characters have different codes and we only make comparisons for equality, just about any scheme will do. In fact, as we have written them, the programs in this book are independent of the internal representation of characters.

We have to face the representation problem with compress and with expand, the inverse of compress, which will be discussed in the next section. For compress, we could represent the count as a bit pattern that fits in one character-sized variable. But this means that our output is not guaranteed to be printable, and we may even get into difficulties with the run-time support with some Pascal systems. Thus, even though it is slightly wasteful, we intend to encode the count in printable characters. The simplest way to do that is to say that the letter 'A' stands for a count of one, the letter 'B' for a count of two, and so on.

Since runs are printed in two places in the program and since the operation promises to be at least slightly complicated, it seems wise to write a procedure to do the job. That leads to a compress like this:

```
{ compress -- compress standard input }
procedure compress;
const
    WARNING = TILDE;     { ~ }
var
    c, lastc : character;
    n : integer;
#include "putrep.p"
begin
    n := 1;
    lastc := getc(lastc);
    while (lastc <> ENDFILE) do begin
        if (getc(c) = ENDFILE) then begin
            if (n > 1) or (lastc = WARNING) then
                putrep(n, lastc)
            else
                putc(lastc)
        end
        else if (c = lastc) then
            n := n + 1
        else if (n > 1) or (lastc = WARNING) then begin
            putrep(n, lastc);
            n := 1
        end
        else
            putc(lastc);
        lastc := c
    end
end;

{ putrep -- put out representation of run of n 'c's }
procedure putrep (n : integer; c : character);
const
    MAXREP = 26;     { assuming 'A'..'Z' }
    THRESH = 4;
begin
    while (n >= THRESH) or ((c = WARNING) and (n > 0)) do begin
        putc(WARNING);
        putc(min(n, MAXREP) - 1 + ord('A'));
        putc(c);
        n := n - MAXREP
    end;
    for n := n downto 1 do
        putc(c)
end;
```

The standard procedure ord converts a char into an integer. The function min computes the minimum of two integers:

```
{ min -- compute minimum of two integers }
function min (x, y : integer) : integer;
begin
    if (x < y) then
        min := x
    else
        min := y
end;
```

We will also add `min` to the standard environment.

There is one potentially dangerous practice here — `putrep` contains an implicit presumption that the letters 'A' through 'Z' are contiguous, or at least that there are 26 innocuous printable characters commencing with 'A'. Pascal does not promise that the letters have contiguous values, just that they sort in increasing order. Given this weak promise, and that the most used character set, ASCII, is safe, we will ignore the danger.

To summarize:

PROGRAM
    `compress`   compress input by encoding repeated characters
USAGE
    `compress`
FUNCTION
    `compress` copies its input to its output, replacing strings of four or more identical characters by a code sequence so that the output generally contains fewer characters than the input. A run of x's is encoded as ~nx, where the count n is a character: 'A' calls for a repetition of one x, 'B' a repetition of two x's, and so on. Runs longer than 26 are broken into several shorter ones. Runs of ~'s of any length are encoded.
EXAMPLE
```
    compress
    Item     Name         Value
    Item~D Name~I Value
    1        car          ~$7,000.00
    1~G car~J ~A~$7,000.00
    <ENDFILE>
```
BUGS
    The implementation assumes 26 legal characters beginning with A.

Now let's go back to our earlier discussion of compression methods, to see what the performance of this program will be. If there are no runs longer than three characters and no occurrences of the warning character, the output exactly matches the input: there is no compression or expansion. Single or double warning characters will be encoded as three characters, a loss of one or two characters. Runs of length 4 up to 26 will be encoded as three characters, so we start saving when there are repetitions of length four or more.

Exercise 2-8. What is the worst possible input for `compress`? What is the maximum inflation for that input? What is the best possible input and amount of compression? □

Exercise 2-9. If your system permits lower case letters, modify `putrep` to encode the length with letters 'a' through 'z' as well, so that runs of length up to 52 require only three characters. How much further can you take this approach? □

Exercise 2-10. How would you take advantage of the redundancy in a dictionary (a sorted word list without definitions) to encode it in minimum space? Test your scheme by encoding the words on page 73 of your favorite dictionary. □

2.4 Text Expansion

Now that we have a way to compress text, we need a companion program to expand it once again so it can be used by other programs. We know what the input looks like: a sequence of characters with occasional runs interspersed. Our first impulse is thus to write

```
while (getc(c) <> ENDFILE)
    if (c = WARNING)
        n := count implied by next char
        c := getc(c)
        for i := 1 to n
            putc(c)
    else
        putc(c)
```

For valid input this works fine, but what happens if an ENDFILE is encountered while reading into the count value? What happens if the count is out of range? The program is unprepared for this, and so produces some random number of repetitions of the next character. It could even make additional calls to getc and putc after ENDFILE is encountered. We have not defined what either of these primitives does under such circumstances. Although they should behave intelligently, it is important to make sure the program that calls them behaves sanely no matter what the input.

We could interpose another function, to be called in place of getc, which would remember an ENDFILE and avoid further calls. With this would go a function that discards ENDFILE's, to be called in place of putc. Or we could modify getc and putc directly. Either choice would ensure correct behavior when reading or writing past end of file. It would permit less careful programming. Such a simple solution is not always possible, however, so we prefer to face the basic issue of error checking.

We could also have the program stop when it finds something wrong, since there is nothing else to do by way of wrapup. Sometimes this is the best, indeed the only, thing to do. But we try to avoid such solutions, convenient as they may at first appear, because they violate a basic principle of top-down design: every function should return to where it is called. This way, strategy is kept visible (and changeable) at the highest level of the code, and execution proceeds strictly from top to bottom.

So our working version of **expand** checks for sensible input after every call on **getc**. It decompresses if possible, but if not, it prints the input as is.

```
{ expand -- uncompress standard input }
procedure expand;
const
    WARNING = TILDE;     { ~ }
var
    c : character;
    n : integer;
begin
    while (getc(c) <> ENDFILE) do
        if (c <> WARNING) then
            putc(c)
        else if (isupper(getc(c))) then begin
            n := c - ord('A') + 1;
            if (getc(c) <> ENDFILE) then
                for n := n downto 1 do
                    putc(c)
            else begin
                putc(WARNING);
                putc(n - 1 + ord('A'))
            end
        end
        else begin
            putc(WARNING);
            if (c <> ENDFILE) then
                putc(c)
        end
end;
```

The function `isupper` tests whether a character is an upper case letter:

```
{ isupper -- true if c is upper case letter }
function isupper (c : character) : boolean;
begin
    isupper := c in [ord('A')..ord('Z')]
end;
```

The construction

```
[ord('A')..ord('Z')]
```

is a *set*, and the test "c in [...]" determines whether the value of c is one of the members of the set. We wrote `isupper` with a set-membership test because it is cleaner, but set tests are not always as fast as range tests like

```
isupper := (n >= ord('A')) and (n <= ord('Z'))
```

Furthermore, there are often limits on how large a set can be, so `isupper` and analogous routines may have to be changed. Finally, in a few character sets, notably EBCDIC, the letters do not have contiguous values. In that case you are better off to spell out the set as

```
[ord('A'), ord('B'), ord('C'),
 { and so on }
 ord('X'), ord('Y'), ord('Z')]
```

Whatever the implementation, `isupper` and some related functions are so useful that we will put them in the standard environment.

Error checking interferes with readability, no question about it, but it is necessary. With the best of languages, error checking obscures the main flow of events because the checks themselves impose a structure on the code which is different from that which expresses the basic job to be done. Programs written from the start with well-thought-out error checks, however, prove to be more reliable and live longer than those where the error checking is pasted on as an afterthought.

The manual page for `expand` follows.

PROGRAM
   expand   expand compressed input
USAGE
   expand
FUNCTION
   expand copies its input, which has presumably been encoded by compress, to its output,
   replacing code sequences ~nc by the repeated characters they stand for so that the text output exactly matches that which was originally encoded. The occurrence of the warning character ~ in the input means that the next character is a repetition count; 'A' calls for one
   instance of the following character, 'B' calls for two, and so on up to 'z.'
EXAMPLE
   ```
   expand
   Item~D Name~I Value
   Item      Name          Value
   1~G car~J ~A-$7,000.00
      1         car          -$7,000.00
   <ENDFILE>
   ```

Exercise 2-11. Delete the error checking from `expand`. How much smaller is it? Does it run any faster? □

Exercise 2-12. Define what `getc` and `putc` should do on `ENDFILE`, so as to simplify routines that call them. Rewrite `expand` to take advantage of this improvement. □

Exercise 2-13. What happens if you send an arbitrary (uncompressed) file to the first version of `expand`? To the final version? What happens if one character gets dropped from a valid compressed file? How long does `expand` take to resynchronize in the worst case? □

Exercise 2-14. Prove that any compression scheme that is reversible, accepts any input, and makes some files smaller must also make some files longer. □

2.5 Command Arguments

If you think back to the programs detab and entab, you will recall that they use the same convention, a tab every four columns. It would be nice, however, if there were an easy way to pass a list of tab settings as arguments to either of these programs at the time the program is run, so the normal settings could be temporarily overridden. Most operating systems make some provision for a program to access the command line or control card that invoked it, so it can pick up options, parameters or other information. We will code in terms of a primitive called getarg, which does whatever is needed to make that argument information available to a program. Most of the programs we present will benefit from having some optional arguments. For a few, arguments are mandatory.

Our specific design for getarg is the following. (Manual pages and sample implementations for all primitives are in the appendix.)

```
function getarg(n : integer; var charstr : string;
        maxsize : integer) : boolean;
```

copies the characters of the nth argument into the character string charstr. (We will describe the type string in a moment.) maxsize specifies the maximum number of characters that we are prepared to deal with; getarg will truncate the argument if necessary to fit it into the space provided. getarg returns true if the nth argument exists and false otherwise.

We haven't really said what kind of object the "string" parameter of getarg is. This raises the thorny problem of how to handle character strings in Pascal. The primary mechanism for storing a sequence of characters is the array. But in standard Pascal (which we intend to stick to), two arrays have the same type only if they have the same element type, and *the same limits on their subscripts*. This is a grave defect of Pascal. We want to be able to write general-purpose routines to handle character strings of widely different sizes, but it just isn't legal: we would need a different routine for each different size. The best we can do is to make *all* strings the same size. This leads to a definition of a string like:

```
type
     string = array [1..MAXSTR] of character;
```

Of course if MAXSTR is too large, we waste space on short strings; if it is too small, we can't handle long strings.

Many versions of Pascal, recognizing the difficulty of using the pure language, provide a special predefined "string" data type that is an array of char that can have any size; objects of this type can be mixed freely. Regrettably, every system seems to handle this extension differently from every other. Furthermore, we want to use our extended type character rather than char. So we will stick to the standard language, plus our portable environment, and pay the price of wasted storage.

Since in general the string stored in a variable of type string will be shorter than MAXSTR, we also need a way to keep track of how big the string is. Two acceptable possibilities spring to mind. One is to make a string a record, with a length and an array for the actual characters:

```
type string =
    record
        length : 0..MAXSTR;
        chars : array [1..MAXSTR] of character
    end;
```

The ith character of such a string s is s.chars[i], and the length is just s.length.

The other organization is to mark the *end* of the array by some special value, one that is not any valid character. In that case, the ith character is just s[i], but the length has to be computed.

Each of these organizations has good and bad points (which you should think about for yourself); there is no "right answer." We have decided to use the mark-at-the-end representation. Every character string in our programs contains as its last element a special marker, which we call ENDSTR. A string of one character has array[1] set to the character and array[2] to an ENDSTR; an empty or *null* string has array[1] an ENDSTR.

Thus one final thing that getarg must do is to ensure that the string it returns is properly terminated with an ENDSTR, and this must fit within the limits of maxsize characters.

To illustrate getarg, here is its most simple use, in a program echo that just echoes its arguments to its output:

PROGRAM
    echo   echo arguments to output
USAGE
    echo [argument ...]
FUNCTION
    echo copies its command line arguments to its output as a line of text with one space between each argument. If there are no arguments, no output is produced.
EXAMPLE
    To see if your system is alive:
        echo hello world!
        hello world!

We use square brackets in manual pages to indicate optional arguments, and ellipses ... for arbitrary repetition.

The code for echo is

```
{ echo -- echo command line arguments to output }
procedure echo;
var
    i, j : integer;
    argstr : string;
begin
    i := 1;
    while (getarg(i, argstr, MAXSTR)) do begin
        if (i > 1) then
            putc(BLANK);
        for j := 1 to length(argstr) do
            putc(argstr[j]);
        i := i + 1
    end;
    if (i > 1) then
        putc(NEWLINE)
end;
```

The function length returns the number of characters in a string, excluding
the ENDSTR that terminates it:

```
{ length -- compute length of string }
function length (var s : string) : integer;
var
    n : integer;
begin
    n := 1;
    while (s[n] <> ENDSTR) do
        n := n + 1;
    length := n - 1
end;
```

Different systems have very different conventions for how arguments are
specified for programs. Some simply separate arguments by blanks or tabs,
which is our preference; others use slashes, commas, and/or parentheses as argument separators. We have written our examples as if blanks were the separators; to provide for an argument with imbedded blanks or tabs, we use optional
quotes, which can be stripped off by getarg if no one else does.

A primitive like getarg helps us to cope with these disparate environments.
Even though each system will have its own conventions about how arguments
are handled, programs that use getarg will work without change once a local
version is written.

Exercise 2-15. A useful companion for getarg is nargs, a function that returns the
number of arguments. nargs should be a primitive just as getarg is, but if it is not,
how would you write it? Rewrite echo using nargs. □

Exercise 2-16. Modify detab and entab to accept a list of tab stops as arguments, so
users can call the program with commands like

```
detab 9 17 25 33 41
entab 10 16 33 73
```

Of course the code that interprets these arguments and fills the `tabs` array should be careful not to overfill the array. Both programs should do something intelligent and useful if there are no arguments. (Later on in this chapter there is a function `ctoi` for converting character strings to integers.) □

Exercise 2-17. Extend `entab` and `detab` to accept shorthand for tab stops, e.g.,

```
entab m +n
```

to mean tab stops every n columns, starting at column m. What is a sensible behavior if m is specified and n is not? □

Exercise 2-18. Another possible representation for character strings is a linked list in which each character (or perhaps group of characters) also has a pointer to the next. What are some of the strengths and weaknesses of such a representation? □

2.6 Character Transliteration

One class of filters *transliterates* certain characters on their way through, passing all other characters through unmodified. We would like to have a program `translit` so that we can write

```
translit x y
```

and have all occurrences of `x` in the standard input be replaced by `y` on the standard output. Multiple translations are also handy:

```
translit xyz XYZ
```

would change all lower case `x`, `y` and `z` to the corresponding upper case letter. It would be nice to have shorthand for alphabets, so

```
translit a-z A-Z
```

would translate all lower case letters to upper case, and

```
translit a-z b-za
```

would produce a Caesar cipher. Even good typists prefer

```
translit A-Z a-z
```

to

```
translit ABCDEFGHIJKLMNOPQRSTUVWXYZ abcdefghijklmnopqrstuvwxyz
```

Once the arguments have been expanded to eliminate any shorthand, the translation loop is straightforward:

```
while (getc(c) <> ENDFILE)
    i := index(fromset, c)
    if (i > 0)   { found a match }
        putc(toset[i])
    else          { no match }
        putc(c)
```

fromset holds the set of characters to be translated and toset the corresponding translations. index returns the index of the character in fromset that matches c, or zero if c isn't in fromset:

```
{ index -- find position of character c in string s }
function index (var s : string; c : character) : integer;
var
    i : integer;
begin
    i := 1;
    while (s[i] <> c) and (s[i] <> ENDSTR) do
        i := i + 1;
    if (s[i] = ENDSTR) then
        index := 0
    else
        index := i
end;
```

There are times when we would like to translate a whole class of characters into just one character, and even to squash runs of that translation into just one instance. For example, translating blanks, tabs, and newlines into newlines and then squashing multiple newlines leaves each of the words in a document on a separate line, ready for further processing. Or we might want to convert all alphabetic symbols in a text into a's and all numbers into n's. We can specify this squashing operation by giving a second argument that is shorter than the first:

```
translit a-zA-Z a
translit 0-9 n
```

The implication is that the last character in the to argument is to be replicated as often as necessary to make it as long as the from argument, and that this replicated character should never appear twice in succession in the output.

The main processing for translit then becomes:

```
lastto := length(toset)
squash := (length(fromset) > lastto);
repeat
    i := index(fromset, getc(c))
    if (squash and i >= lastto) { squash }
        putc(toset[lastto])
        repeat
            i := index(fromset, getc(c))
        until (i < lastto)
    if (c <> ENDFILE)
        if (i > 0)          { translate }
            putc(toset[i])
        else                { copy }
            putc(c)
until (c = ENDFILE)
```

Note that the while has become a repeat-until, since there may be some work to do now even when an ENDFILE is read. We use length to decide how to set squash, which indicates whether or not squashing is to take place.

translit leaves open the possibility that some characters can be translated while others are squashed, not so much because it is likely to be a heavily used option but so that the program behaves in a sane and predictable fashion no matter what the arguments. Esoteric cases should do something reasonable.

Only characters corresponding to the last translation character (or beyond) are subject to squashing, and squashing is operative only if toset is shorter than fromset.

But there is a bug: if toset is missing or empty, containing only an ENDSTR, any translation will reference toset[0]. (You might want to verify this.) We could give an error message when the second argument of translit is empty, but we could also take this condition as a request to *delete* all occurrences of characters in the first string, since that is a useful and sensible interpretation. The changes to implement this are straightforward if we keep firmly in mind that the condition lastto=0 always calls for the matched character to be deleted. The matched character is one whose index is greater than zero.

One final capability is worth adding: sometimes we would like to be able to translate and compress *all but* a set of characters. For instance

```
translit ^a-z -
```

would replace strings of non-letters with a dash (minus). The leading ^ in the fromset string reads as a "not." And

```
translit ^a-z
```

would delete all but lower case letters.

The addition is once again easy because of the way the program is partitioned into modules. We need only introduce a flag allbut, set to true when we wish to deal with *all but* a specified set of characters, and a new function `xindex` that interfaces between `index` and the rest of the program.

```
{ xindex -- conditionally invert value from index }
function xindex (var inset : string; c : character;
        allbut : boolean; lastto : integer) : integer;
begin
    if (c = ENDFILE) then
        xindex := 0
    else if (not allbut) then
        xindex := index(inset, c)
    else if (index(inset, c) > 0) then
        xindex := 0
    else
        xindex := lastto + 1
end;
```

When `allbut` is `false`, `xindex` returns the value returned by `index`. When `allbut` is `true`, however, `xindex` tells a lie: if `index` says the character was found, `xindex` says it wasn't; if `index` says it wasn't found, `xindex` says it was. Furthermore, we presume that the set of *all but* a few characters is so huge that it only makes sense to map them all into one character (or delete them), so if `allbut` is `true`, `xindex` returns an index that is guaranteed to be squashed if the character is in the set, zero if it is not, or the normal result of `index` if `allbut` is `false`. `xindex` is also careful never to report `ENDFILE` as a matched character. Got that?

With this organization, `index` remains simple, and so does the program that uses it through `xindex`. Imagine what the logic would be like if the equivalent decisions were scattered throughout the main routine instead of localized in `xindex`.

By the way, we could have written `xindex` as

```
xindex := index(inset, c);
if (c = ENDFILE) or (allbut and (xindex > 0)) then
    xindex = 0
else if (allbut) and (xindex = 0) then
    xindex := lastto + 1
```

This is shorter but less clear. Logical decisions that intermix and's and or's, or that require parentheses, seem to be hard to grasp, so we avoid them. The version we used shows clearly that exactly one of four cases is to be chosen. When in doubt, try the "telephone test" — if you can understand a logical expression when it's read aloud, then it is acceptably clear. Otherwise, it should be rewritten.

All that remains is to add the argument-interpreting code and we have a powerful character translator:

```
{ translit -- map characters }
procedure translit;
const
    NEGATE = CARET; { ^ }
var
    arg, fromset, toset : string;
    c : character;
    i, lastto : 0..MAXSTR;
    allbut, squash : boolean;
#include "makeset.p"
#include "xindex.p"
begin
    if (not getarg(1, arg, MAXSTR)) then
        error('usage: translit from to');
    allbut := (arg[1] = NEGATE);
    if (allbut) then
        i := 2
    else
        i := 1;
    if (not makeset(arg, i, fromset, MAXSTR)) then
        error('translit: "from" set too large');
    if (not getarg(2, arg, MAXSTR)) then
        toset[1] := ENDSTR
    else if (not makeset(arg, 1, toset, MAXSTR)) then
        error('translit: "to" set too large')
    else if (length(fromset) < length(toset)) then
        error('translit: "from" shorter than "to"');

    lastto := length(toset);
    squash := (length(fromset) > lastto) or (allbut);
    repeat
        i := xindex(fromset, getc(c), allbut, lastto);
        if (squash) and (i>=lastto) and (lastto>0) then begin
            putc(toset[lastto]);
            repeat
                i := xindex(fromset, getc(c), allbut, lastto)
            until (i < lastto)
        end;
        if (c <> ENDFILE) then begin
            if (i > 0) and (lastto > 0) then    { translate }
                putc(toset[i])
            else if (i = 0) then    { copy }
                putc(c)
            { else delete }
        end
    until (c = ENDFILE)
end;
```

The procedure error is another primitive, of a special kind. It prints the message and then causes the program to terminate. We will use it henceforth to report fatal errors in programs.

error cannot be written in standard Pascal, since there is no way to declare an argument that is a variable-length packed array of char's, i.e., a literal string, nor is there an official way to get early termination of a program. We will discuss ways of implementing error in Chapter 8; for now you can treat it as a primitive that provides a nicer way of writing diagnostics than

```
begin
    writeln('the sky has fallen');
    goto 9999    { branch to end of program }
end
```

Notice, by the way, that the message printed out when there are no arguments is not just "no arguments" or "the sky has fallen." Instead, a prompt is given reminding the user how to use the program properly. Better to tell people concisely how to do things right than tell them only that they did something wrong. The error message contains the name of the program too, so that when it appears out of nowhere, the user knows who said it.

Other than that, we wrote translit so that it produces few error messages. An unusual argument is given some reasonable interpretation whenever possible, and a harmless interpretation otherwise. For a general-purpose tool, this is a good design principle. Otherwise, we might inadvertently head off a useful application we didn't think of at the start. It also minimizes the confusion introduced by a welter of error checks.

The function makeset creates the from and to sets, by calling dodash and addstr.

```
{ makeset -- make set from inset[k] in outset }
function makeset (var inset : string; k : integer;
        var outset : string; maxset : integer) : boolean;
var
    j : integer;
#include "dodash.p"
begin
    j := 1;
    dodash(ENDSTR, inset, k, outset, j, maxset);
    makeset := addstr(ENDSTR, outset, j, maxset)
end;
```

addstr adds a character at a time to a specified position of an array and increments the index. It also checks that there's enough room to do so. We will use this function extensively in later programs, so we will add it to our standard context for all programs.

```
    { addstr -- put c in outset[j] if it fits, increment j }
    function addstr(c : character; var outset : string;
            var j : integer; maxset : integer) : boolean;
    begin
        if (j > maxset) then
            addstr := false
        else begin
            outset[j] := c;
            j := j + 1;
            addstr := true
        end
    end;
```

   translit provides shorthand for consecutive lower case letters, upper case
letters and digits. dodash does all the work of building a translation set,
expanding shorthand as necessary, with the help of addstr, esc and index.
We wrote dodash in a general fashion, looking for an arbitrary delimiter and
returning updated indices, because it will be used in later dealings with sets of
characters.

```
    { dodash - expand set at src[i] into dest[j], stop at delim }
    procedure dodash (delim : character; var src : string;
            var i : integer; var dest : string;
            var j : integer; maxset : integer);
    var
        k : integer;
        junk : boolean;
    begin
        while (src[i] <> delim) and (src[i] <> ENDSTR) do begin
            if (src[i] = ESCAPE) then
                junk := addstr(esc(src, i), dest, j, maxset)
            else if (src[i] <> DASH) then
                junk := addstr(src[i], dest, j, maxset)
            else if (j <= 1) or (src[i+1] = ENDSTR) then
                junk := addstr(DASH,dest,j,maxset) { literal - }
            else if (isalphanum(src[i-1]))
              and (isalphanum(src[i+1]))
              and (src[i-1] <= src[i+1]) then begin
                for k := src[i-1]+1 to src[i+1] do
                    junk := addstr(k, dest, j, maxset);
                i := i + 1
            end
            else
                junk := addstr(DASH, dest, j, maxset);
            i := i + 1
        end
    end;
```

Most of the code in dodash is a multi-way branch. If the character under consideration is escaped or not a dash, it is added to the set immediately, as is a

dash that occurs as first or last character, or not preceded by a letter or digit. Only if a dash appears between letters or digits that could represent shorthand is it expanded.

dodash introduces a new boolean function called isalphanum, which returns true if its argument is a letter or number, and false otherwise. One implementation parallels isupper:

```
{ isalphanum -- true if c is letter or digit }
function isalphanum (c : character) : boolean;
begin
    isalphanum := c in
        [ord('a')..ord('z'),
         ord('A')..ord('Z'),
         ord('0')..ord('9')]
end;
```

By the way, this set has 62 elements. If your Pascal system requires sets to be smaller, you can split isalphanum into separate range tests on letters and digits; it may even run faster. You should also think about the issues of character set mentioned in the discussion of isupper a few pages ago.

The other new thing in dodash is the set of calls of the form

```
junk := addstr(...)
```

Since dodash has no interest in the value returned by addstr (final checking is done by makeset), we have to toss it away. We will always assign unwanted function values to junk to show that they are explicitly discarded.

translit also provides a convention for writing tabs and newlines so that they are visible and cause a minimum of grief for any program that must inspect the arguments. We use the at-sign @ as an *escape character*: whatever character follows the escape character is in some way special. In particular, we define @t to be a tab and @n to be a newline, so we can write:

```
translit " @t@n" @n
```

to change each run of blanks, tabs, and newlines to just one newline and thus leave one word per line. (Note the use of quotes, which we mentioned earlier, to include a blank in the first argument string.) Other special codes can be added easily, if need be. The escape character also turns off the special meaning of any character following, including blanks and quotes and the escape itself, so that special characters can be used literally. The example above could also be written

```
translit @ @t@n @n
```

provided getarg also knows about escapes.

The escape convention provides a clean and uniform mechanism for altering the meaning of special characters. Checking for an escape, and returning the appropriate character and the proper index is done by esc:

```
    { esc -- map s[i] into escaped character, increment i }
    function esc (var s : string; var i : integer) : character;
    begin
        if (s[i] <> ESCAPE) then
            esc := s[i]
        else if (s[i+1] = ENDSTR) then   { @ not special at end }
            esc := ESCAPE
        else begin
            i := i + 1;
            if (s[i] = ord('n')) then
                esc := NEWLINE
            else if (s[i] = ord('t')) then
                esc := TAB
            else
                esc := s[i]
        end
    end;
```

Like **xindex**, `esc` conceals complexity in a simple interface, instead of spreading decisions throughout the code. We will add `esc` to the standard environment.

translit is not an easy program to understand, because it does many things, yet the functions are worth combining because they all address similar problems. You learn the most useful formats, like

```
    translit A-Z a-z
```

for case conversion, and study the formation rules only when you encounter a new application. The program itself is not complicated, however, because it was constructed in a modular fashion beginning with the simplest applications. The added complexity is confined to separate new modules and does not clutter up the original structure.

Here is where the idea of a manual page really pays off. All the features we accumulated along the way to a final version of **translit** can now be neatly summarized. (The brackets [...] in the USAGE section indicate optional material.)

PROGRAM
    `translit`   transliterate characters
USAGE
    `translit [^]src [dest]`
FUNCTION
    `translit` maps its input, on a character by character basis, and writes the translated version to its output. In the simplest case, each character in the argument `src` is translated to the corresponding character in the argument `dest`; all other characters are copied as is. Both `src` and `dest` may contain substrings of the form *c1-c2* as shorthand for all of the characters in the range *c1..c2*. *c1* and *c2* must both be digits, or both be letters of the same case.

    If `dest` is absent, all characters represented by `src` are deleted. Otherwise, if `dest` is shorter than `src`, all characters in `src` that would map to or beyond the last character in `dest` are mapped to the last character in `dest`; moreover adjacent instances of such characters in the input are represented in the output by a single instance of the last character in `dest`. Thus
        `translit 0-9 9`
    converts each string of digits to the single digit 9.

    Finally, if `src` is preceded by a ^, then *all but* the characters represented by `src` are taken as the source string; i.e., they are all deleted if `dest` is absent, or they are all collapsed if the last character in `dest` is present.
EXAMPLE
    To convert upper case to lower:
        `translit A-Z a-z`
    To discard punctuation and isolate words by spaces on each line:
        `translit ^a-zA-Z@n " "`
        `This is a simple-minded test, i.e., a test of translit.`
        This is a simple minded test i e a test of translit

What determines the running time of `translit`? Somewhat unexpectedly, it is *not* all input and output. `index`, deciding whether an input character is in `fromset`, is actually just as important. In our case, translating the `translit` program itself into upper case, took 9 seconds for 13,400 characters (608 lines). `index` took 50.2 percent of that time.

Naturally, input and output are not free: `getc` itself took 10.7 percent, and lower-level routines that it calls took 3.4 percent. `putc` and its subordinates took 20.8 percent. Handling characters one at a time with `getc` and `putc` is not nearly as bad as might be thought. Most of the rest was in `xindex` (5.4 percent) and `translit` (7.2 percent).

Clearly, `index` is the routine to speed up, both because of the fraction of the time it consumes and because its time varies with both the number of input characters and the size of `fromset`. To answer the obvious question raised by this experiment, we did not use sets for `fromset` and `toset` because sets that are large enough are not always available. The mapping array suggested in one of the following exercises should make `translit` run faster, but it does not mesh well with some other uses we have planned for `dodash` in Chapters 5 and 6.

Exercise 2-19. Modify `translit` so that `fromset` and `toset` are true Pascal sets, not arrays (assuming that sets this large are permitted). Measure the change in run time. □

Exercise 2-20. Rewrite `translit` to use a character map, i.e.,

```
var map : array [character] of character;
```

which is initialized to map all characters into themselves, then modified once, at the outset, to provide all translations requested. Compare its run time to the previous version. □

Exercise 2-21. Describe the actions performed by the following commands.

```
translit a-b-d abcd
translit a-c xyz
translit -ac xyz
translit @@
translit ^^ x
translit @^ x
translit @^^ x
```

How would you convert runs of blanks into single occurrences? □

Exercise 2-22. One purpose of the escape mechanism is to input characters that are difficult to type, or hard to read, or that have special meaning. Extend `esc` to recognize s for space, b for backspace, and perhaps a string of 2 or 3 octal or hexadecimal digits to represent an arbitrary character-sized bit pattern. Other useful control characters you might include are f for formfeed, v for vertical tab, and r for carriage return. □

2.7 Numbers

`translit` is used frequently to filter files before counting things in them, as with `charcount` introduced in the previous chapter. Since we were primarily concerned then with introducing Pascal and simple tools, we postponed the description of `putdec`, the procedure that printed the final count. Before going any further, here it is.

`putdec(n, w)` puts out the number n as a string of at least w characters, including a sign if n is negative. If fewer than w characters are needed, blanks are inserted to the left to make up the count; if more than w are needed, more are provided. It is this feature that makes `putdec` more useful than conventional output options in most languages; it is generally equivalent to the Pascal `write(n:w)`, except that it works through our standard interface.

```
{ putdec -- put decimal integer n in field width >= w }
procedure putdec (n, w : integer);
var
    i, nd : integer;
    s : string;
begin
    nd := itoc(n, s, 1);
    for i := nd to w do
        putc(BLANK);
    for i := 1 to nd-1 do
        putc(s[i])
end;
```

putdec in turn calls on itoc to do the conversion. itoc converts an integer to characters in an array provided by the caller, and returns the index of the ENDSTR that terminates the resulting string.

```
{ itoc - convert integer n to char string in s[i]... }
function itoc (n : integer; var s : string; i : integer)
        : integer;  { returns end of s }
begin
    if (n < 0) then begin
        s[i] := ord('-');
        itoc := itoc(-n, s, i+1)
    end
    else begin
        if (n >= 10) then
            i := itoc(n div 10, s, i);
        s[i] := n mod 10 + ord('0');
        s[i+1] := ENDSTR;
        itoc := i + 1
    end
end;
```

This is a recursive routine that, on each invocation, if necessary calls itself to print all but the last digit, then adds the last digit to the end.

The complement of itoc is of course ctoi, a routine for converting a character string to an integer. A useful design is this: the call

```
n := ctoi(c, i)
```

starts looking at position i of c. Leading blanks and tabs are ignored; an optional sign is permitted; any subsequent digits are converted to the correct numeric value. The first non-digit seen terminates the scan; upon return i points to this position and n is the value of the integer. Note that, unlike integer conversions in the standard Pascal read, ctoi does not cause an error condition when an unexpected character is encountered, so the program can stay in control. We will use ctoi regularly throughout the book, so we have added it (and itoc and putdec) to the standard environment.

```
{ ctoi -- convert string at s[i] to integer, increment i }
function ctoi (var s : string; var i : integer) : integer;
var
    n, sign : integer;
begin
    while (s[i] = BLANK) or (s[i] = TAB) do
        i := i + 1;
    if (s[i] = MINUS) then
        sign := -1
    else
        sign := 1;
    if (s[i] = PLUS) or (s[i] = MINUS) then
        i := i + 1;
    n := 0;
    while (isdigit(s[i])) do begin
        n := 10 * n + s[i] - ord('0');
        i := i + 1
    end;
    ctoi := sign * n
end;
```

Of course isdigit is just like isupper and isalphanum:

```
{ isdigit -- true if c is a digit }
function isdigit (c : character) : boolean;
begin
    isdigit := c in [ord('0')..ord('9')]
end;
```

Now for the payoff. We can use charcount in series with translit to provide all sorts of useful information. Let's invent some job control language: we say that the notation ¦ indicates a series connection of two programs.

```
translit ^@n ¦ charcount
```

means "take the output produced by translit and feed it as input to charcount." We'll call this construction a *pipeline*. Whether a pipeline is a direct connection between simultaneously executing processes, or just a prescription for what intermediate temporary files to write and read, is not relevant for most applications. Our concern rests with what we can *do* with such pipelines.

The example we just gave, for instance, deletes everything but the newlines in a file, then counts them up. We have a line counting program directly equivalent to linecount. Counting words is only a little harder:

```
translit " @t@n" @n ¦ translit ^@n ¦ charcount
```

First we put one word per line by compressing white space, then count lines as before. We can even count all the decimal digit strings in a program:

```
translit 0-9 9 | translit ^9 | charcount
```

This converts each string of digits into a single 9, deletes all other characters, then counts the 9's.

Writing a program to do what this last pipeline does is a nuisance; it is not likely that you would want to stockpile such an odd assortment of gadgets against the likelihood of eventually having a need for them. But having a single tool as powerful as `translit` makes sense. You can use it alone or in conjunction with other filters like `charcount` to perform a host of variations. This is what tool building is all about.

Exercise 2-23. Many computers store integers in *two's complement* notation, which has one more negative number than it has positive numbers. Pascal excludes this extra negative number, but it frequently crops up anyway. Other representations have as many negative numbers as positive numbers but also have two representations of zero. Rewrite `putdec` to handle two's complement arithmetic properly. (Do you know where the current version fails?) □

Exercise 2-24. Write `ctof`, which converts a character string to a floating point number (type `real` in Pascal); it should recognize an optional sign, an optional decimal point, and scientific notation for an exponent, as in

```
-1.23E-4
```

How about `ftoc` for floating point output conversion? □

Exercise 2-25. Design and implement a filter `calc` to simulate a pocket calculator. `calc` should deal with at least +, -, and =, so an expression like

```
1 + 2 - 3 =
```

can be evaluated. Refinements include more operators, parentheses, memory, and the like. (See Chapter 8 for the rudiments of expression evaluation.) How would you modify `calc` to handle numbers too large to fit in one machine word? □

Exercise 2-26. Write a filter `tail` that produces only the last n lines of its input as output, where n is an optional argument. That is,

```
program | tail 10
```

prints the last ten lines produced by `program`. Of course there is a limit on how large n can be in a practical implementation. If no value of n is specified, what is a reasonable default? □

Exercise 2-27. There are many useful variations on `tail`. You might try an option to print the tail in reverse order; one to start printing at line n; one to change the units to characters instead of lines. You could also write `head`, which prints the first so many lines or characters of its input. □

Exercise 2-28. Write a filter `screen` that will print its input in small chunks on the screen of a terminal, waiting after each page for a signal before proceeding. Adapt code from `tail` to permits users to move backward in the input as well as forward. □

Exercise 2-29. Write a program that will print every character in a file whether or not it is a graphic. The notation @*nnn* is a convenient way to present the octal or hexadecimal value of non-graphics. □

Exercise 2-30. Write a program to take arbitrary bit patterns and interpret them as octal or hexadecimal numbers, as characters, and perhaps as machine instructions, as appropriate for your particular computer, and as specified by various optional arguments. Implement it as a filter. How much of it has to be machine-dependent? □

2.8 Summary

The filters presented in this chapter are diverse, but most share an important feature. Each encourages, in its own way, a standard representation for text to be passed between programs or to be stored in files for later use. By pushing information about particular devices as far out to the edges of a system as possible, we expand the range of programs that can freely cooperate. And by writing filters to interface these devices to standard format files, we isolate and contain device-dependent information. That way, radical changes can be made in the peripherals attached to a machine without affecting more than a module or two. It also means that you can have considerable assurance that each new device can be put to use with little reprogramming. This is an important consideration in planning for painless growth.

`translit` is an even more general tool. Having it around, you can ignore many of the little character-set dependencies that so often haunt a computer center and make it difficult to combine software packages. You can use `translit` to take up the slack between two programs that don't quite cooperate, and thus avoid the messy problem of recoding one (or both). And besides, it's useful all by itself.

Once you learn that you can isolate and adapt by introducing filters, you begin to think more freely in terms of combining existing programs instead of writing new ones. You overcome much of the temptation to build a whole new package; instead you adapt pieces that already exist. You become, in short, more of a tool user.

Bibliographic Notes

The idea of pipelines and filters — a uniform mechanism for connecting the input of one program to the output of another — was conceived by M. D. McIlroy. It was anticipated in a somewhat less general way in the "communication files" of the Dartmouth Time-sharing System. Pipelines have an especially clean implementation in the Unix operating system developed at Bell Labs by K. L. Thompson and D. M. Ritchie. Here the programs in the pipeline run concurrently, with sufficient interlocks to ensure that the receiving program never reads information that isn't there, and that the sending program never creates too much information before the receiver has read some. The vertical bar is the Unix syntax for a pipeline, and is due to Thompson. See "The Unix time-sharing system," *Communications of the ACM,* July, 1974, or "The Unix Programming Environment," by B. W. Kernighan and J. R. Mashey, *Software*

Practice and Experience, January, 1979.

Data compression techniques are not often covered in basic textbooks. One exception is a discussion of Huffman encoding in *Data Structures Using Pascal*, by A. M. Tenenbaum and M. J. Augenstein (Prentice-Hall, 1981).

Timing data for `translit`, and for the other programs as well, was obtained on a DEC VAX 11/780 using profiling code from W. N. Joy of the University of California at Berkeley.

Up to this point we have talked about programs that read one input and write one output, without really worrying about how to get the input and output where we want them. Although many useful programs need only one input and one output, this is hardly adequate in general; and even for them, some provision must be made for redirecting input or output, or the programs have very limited utility. In this chapter we will discuss programs that have more complicated interactions with their environment — reading or writing more than one file, and creating and deleting files as they run. These programs are mainly intended for an operating system that provides some kind of permanent file system where information can be kept for extended periods on secondary storage and can be easily accessed by running programs.

Sadly, operations like these are hard even to talk about, let alone program. Each operating system has its own jargon for describing system actions. Each operating system has its own capabilities and limitations. Some of the things we want to do can't be done easily on some operating systems. The Pascal standard itself simply does not address most of the serious issues in communicating with an operating system.

As we did in the previous chapters, we will try to avoid these difficulties by organizing our discussion and programs around *primitives* — operations like getc, putc, and getarg, which are conceptually simple, each performing a well-defined task. The mechanics of how a primitive is accomplished will vary from system to system, but the basic functions will be easy to understand, and easy to implement, on most systems, in terms of existing functions. Defining and using primitive functions to localize operating system dependencies is a crucial form of modularization. It is the only way to write portable software for real systems.

3.1 File Comparison

One tool that illustrates a more complicated relationship with the operating system is compare, a program that compares two files and lists the places where they differ. compare has to access two input files to do its job.

compare is used for comparing the output of one program with another, for

63

example, or for comparing two versions of a text. It mechanizes a task all too often done manually.

The design of compare depends on what is to be compared. We will write a version that compares two text files; variations are left as exercises. For text the natural unit of comparison is the line — if two lines differ in length, we can resynchronize at the next line. Of course a missing line in one of the files will destroy synchronization for the rest of the input, so this is not the best comparison imaginable, but it is a beginning. In outline the program is

```
repeat
    get a line from file 1
    get a line from file 2
    if (not ENDFILE on either one)
        if (line1 <> line2)
            print line number and offending lines
until (ENDFILE on either file)
if (only one file is ended)
    print message about which file terminated early
```

First we check the general flow of control by examining some critical boundary cases. As long as the two files are identical, no output will be produced; if they end together, all is well, even if both are empty. If one file is a prefix of the other, then a message to that effect is printed. Finally, if the files differ anywhere in some line, the differing lines will be printed.

Now we can begin to fill in details. Comparing two lines is a self-contained task that should be isolated in a separate routine. The function equal compares two strings; it returns true if they are identical, false if they differ. Each string must of course be terminated by an ENDSTR. We compare strings terminated by ENDSTR, not lines terminated by NEWLINE, because the more general routine costs nothing extra, yet is much more likely to be useful in other programs.

```
{ equal -- test two strings for equality }
function equal (var str1, str2 : string) : boolean;
var
    i : integer;
begin
    i := 1;
    while (str1[i] = str2[i]) and (str1[i] <> ENDSTR) do
        i := i + 1;
    equal := (str1[i] = str2[i])
end;
```

The next problem, and the one which is the principal subject of this chapter, is how to connect the program to its sources of input — how to arrange for the operations

```
get a line from file 1
get a line from file 2
```

Up to now, we have assumed that a program has some default standard input and standard output connected to it when it runs, which `getc` and `putc` use implicitly. These are often the user's terminal keyboard and printer in an interactive environment, or a card reader and line printer in a batch system. Almost all operating systems provide some way to change these default assignments, and to add other inputs and outputs. For example, most batch systems have a control card that says (in effect)

```
Connect Pascal internal file f to external file X
```

so that I/O statements like

```
read(f, ...)
```

and

```
write(f, ...)
```

will operate on X. Control card syntax varies wildly from system to system, but the function is always available. Interactive systems typically perform the same function on the command line, the line you type to invoke the program and specify its arguments as well.

In Pascal, the internal file names are often specified in the `program` line, as in

```
program outer (input, output, file1, file2);
```

perhaps with some further command, outside the program proper, needed to relate these to external files.

Thus a rudimentary version of `compare` could read from two input streams, with internal names by convention `file1` and `file2`, and require the *user* to connect the right external files to these internal names by control card or command. Such a `compare` would not take any explicit action to connect itself to its sources — someone else would have to do the work. Here is a version of `compare` that is intentionally vague about how it gets connected; we will deal with that issue once the basic comparison machinery is presented:

```
{ compare (simple version) -- compare two files for equality }
procedure compare;
var
    line1, line2 : string;
    lineno : integer;
    f1, f2 : boolean;
#include "diffmsg.p"
begin
    lineno := 0;
    repeat
        lineno := lineno + 1;
        f1 := getline(line1, infile1, MAXSTR);
        f2 := getline(line2, infile2, MAXSTR);
        if (f1 and f2) then
            if (not equal(line1, line2)) then
                diffmsg(lineno, line1, line2)
    until (f1 = false) or (f2 = false);
    if (f2 and not f1) then
        message('compare: end of file on file1')
    else if (f1 and not f2) then
        message('compare: end of file on file2')
end;
```

`message` is a general-purpose message printer, identical to `error` in Chapter 2, except that it returns after printing, instead of stopping. It presents the same implementation problems as `error`, and hence will be discussed in detail later on. Notice that `compare` produces no message if the files are identical. Generally a program should say nothing unless and until it has something to say.

If there are any discrepancies between the two files, `diffmsg` prints the line number and the differing lines:

```
{ diffmsg -- print line numbers and differing lines }
procedure diffmsg (n : integer; var line1, line2 : string);
begin
    putdec(n, 1);
    putc(COLON);
    putc(NEWLINE);
    putstr(line1, STDOUT);
    putstr(line2, STDOUT)
end;
```

The function call

```
getline(line, infile, MAXSTR)
```

copies the next line from the file with the "internal name" `infile` into the character string `line`. Copying ends either when a NEWLINE is encountered or when the string gets to MAXSTR characters, including the terminating ENDSTR, which will always be provided. `getline` returns `true` as long as there is data, and `false` when end of file is encountered. Like `getc`, `getline` maps characters into their internal representation as necessary.

It is clear that `getline` can be written in terms of `getc` (try it), but for the sake of efficiency it may well be the lower level primitive that `getc` calls! Like certain groups of elementary particles in physics, it is hard to say which is fundamental and which is derived from the other. We will call both `getc` and `getline` primitives.

`putstr` is likewise a primitive, to output a string onto a given file. It performs whatever character translation is needed to match `getline` and `getc`. (We call it `putstr` instead of `putline` because there is no implication of "line"; the string needn't end with a NEWLINE, though it often will. It might even contain one in the middle.) We require that output produced by interleaved calls to `putc` and `putstr` goes out in the proper order.

STDOUT is the internal name for the standard output; as you might expect, there is a corresponding STDIN for the standard input, and a STDERR for the output stream used by `error` and `message`. Although STDERR might be synonymous with STDOUT, generally it should be distinct; this way informative but not disastrous messages can appear without cluttering up the main output of a program or disappearing down a pipeline. The system must arrange that these streams are ready when the program begins to run, just as `input` and `output` are in conventional Pascal.

The internal names used by `getline` and `putstr` are typically a subrange of integers. Our Pascal environment (described in the appendix) contains a type definition for `filedesc`, for "file descriptor," that can be used to typify all internal names:

```
const
    IOERROR = 0;
    MAXOPEN = 10;    { for instance }
type
    filedesc = IOERROR..MAXOPEN;
```

IOERROR is the value of type `filedesc` that will be used to signal error conditions. MAXOPEN is the maximum number of files that may be simultaneously open; it is very system dependent.

Exercise 3-1. How would you implement `getline` and `putstr` in terms of `getc` and `putc`? How would you implement `getc` and `putc` using `getline` and `putstr`? □

Exercise 3-2. In a non-interactive environment, `compare` should not print much output for files that are very different. Add an optional argument so the comparison terminates after a specified number of mismatched lines has occurred. An alternate design is to have `compare` stop after the first mismatch. In that case, the optional argument would allow more than one mismatch. □

Exercise 3-3. Construct a version of `compare` such that two lines are considered to be the same if they are the same after each run of blanks and tabs is replaced by a single blank. Can you achieve the same effect by using `translit`? Can you steal any code from `translit`? □

Exercise 3-4. (Hard) Our `compare` is rudimentary. It is useful for finding out the first place where two files have become different, but it breaks down quickly after that, producing voluminous but uninformative output. Invent a scheme that can cope with missing and transposed lines. How much space and time does your method take, as a function of the file sizes? Can it break down completely? (See the bibliographic notes at the end of this chapter.) □

3.2 Connecting Files by Name

Let us return to the question of how to connect the external name of a file to the name used within the program. Normally the external name will be the name of a file in a file system, or perhaps some temporary file assigned for the duration of the job. Less frequently it will be an I/O device such as a tape or a disk. As we said, the traditional batch way to connect the external name and internal name is by a control card; even in some interactive environments this is all that is possible. But no one wants to have to say

```
connect file1 to name1
connect file2 to name2
compare
```

just because `compare` can only read the internal streams `file1` and `file2`. It's not even the extra work of preparing the `connect` commands that makes this bad, although that is nuisance enough; it's that you have to remember the internal names the program uses. How much more natural to say

```
compare name1 name2
```

and let `compare` worry about accessing the files.

Suppose we pass the actual name of the file to the program and let the program itself arrange the correspondence between external name and internal stream. We will call the primitive that performs this task `open`. `open` does whatever is necessary to access the file, and assigns it an internal file name or file descriptor, which is returned as the function value:

internal-name := open(*external-name*, *access-mode*)

This *internal-name* is now used for subsequent calls to `getline` and `putstr`.

Depending on the local environment, `open` may need other information in addition to the external name — buffer space, access mode, and so on. We will summarize all this extra material as *access-mode*, which in our programs will always be one of the integer constants `IOREAD` or `IOWRITE`, to indicate how the program intends to use the file. Of course if the system you are using provides file security in some form, `open` may have to negotiate for the access you wish.

`open` signals any kind of error by returning the value `IOERROR` instead of a legal internal name. As shown above, a convenient implementation is to have the internal names be small positive integers; `open` simply returns the first unassigned value. In this case zero is a natural value for IOERROR.

The primitive open is *not* the same as Pascal's reset. In some systems, the nonstandard call reset(f,s) in fact opens external file s so that subsequent read(f,...) statements operate on it. Since this is not a standard mechanism, it comes in a variety of forms, or may not be present at all. If present, it provides a perfectly good basis for implementing the primitive open to our specifications. The appendix contains a manual page for open.

One final point: no restrictions are imposed on external names, as used by open, other than the limitations of the string data type, which seldom gets in the way. It is up to the host operating system to interpret these names. Our practice for Pascal source file names is to use only one case of letters, plus digits; to begin all file names with a letter; and to end each name with .p. We have also taken care that all file names are unique in the first six characters; if your system prefers short names, ours can be chopped without risk.

Given open, compare can now be written as

```
{ compare -- compare two files for equality }
procedure compare;
var
    line1, line2 : string;
    arg1, arg2 : string;
    lineno : integer;
    infile1, infile2 : filedesc;
    f1, f2 : boolean;
#include "diffmsg.p"
begin
    if (not getarg(1, arg1, MAXSTR))
      or (not getarg(2, arg2, MAXSTR)) then
        error('usage: compare file1 file2');
    infile1 := mustopen(arg1, IOREAD);
    infile2 := mustopen(arg2, IOREAD);
    lineno := 0;
    repeat
        lineno := lineno + 1;
        f1 := getline(line1, infile1, MAXSTR);
        f2 := getline(line2, infile2, MAXSTR);
        if (f1 and f2) then
            if (not equal(line1, line2)) then
                diffmsg(lineno, line1, line2)
    until (f1 = false) or (f2 = false);
    if (f2 and not f1) then
        message('compare: end of file on file1')
    else if (f1 and not f2) then
        message('compare: end of file on file2')
end;
```

compare doesn't call open directly, but through an agent mustopen. mustopen tries to open the file with the indicated mode. If it succeeds, it returns the value returned by open; otherwise it prints a message (with error) and terminates the program. Even though this is a trifling task, it occurs often enough to warrant a separate routine.

```
{ mustopen -- open file or die }
function mustopen (var name : string; mode : integer)
        : filedesc;
var
    fd : filedesc;
begin
    fd := open(name, mode);
    if (fd = IOERROR) then begin
        putstr(name, STDERR);
        error(': can''t open file')
    end;
    mustopen := fd
end;
```

Most interactive systems provide the connection ability (with varying degrees of grace); it is less common in batch environments. Clearly the function must exist as part of *any* operating system that provides a way to store files by name, for how else could the program that interprets the command language operate? Yet all too often the operation is arbitrarily restricted to "system" programs and forbidden to ordinary users. This is regrettable, for it is important that a program be able to attach input sources dynamically. Programs should be easy to use, as a matter of good human engineering. You should only have to say "compare these files," and let the program do *all* the work. The less setup you have to do before actually using a program, the more likely you are to think of it as a tool.

PROGRAM
    compare   compare files for equality
USAGE
    compare file1 file2
FUNCTION
    compare performs a line-by-line comparison of file1 and file2, printing each pair of differing lines, preceded by a line containing the offending line number and a colon. If the files are identical, no output is produced. If one file is a prefix of the other, compare reports end of file on the shorter file.
EXAMPLE
        compare old new
BUGS
    compare can produce voluminous output for small differences.

Exercise 3-5. Does

```
compare f f
```

work on your system? If not, why not? Should it? Why would you want to do such an operation? □

Exercise 3-6. Modify `compare` so that if it is called with a single argument, it assumes the other file is the standard input. Then you can use `compare` in pipelines, like this

```
expand | compare f
```

Is this design of any value when pipelines must be implemented with temporary files? □

Exercise 3-7. Extend the syntax and semantics of pipelines so *both* sources for `compare` can be the outputs of programs. □

3.3 File Inclusion

Once `open` exists, we can conveniently build tools that access any number of files. One example is `include`, which just copies its standard input to its standard output, except that any input line that begins

```
#include "filename"
```

is replaced by the entire contents of the file `filename`.

We have used `include` to assemble most of the programs in this book. This enables us to keep the source files of the program separate for easy editing, present them separately for better comprehension, yet collect them together for compilation. We also pick up definitions of constants with `#include`. Since we tend to use symbolic constants wherever possible, most of our programs include a standard set of things like `ENDFILE` and `ENDSTR`, and perhaps another set peculiar to a given set of routines. That is, to compile a Pascal program we actually run `include` on a small control file that looks like this:

```
program outer (input, output);
    #include "global definitions"
    #include "i/o primitives"
    #include "utility functions"
begin
    #include "initialize the i/o system"
    #include "main program"
end.
```

`include` is analogous to a facility found in the PL/I preprocessor, where lines of the form

```
% include file;
```

are replaced by the contents of `file`. Similar capabilities exist in other languages. Our version can be used for any text files.

The general outline of `include` is

```
while (getline(line, file, MAXSTR))
    if (line starts with "#include")
        include new file
    else
        output line
```

If the included file can contain further include's, this is obviously a recursive procedure, that is, the operation can be defined in terms of itself. As it turns out, nested include's are useful and not at all difficult to deal with. Since Pascal procedures may be called recursively, we will use one to provide this service.

The other question is how to decide if the line contains #include. This is best broken into two steps — finding the first word on the line, then comparing it to "#include." We write a routine getword which isolates the next word on the input line, a "word" being a string of non-blank characters delimited by blanks, tabs or newlines. getword skips any leading blanks, tabs and newlines and copies the word into the string named by the third argument. getword returns the index of the first character past the end of the word, so if the word is #include, we can use getword again to find the file name, by starting to look right after the #include. getword returns zero when ENDSTR is encountered.

```
{ getword -- get word from s[i] into out }
function getword (var s : string; i : integer;
         var out : string) : integer;
var
    j : integer;
begin
    while (s[i] in [BLANK, TAB, NEWLINE]) do
        i := i + 1;
    j := 1;
    while (not (s[i] in [ENDSTR,BLANK,TAB,NEWLINE])) do begin
        out[j] := s[i];
        i := i + 1;
        j := j + 1
    end;
    out[j] := ENDSTR;
    if (s[i] = ENDSTR) then
        getword := 0
    else
        getword := i
end;
```

The main routine looks like this:

```
    { include -- replace #include "file" by contents of file }
    procedure include;
    var
        incl : string;  { value is '#include' }
    #include "finclude.p"
    begin
        { setstring(incl, '#include'); }
            incl[1] := ord('#');
            incl[2] := ord('i');
            incl[3] := ord('n');
            incl[4] := ord('c');
            incl[5] := ord('l');
            incl[6] := ord('u');
            incl[7] := ord('d');
            incl[8] := ord('e');
            incl[9] := ENDSTR;
        finclude(STDIN)
    end;
```

Obviously the real work is done in the recursive procedure finclude:

```
    { finclude -- include file desc f }
    procedure finclude (f : filedesc);
    var
        line, str : string;
        loc, i : integer;
        f1 : filedesc;
    #include "getword.p"
    begin
        while (getline(line, f, MAXSTR)) do begin
            loc := getword(line, 1, str);
            if (not equal(str, incl)) then
                putstr(line, STDOUT)
            else begin
                loc := getword(line, loc, str);
                str[length(str)] := ENDSTR; { remove quotes }
                for i := 1 to length(str) do
                    str[i] := str[i+1];
                f1 := mustopen(str, IOREAD);
                finclude(f1);
                close(f1)
            end
        end
    end;
```

equal decides if the word is #include; we wrote it early in this chapter. Notice that it is used to compare strings, not lines — generality has paid off already.

We turned the if-else around from our pseudo-code version of include, because we find it is better to associate shorter segments of code with the if and save the longer alternative for the `else`. That way we don't lose track of a tiny trailing `else` clause halfway down the page.

By the way, the comment

```
{ setstring(incl, '#include'); }
```

is a shorthand for the tedious sequence of assignments that follow it. What we would love to say, of course, is

```
if (str = '#include') then ...
```

but our type `string` is incompatible with the type of literal strings. Next best would be to write

```
if (equal(str, '#include')) then ...
```

but once again there is no way to declare `equal` to accept more than one literal string length. Nor can we write

```
incl := '#include';
if (equal(str, incl)) then ...
```

for much the same reasons.

So we need some way to initialize an array of our type `string` with the characters of '#include.' Since Pascal doesn't provide for initialization of variables as the program is compiled, we have to do it with executable code when it's run.

We have written all of our code in terms of the "procedure" `setstring` as if it worked properly. In some Pascal implementations, this can be done by calling a true procedure; in others, it is possible to expand the `setstring` notation as a text macro, the topic of Chapter 8. If neither of these courses is available to you, then you will have to do what we have done — translate it into the equivalent shown here. (Naturally we wrote a program to do the work.)

The primitive operation `close` is the opposite of `open`: it breaks the connection between an external name and an internal one, and frees the internal name and any associated resources for some other use. (`close` is *not* the `reset` operation familiar to Pascal programmers, which repositions without closing.) The reason for using `close` here is that we do not know how many times a particular file will be used nor how many different files there will be. Since most systems have a limit on the number of simultaneously open files, we must explicitly close them to avoid running out of internal names.

Although our programs are careful to close files when finished, it is convenient if the system closes all open files when a program terminates. This simplifies the handling of abnormal terminations. If necessary, a cleanup operation can be added to the outer block to close all open files in the list, according to whatever local rules are appropriate.

`include` also assumes a property of `open` that we didn't mention earlier —

when a file is opened, it must be positioned at its beginning, just as with
reset. This behavior is vital for include, since the same file may be
included several times.

PROGRAM
    include   include copies of subfiles
USAGE
    include
FUNCTION
    include copies its input to its output unchanged, except that each line beginning
        #include "filename"
    is replaced by the contents of the file whose name is filename. included files may con-
    tain further #include lines, to arbitrary depth.
EXAMPLE
    To piece together a Pascal program such as include:
        #include "include.p"
BUGS
    A file that includes itself will not be diagnosed, but will eventually cause something to break.

Exercise 3-8. Modify include for a system or language where files cannot be opened
by name. Describe a systematic way to use it. □

3.4 File Concatenation

The next program we will write is concat, which concatenates a set of
named input files onto its standard output. A common use for concat is to
combine multiple files into one, for use by another program that can only read
its standard input, like the filters of Chapter 2. It is also the easiest way to
print the contents of a file without reformatting or any other interpretation.

```
{ concat -- concatenate files onto standard output }
procedure concat;
var
    i : integer;
    junk : boolean;
    fd : filedesc;
    s : string;
begin
    for i := 1 to nargs do begin
        junk := getarg(i, s, MAXSTR);
        fd := mustopen(s, IOREAD);
        fcopy(fd, STDOUT);
        close(fd)
    end
end;
```

We mentioned the primitive nargs in Chapter 2. It returns the number of
arguments that a program was called with.

If there are no input files, concat does the right thing — it produces no
output whatsoever. The actual copying is done by fcopy, which is just the

example we began with in Chapter 1. The only difference is that the program reads or writes specified files instead of using the standard input and standard output.

```
{ fcopy -- copy file fin to file fout }
procedure fcopy (fin, fout : filedesc);
var
    c : character;
begin
    while (getcf(c, fin) <> ENDFILE) do
        putcf(c, fout)
end;
```

getcf and putcf are versions of getc and putc that access explicit file descriptors instead of STDIN and STDOUT. Thus getc(c) is identical to getcf(c,STDIN), and in fact getc might well be implemented as a call to getcf.

fcopy assumes that its files are all opened, positioned and ready to go; it simply copies. This way we can use it to copy *parts* of files. If fcopy carefully opened and closed its files, that would limit its usefulness. You should avoid putting arbitrary restrictions on programs, particularly by making them try do too many things. If you want to open and close files, wrap another layer around fcopy, just as we did.

PROGRAM
    concat   concatenate files
USAGE
    concat file ...
FUNCTION
    concat writes the contents of each of its file arguments in turn to its output, thus con-
    catenating them into one larger file. Since concat performs no reformatting or interpreta-
    tion of the input files, it is useful for displaying the contents of a file.
EXAMPLE
    To examine a file:
        concat file

3.5 File Printer

One of the most useful programs that has the form "indeterminate number of inputs, one output" is a file printer or lister. print is invoked with one or more files as arguments; it prints the files with top and bottom margins, and, at the top of each page, the file name and page number. Each new file begins on a new page. print is used instead of concat when you want a neat, self-identifying listing of a set of files.

In outline, the program is

```
for each file
    get name
    open(name)
    fprint(name, fin)
    close(fin)

fprint(name, fin)
    initialize
    while (getline(line, fin, MAXSTR))
        if (at top)
            print page header
        print line
        if (page full)
            space to bottom
    if (page partially full)
        space to bottom
```

This organization puts all of the code for stepping through the argument list at one level, and all the details of counting lines for an individual file at a lower level.

The actual code for print is identical to concat except for calling fprint instead of fcopy.

```
{ print -- print files with headings }
procedure print;
var
    name : string;
    i : integer;
    fin : filedesc;
    junk : boolean;
#include "fprint.p"
begin
    for i := 1 to nargs do begin
        junk := getarg(i, name, MAXSTR);
        fin := mustopen(name, IOREAD);
        fprint(name, fin);
        close(fin)
    end
end;
```

fprint has to be carefully thought out so it doesn't botch its boundary conditions. The most obvious pitfall is that the right number of lines must be printed on each page, or the output will gradually drift up or down successive pages. Less obvious, if a file exactly fills the last page, the next file should begin at the top of the next page, with no intervening blank page (or worse, a page with just a heading on it).

```
{ fprint -- print file "name" from fin }
procedure fprint (var name : string; fin : filedesc);
const
    MARGIN1 = 2;
    MARGIN2 = 2;
    BOTTOM = 64;
    PAGELEN = 66;
var
    line : string;
    lineno, pageno : integer;
#include "skip.p"
#include "head.p"
begin
    pageno := 1;
    skip(MARGIN1);
    head(name, pageno);
    skip(MARGIN2);
    lineno := MARGIN1 + MARGIN2 + 1;
    while (getline(line, fin, MAXSTR)) do begin
        if (lineno = 0) then begin
            skip(MARGIN1);
            pageno := pageno + 1;
            head(name, pageno);
            skip(MARGIN2);
            lineno := MARGIN1 + MARGIN2 + 1
        end;
        putstr(line, STDOUT);
        lineno := lineno + 1;
        if (lineno >= BOTTOM) then begin
            skip(PAGELEN-lineno);
            lineno := 0
        end
    end;
    if (lineno > 0) then
        skip(PAGELEN-lineno)
end;
```

The constants MARGIN1 and MARGIN2 are the number of lines before and after the heading line. BOTTOM is the line number of the last text line on a page; PAGELEN is the number of lines on a page. For standard 8½×11 inch paper with 6 lines per inch, PAGELEN is 66. The margins will usually be two or three lines each.

skip produces n blank lines; we use a tiny separate routine rather than clutter up fprint with six occurrences of the loop.

```
{ skip -- output n blank lines }
procedure skip (n : integer);
var
    i : integer;
begin
    for i := 1 to n do
        putc(NEWLINE)
end;
```

Since we want the `printed` listing to identify the files by name, it is natural and convenient to attach files to the program dynamically by name instead of by some control card mechanism. At the least, procedure `head` should print a single line with the file name and page number, as ours does. It might also print the date and time if they are available.

```
{ head -- print top of page header }
procedure head (var name : string; pageno : integer);
var
    page : string;   { set to ' Page ' }
begin
    { setstring(page, ' Page '); }
        page[1] := ord(' ');
        page[2] := ord('P');
        page[3] := ord('a');
        page[4] := ord('g');
        page[5] := ord('e');
        page[6] := ord(' ');
        page[7] := ENDSTR;
    putstr(name, STDOUT);
    putstr(page, STDOUT);
    putdec(pageno, 1);
    putc(NEWLINE)
end;
```

Since `putstr` and `putdec` do *not* add a newline at the end of the string they are putting out, you can make several calls to them to build up one output line, as we did here to get the name and page number on the same line.

Once the basic tool is working, many refinements are possible, and some are even desirable. You might consider adding the capability to

- convert tabs to spaces
- change default paper length, margins, line spacing, tab stops, etc.
- fold long lines
- number lines
- start and stop on specified pages
- print multiple files in parallel
- print multi-column output

All of these are easy except for the last, multi-column printing. That can be done, of course, by accumulating a whole page before printing any of it.

When you write a program, there is a great temptation to add more and more "features" like these, little things that it will do for you. But beware — unless the features work together in a uniform way, the result is going to be a grab-bag of unrelated capabilities, most of which won't get used because nobody can remember them. If you have to look up how to use a program for even the simplest applications, you know you've gone too far. When in doubt, treat "feature" as a pejorative. (Think of a hundred-bladed Swiss army knife.)

We have found the following syntax for optional arguments to be convenient. Optional arguments are usually a single letter, or at least a short string. They are introduced by a character which is unlikely to begin a file name, so arguments can be distinguished from file names. (We use a minus sign.) If `print` provides multi-column output, for example, it might be specified by the argument -cn where n is the number of columns, so

```
    print -c4 file1 file2 ...
```

calls for printing of the files in 4-column format. By processing the arguments strictly left to right, the program could set up parameters for a file, print it, then selectively alter them for the next file.

Once you have options, the question arises of what to do when a particular option is left unspecified. This should *never* be considered an error; instead some default value should be chosen. Selecting the right default behavior of a program may seem like a trivial concern, but if you do it wrong, everyone suffers (or your program isn't used). Sometimes the decision is obvious: page lengths are pretty much standardized, for example. But others are less clear: should `print` fold very long lines into several shorter ones by default? If so, where? Keep in mind that you are building tools, and make them as useful and as easy to use as possible. Things that are said often should be concise; therefore the defaults should reflect the most common usage. Furthermore, defaults should be set so the user who doesn't know any options gets reasonable behavior. Try not to surprise your users, and don't limit *their* options.

Exercise 3-9. Implement some of the enhancements of `print`, making them accessible through optional arguments. Before you do, try to predict which will be heavily used and which not at all. Write the new manual page first to see how easy the new features are to explain. After your new version has been used for a while, determine how accurate your predictions were. What options should `print` choose by default? □

3.6 Multi-stage Processing: Pipelines

This book is about tools, so by now it has probably occurred to you that with a little care you could use `print` as a tool to print the output from any program. If this were easy, then no other program would ever have to contain code for things like multi-column printing — one version of `print` could serve all comers.

Suppose we modify `print` slightly so that if it has no file name arguments, it reverts to taking its input from the standard input. This is an easy task because of the way we organized it in the first place. We need only add a test for no arguments and an empty file name for the standard input.

```
{ print (default input STDIN) -- print files with headings }
procedure print;
var
    name : string;
    null : string;  { value '' }
    i : integer;
    fin : filedesc;
    junk : boolean;
#include "fprint.p"
begin
    { setstring(null, ''); }
        null[1] := ENDSTR;
    if (nargs = 0) then
        fprint(null, STDIN)
    else
        for i := 1 to nargs do begin
            junk := getarg(i, name, MAXSTR);
            fin := mustopen(name, IOREAD);
            fprint(name, fin);
            close(fin)
        end
end;
```

The manual page for `print` is thus:

PROGRAM
    print   print files with headings
USAGE
    print [file ...]
FUNCTION
    print copies each of its argument files in turn to its output, inserting page headers and footers and filling the last page of each file to full length. A header consists of two blank lines, a line giving the filename and page number, and two more blank lines; a footer consists of two blank lines. Pages for each file are numbered starting at one. If no arguments are specified, print prints its standard input; the file name is null.
    The text of each file is unmodified — no attempt is made to fold long lines or expand tabs to spaces.
EXAMPLE
        print print.p fprint.p

Any program which wants to use `print` as a post-processor need only arrange that its output be directed to the standard input of `print`. `print` itself should not know or care that it is being used by some other program. With the pipeline notation introduced in Chapter 2, for instance, we merely say

•

```
program ... | print
```

This lets any program have formatted output, within the capabilities of `print`. And since `print` will have wide use, some effort can be lavished on enhancing its capabilities and making it efficient.

Just how to arrange a pipeline varies quite a bit from system to system. Ideally, `program` and `print` should be concurrent processes, connected by the system, neither knowing that the other is running. Less desirable, but more likely to be feasible, they can communicate via temporary files. Our standard interface does *not* provide pipelines.

Even when pipelines are not directly supported, however, the notion of *input-output redirection* can be used to obtain the same effect. We use the notation

```
wordcount <paper
```

to mean that the standard input of `wordcount` is to be taken from the file `paper` rather than the terminal. Similarly,

```
compress >small
```

means that the standard output of `compress` is to be collected on the file `small`, which is created or made empty as necessary before the program is run.

Needless to say, the programs presented in Chapters 1 and 2 become *much* more useful in an environment that provides input-output redirection. Put another way, they are largely worthless without it, for how often do you want to type at `compress` and watch the compressed text come back to your terminal? Tools are useful only if they are easily applied.

Give input-output redirection, the pipeline

```
prog | print
```

can be simulated by the three separate commands

```
prog >tempfile
print <tempfile
remove tempfile
```

where `remove` is a program (which we don't supply in this book) that causes `tempfile` to be discarded. Temporaries are clumsier than pipes, but you can live with them.

Readers who are sensitive to questions of efficiency may wonder if it is economical to use two programs when one would serve. The answer depends on the true costs involved, which are often not properly estimated. Most people who talk about "efficiency" are concerned primarily with how much machine resources are used in the final run or in hands-off production, not with how much "people" and machine time is consumed in all the compilations, debugging and other false starts that prepare for the final run. Throughout this book we consistently take the view that people cost a great deal more than machines, and that the disparity will increase in the future. Therefore the most important consideration is that people get their jobs done with a minimum of fuss and bother.

One way to help this happen is to provide tools. It is not sufficient, however, to have a large collection of "utilities," if each is hard to use, deals with just one special case (even though it has a lot of "features"), and cannot be connected to other tools in any useful way. Tools must work together. One advantage of the pipeline is that it encourages people who build programs to think in terms of how programs can be connected to other programs. This in turn forces a certain degree of standardization, for a program which will not interface cleanly to other programs cannot share a pipeline with them.

A second consideration in favor of the pipeline is that it encourages the construction of smaller programs to do simpler functions. These smaller programs are much easier to write, debug, document, maintain and improve independently than they would be if combined into a single monster. Furthermore, separate programs can be combined in novel ways, something which is rarely possible if they have already been combined in some "obvious" way.

A final consideration is that many jobs will not get done at all unless they can be done quickly. Efficiency is hardly of importance for a temporary hookup meant to be used only a few times. Should a particular combination of tools prove so useful that it begins to consume significant resources, *then* you can consider replacing it with a more efficient version. And you are way ahead at this point, for you are writing a program that has precise specifications and that has been shown to be useful. This is the best formula known for ensuring the success of a programming effort.

Exercise 3-10. Determine if it is possible in your operating system to construct a program which reads an input line describing a pipeline and arranges the necessary operating system commands to make the operation happen. Build it if possible. If not, what facilities are lacking, and how would you provide them most easily? □

Exercise 3-11. How would you organize the outer block to interpret arguments with < and >? □

3.7 Creating Files Dynamically

We come now to an area which is of great importance in programs that interact with their environment — the ability to *create* files or information streams dynamically, that is, while the program runs. Clearly, our standard interface must have this ability, to implement redirection of the form

```
    prog >file
```

makecopy further illustrates the problems.

```
    makecopy f g
```

copies file f to file g. g is created if necessary; if it already exists, its contents are overwritten.

How do we create the output file? Since each operating system has a different syntax for this operation, we will assume that the operation of creating a file is done by a primitive function `create`, which you will have to provide in the appropriate form on your machine. Its use is

internal-name := create(*external-name*, *access-mode*)

`create` and `open` are very similar: the external name is the name that the file is to have in the external world, and the internal name is a file descriptor for use by `getline` and `putstr`. As with `open`, `create` may well need further information, such as access permissions; we summarize all this in *access-mode*. A `create` of a file that already exists should first remove the old version or truncate it to zero length; this ensures that re-using a file is not a special case. If the file creation fails for any reason, `create` returns `IOERROR`.

The `create` primitive is *not* the `rewrite` operation of Pascal. As with `open` and `reset`, however, some non-standard implementations of `rewrite` can be used to implement `create` as defined here.

```
{ makecopy -- copy one file to another }
procedure makecopy;
var
    inname, outname : string;
    fin, fout : filedesc;
begin
    if (not getarg(1, inname, MAXSTR))
      or (not getarg(2, outname, MAXSTR)) then
        error('usage: makecopy old new');
    fin := mustopen(inname, IOREAD);
    fout := mustcreate(outname, IOWRITE);
    fcopy(fin, fout);
    close(fin);
    close(fout)
end;
```

`fcopy` is from `concat` earlier in this chapter; `mustcreate` is like `mustopen`:

```
    { mustcreate -- create file or die }
    function mustcreate (var name : string; mode : integer)
            : filedesc;
    var
        fd : filedesc;
    begin
        fd := create(name, mode);
        if (fd = IOERROR) then begin
            putstr(name, STDERR);
            error(': can''t create file')
        end;
        mustcreate := fd
    end;
```

PROGRAM
    `makecopy`   copy a file to new file
USAGE
    `makecopy old new`
FUNCTION
    `makecopy` copies the file `old` to a new instance of the file new, i.e., if new already exists it
    is truncated and rewritten, otherwise it is made to exist. The new file is an exact replica of
    the old.
EXAMPLE
    To make a backup copy of a precious file:
        `makecopy precious backup`
BUGS
    Copying a file onto itself is very system dependent and usually disastrous.

Exercise 3-12. Many operating systems offer a "copy" command like `makecopy`. Sometimes if the target file already exists, the command either refuses to proceed, or requests confirmation before destroying the old contents. Is this desirable behavior? Modify `makecopy` to deal sensibly with

      `makecopy f f`

□

3.8 Putting it All Together: archive

As the final example of this chapter, let us construct a program which requires *all* of the file system primitives we have discussed, and which could profit from a few others not yet mentioned. `archive` is a library maintainer whose purpose is to collect sets of arbitrary files into one big file and to maintain that file as an "archive." This often saves storage space and, more important, gives you a handle by which you can deal with a whole group of related files at once. Files can be extracted from the archive, new ones can be added, old ones can be deleted or replaced by updated versions, and data about the contents can be listed. There are no restrictions on what kinds of files can be archived. Thus an archive can provide a library service for other programs like loaders, compilers, and so on. It's also a convenient way to identify files on magnetic tape.

archive is invoked by the command line

        archive   -command archname [filenames]

command is a single letter which specifies what operation we want to perform on the archive archname. The optional filenames specify individual files that participate in the action. The possible commands are

    -c   create a new archive with named members
    -d   delete named members from archive
    -p   print named members on standard output
    -t   print table of archive contents
    -u   update named archive members or add at end
    -x   extract named members from archive

To make archive easy to use, we adopt the rule that if no files are named, the action is done on all files in the archive:

        archive -t arch

lists the entire table of contents. But if any files are explicitly named, they are the only ones that take part in the action. For instance,

        archive -t arch f g

lists only information about f and g. archive also provides a warning for each explicitly named file that doesn't exist in the archive. These are services that cost little to implement but add much to the human engineering of the program.

Here is the manual page for archive:

PROGRAM
    `archive`   maintain file archive
USAGE
    `archive -cmd aname [ file ... ]`
FUNCTION
    `archive` manages any number of member files in a single file, `aname`, with sufficient information that members may be selectively added, extracted, replaced, or deleted from the collection. `-cmd` is a code that determines the operation to be performed:

        `-c`   create a new archive with named members
        `-d`   delete named members from archive
        `-p`   print named members on standard output
        `-t`   print table of archive contents
        `-u`   update named members or add at end
        `-x`   extract named members from archive

    In each case, the "named members" are the zero or more filenames given as arguments following `aname`. If no arguments follow, then the "named members" are taken as *all* of the files in the archive, except for the delete command `-d`, which is not so rash. `archive` complains if a file is named twice or cannot be accessed.
    The `-t` command writes one line to the output for each named member, consisting of the member name and a string representation of the file length, separated by a blank.
    The create command `-c` makes a new archive containing the named files. The update command `-u` replaces existing named members and adds new files onto the end of an existing archive. Create and update read from, and extract writes to, files whose names are the same as the member names in the archive. An intermediate version of the new archive file is first written to the file `artemp`; hence this filename should be avoided.
    An archive is a concatenation of zero or more entries, each consisting of a header and an exact copy of the original file. The header format is
        `-h-` *name length*
EXAMPLE
    To replace two files in an existing archive, add a new one, then print the table of contents:
        `archive -u archfile old1 old2 new1`
        `archive -t archfile`

The manual page documents the format of files produced and manipulated by `archive`. Often this information is not provided to the user, sometimes because it is "internal" information that the user need not know, but sometimes because of a confusion between information hiding and secrecy. A file is very much an external creature, one that may have to be manipulated by other tools from time to time. Hence it is important that file formats be clearly documented, preferably in conjunction with the program that *writes* the file.

The archive program is a natural for what we like to call "left-corner" construction. The idea is to nibble off a small, manageable corner of the program — a part that does something useful — and make that work. Once it does, more and more pieces are added until the whole thing is done. If care is taken with the original design, later pieces should fit in relatively smoothly. Debugging and testing are easier, for the pieces are only added one at a time. Furthermore, if you decide to scrap the whole thing at some point, you are scrapping only that fraction built so far.

The beauty of left-corner construction is that the program does some part of its job very early in the game. By implementing the most useful functions first,

you get an idea of how valuable the program will be before investing any time
in the difficult or esoteric services (which often prove to be unnecessary or
unwanted anyway). You also ensure that the simpler and more common functions are handled simply, which leads to greater efficiency in the end.

The first function to consider is adding files to an archive. (Creating a new
archive is the same job, done on a virgin file.) Until we can create and add to
an archive, no other operation is very interesting anyway. Thus we come naturally to the question of what the format of an archive file should be. There are
at least two possibilities. The first is to have a "directory" at the beginning of
the archive, which lists the files contained, plus other useful information about
them — where they are in the archive, how big they are, when they were
archived, and so on. The second method, which we will use, is to distribute
this directory information throughout the file, one piece per file. Each
approach has its advantages and disadvantages; one of the exercises is concerned
with making a detailed comparison. Before reading further, you might think
about what is likely to be easy and what will be hard for each organization.

As always, the local environment can radically affect the merits of the two
organizations, by helping or hindering various operations. Furthermore, any
conclusions we draw must take into account how the program is actually used,
which often depends on what it does well, which depends in turn on the organization, and so on.

With the centralized directory, an operation like listing the table of contents
is likely to be faster, because the information is concentrated. This may also
allow better error checking, because all the information is available at one time.
It also simplifies any task in which the members must be accessed in a different
order from the one in which they are stored. On the negative side, however,
you really have to be prepared to deal with the directory all at once, which can
limit the number of members in an archive.

With a distributed directory, operations on the table of contents will in all
probability be slower, unless your system lets you move quickly to any point in a
file without reading the intervening data. Even with this facility the time to
access a particular file will be longer than with the centralized directory, because
you have to at least look at directory entries until you find the one you want.
But this slowdown will be small in comparison to the time required to actually
process the file.

Having built both kinds in the past, we feel that the distributed directory is a
clearer and less complicated organization. And of course you can always make
a copy of the directory in a file, then add that to the archive.

Since we are using a distributed directory, each entry in an archive begins
with a header, containing as a bare minimum the file name and some reliable
way to distinguish a header from the contents of an archive member. The
archive looks like this:

```
header for file 1
file 1
header for file 2
file 2
...
```

Given this picture, we can see immediately how to implement some operations. For example, to list the file names, we need merely find the headers and print the relevant parts. Other operations are harder, and depend on what services are provided by the local operating system.

The top level of archive is a multi-way branch that gets the command argument and archive name, then calls the routine appropriate for the command. We will show it all later; for now, here is the executable body:

```
begin
    initarch;
    if (not getarg(1, cmd, MAXSTR))
        or (not getarg(2, aname, MAXSTR)) then
            help;
    getfns;
    if (length(cmd) <> 2) or (cmd[1] <> ord('-')) then
            help
    else if (cmd[2] = ord('c')) or (cmd[2] = ord('u')) then
            update(aname, cmd[2])
    else if (cmd[2] = ord('t')) then
            table(aname)
    else if (cmd[2] = ord('x')) or (cmd[2] = ord('p')) then
            extract(aname, cmd[2])
    else if (cmd[2] = ord('d')) then
            delete(aname)
    else
            help
end;
```

The create and update operations are combined in one routine because they differ only in how the archive is accessed. Similarly, extract and print differ only in what file the output is to be sent to.

help is called when archive has been used incorrectly. For a program that is easy to describe, the most useful diagnostic is a brief synopsis of how to use it properly.

```
{ help -- print diagnostic for archive }
procedure help;
begin
    error('usage: archive -[cdptux] archname [files...]')
end;
```

This message is usually enough to remind the user of what to say.

The routine getfns fetches the file name arguments from the command

line and collects them in an array fname; nfiles is the number of file arguments. getfns also checks the argument list for duplicates and overflow.

```
{ getfns -- get filenames into fname, look for duplicates }
procedure getfns;
var
    i, j : integer;
    junk : boolean;
begin
    errcount := 0;
    nfiles := nargs - 2;
    if (nfiles > MAXFILES) then
        error('archive: too many file names');
    for i := 1 to nfiles do
        junk := getarg(i+2, fname[i], MAXSTR);
    for i := 1 to nfiles do
        fstat[i] := false;
    for i := 1 to nfiles - 1 do
        for j := i + 1 to nfiles do
            if (equal(fname[i], fname[j])) then begin
                putstr(fname[i], STDERR);
                error(': duplicate file name')
            end
end;
```

archive is eventually going to print a message about any files which have
been referred to in the argument list but not seen in the archive. fstat is used
to record this information: if fstat[i] is false, the ith file has not yet been
seen in the archive. These variables are needed by several routines, so they are
declared at the beginning of the procedure archive itself; there are too many
to pass around to each routine that needs them.

```
const
    MAXFILES = 100; { or whatever }
var
    aname : string;      { archive name }
    cmd : string;        { command type }
    fname : array [1..MAXFILES] of string;  { filename args }
    fstat : array [1..MAXFILES] of boolean; { true=in archive }
    nfiles : integer;    { number of filename arguments }
    errcount : integer;  { number of errors }
    archtemp : string;   { temp file name 'artemp' }
    archhdr : string;    { header string '-h-' }
```

errcount is used to count errors; it is used by several routines, and is thus
best kept visible as well. We also put the name for the archive temporary file
and the header string in global variables so they can be initialized.

Notice that the main routine of archive knows about these variables even
though it makes no use of most of them, because some of its subordinates do,
and because initialization is needed. Block structure inheritance is a convenient

way to deal with a group of related variables, but it is also dangerous since it is less disciplined than passing arguments and can make it hard to determine what routines are using what variables. An alternative is to put a group of related variables in a record, and pass that as a single argument to routines that need access. That doesn't really solve the problem either, if different routines need different parts of the record. We do try to restrict as much as possible the scope of variables to those routines that "need to know," but the decision as to whether to use inheritance or an argument has to be made in each individual case; there is no automatic way to decide.

Updating an archive breaks cleanly into two stages: replacing existing members with new versions, and adding to the end any files named as arguments but not present in the archive. We assume that the only way to add data to the end of a file is to copy the existing information to a new file, add the new data to the end of that, then copy the whole thing back to the original. Even though some systems allow you to add at the end or rewrite in the middle of a file, it is unwise to do so. It is safer not to alter an existing archive until you're sure that the replacement is complete and correct.

The process of updating can be summarized as

```
open archive (create if new)
create temporary file
update existing archive contents onto temporary
for each new file
    create header and copy it to temporary
    copy file to temporary
if no errors
    move temporary back to archive
```

These operations are controlled by update.

```
{ update -- update existing files, add new ones at end }
procedure update (var aname : string; cmd : character);
var
    i : integer;
    afd, tfd : filedesc;
begin
    tfd := mustcreate(archtemp, IOWRITE);
    if (cmd = ord('u')) then begin
        afd := mustopen(aname, IOREAD);
        replace(afd, tfd, ord('u'));     { update existing }
        close(afd)
    end;
    for i := 1 to nfiles do      { add new ones }
        if (fstat[i] = false) then begin
            addfile(fname[i], tfd);
            fstat[i] := true
        end;
    close(tfd);
    if (errcount = 0) then
        fmove(archtemp, aname)
    else
        message('fatal errors - archive not altered');
    remove(archtemp)
end;
```

archive is designed to identify as many errors as possible per run. update processes all the files in the argument list, even though it may have encountered an error trying to open one of them. errcount counts the errors; the archive is updated only if errcount is zero at the end of the run. replace copies an archive onto the temporary, updating any files specified. addfile adds a single file to the end of the temporary if it can. (We will return to replace and addfile shortly.)

remove is the complement of create, a primitive for removing a file forever.

fmove moves the information from the temporary back onto the archive file if no errors have occurred. In the worst case, this has to be done by physically removing the old archive, creating a new one, then copying the temporary back onto it, like this:

```
{ fmove -- move file name1 to name2 }
procedure fmove (var name1, name2 : string);
var
    fd1, fd2 : filedesc;
begin
    fd1 := mustopen(name1, IOREAD);
    fd2 := mustcreate(name2, IOWRITE);
    fcopy(fd1, fd2);
    close(fd1);
    close(fd2)
end;
```

In a different environment, you might be able merely to *rename* the temporary to be the new archive. This is a useful primitive to have available, for it is clearly more efficient than physically copying the entire file, and it also minimizes the length of time during which the permanent copy of the archive is in an incomplete state. We use "move" for any file transfer that could be effected by renaming, and "copy" only when we explicitly want the source to remain where it is.

Let us deal with addfile next, since it is relatively self-contained.

```
{ addfile -- add file "name" to archive }
procedure addfile (var name : string; fd : filedesc);
var
    head : string;
    nfd : filedesc;
#include "makehdr.p"
begin
    nfd := open(name, IOREAD);
    if (nfd = IOERROR) then begin
        putstr(name, STDERR);
        message(': can''t add');
        errcount := errcount + 1
    end;
    if (errcount = 0) then begin
        makehdr(name, head);
        putstr(head, fd);
        fcopy(nfd, fd);
        close(nfd)
    end
end;
```

makehdr makes the uniquely identifiable header record that precedes each archived file. For testing, any printable string is quite adequate. We use -h-, followed by a blank, the filename, another blank, and the file length. For ultimate use, it would be nice to add things like the date and time the file was archived, if that is available.

Further contents depend on the local system. The main consideration is to eliminate any possibility of confusing a header with the contents of an archive member. If it is easy and fast to find out the size of a file in convenient units, such as the number of characters or the number of records, the header can contain the file size as one of its entries, and there is no difficulty in deciding what is a header and what is text inside an archive. Our version of makehdr includes a character count in the header, separated from the file name by a blank. We put the character count into the file as a character string, not in binary, because that representation is portable and because the archive can thus remain a text file (if its members are) and amenable to processing by other tools.

```
{ makehdr -- make header line for archive member }
procedure makehdr (var name, head : string);
var
     i : integer;
#include "fsize.p"
begin
     scopy(archhdr, 1, head, 1);
     i := length(head) + 1;
     head[i] := BLANK;
     scopy(name, 1, head, i+1);
     i := length(head) + 1;
     head[i] := BLANK;
     i := itoc(fsize(name), head, i+1);
     head[i] := NEWLINE;
     head[i+1] := ENDSTR
end;
```

   makehdr uses length and itoc, which we wrote in Chapter 2. scopy is a basic string copying routine:

```
scopy(src, i, dest, j)
```

copies the (sub)string of src that starts at i to dest[j].

```
{ scopy -- copy string at src[i] to dest[j] }
procedure scopy (var src : string; i : integer;
        var dest : string; j : integer);
begin
    while (src[i] <> ENDSTR) do begin
        dest[j] := src[i];
        i := i + 1;
        j := j + 1
    end;
    dest[j] := ENDSTR
end;
```

   The function fsize returns the size of a file in characters. Ideally this will be a primitive, a service of the local file system. The less favorable (but common) case is that you can only find out how big a file is by reading through it. Although this is costly, if you extract contents more than you replace them you can endure the extra overhead even with double reading. Remember, archive reads and writes the *entire* archive twice to update it; the incremental cost of reading a few of the members one more time is small in comparison.

```
{ fsize -- size of file in characters }
function fsize (var name : string) : integer;
var
    c : character;
    fd : filedesc;
    n : integer;
begin
    n := 0;
    fd := mustopen(name, IOREAD);
    while (getcf(c, fd) <> ENDFILE) do
        n := n + 1;
    close(fd);
    fsize := n
end;
```

Exercise 3-13. How would you test the part of archive built so far? What are some critical boundaries? □

Exercise 3-14. fsize opens the file anew, even though it has already been opened by addfile. Does this work on your system? Should it? If it doesn't, how would you rewrite fsize to get around the problem? What primitive operations are needed? □

Exercise 3-15. An alternate approach which eliminates the file size computation is to end each archive member with a "trailer" analogous to the header. Implement this variation. □

Exercise 3-16. The procedure update tries to copy a file that has been created but which has never had anything written on it. What is a reasonable behavior in this case? What happens on your system? What primitive should deal with the situation if the system does something unreasonable? □

Exercise 3-17. Modify archive to use a linked list instead of an array to store the information in fstat. □

3.9 More Archive Commands

Now that we can create an archive and put files in it (and presumably have carefully tested that much), can we print the table of contents? That seems to be the next easiest function to add in a left-corner approach. archive is to list the files named as arguments, or all the files if there are no file arguments, so the table of contents operation is basically this:

```
    open archive
    for each file in archive
        if (header matches any argument)
            print header information
        skip over archived file
    warn about any that couldn't be found
```

This is done by `table`:

```
{ table -- print table of archive contents }
procedure table (var aname : string);
var
    head, name : string;
    size : integer;
    afd : filedesc;
#include "tprint.p"
begin
    afd := mustopen(aname, IOREAD);
    while (gethdr(afd, head, name, size)) do begin
        if (filearg(name)) then
            tprint(head);
        fskip(afd, size)
    end;
    notfound
end;
```

`table` opens the archive for reading only, so you can read an archive that you might not have permission to alter.

`tprint` prints the desired information from the header; our dummy version prints the member name and size, which is all we need for testing the program.

```
{ tprint -- print table entry for one member }
procedure tprint (var buf : string);
var
    i : integer;
    temp : string;
begin
    i := getword(buf, 1, temp); { header }
    i := getword(buf, i, temp); { name }
    putstr(temp, STDOUT);
    putc(BLANK);
    i := getword(buf, i, temp); { size }
    putstr(temp, STDOUT);
    putc(NEWLINE)
end;
```

`gethdr` tests whether the next input is a header; if so, it returns the header, the file name and the size. If `gethdr` fails to see an archive header immediately, something has gone awry: either the file in question is not an archive or its contents have been corrupted. In any case, `archive` can proceed no further, so gethdr exits with an error message.

```
{ gethdr -- get header info from fd }
function gethdr (fd : filedesc; var buf, name : string;
        var size : integer) : boolean;
var
    temp : string;
    i : integer;
begin
    if (getline(buf, fd, MAXSTR) = false) then
        gethdr := false
    else begin
        i := getword(buf, 1, temp);
        if (not equal(temp, archhdr)) then
            error('archive not in proper format');
        i := getword(buf, i, name);
        size := ctoi(buf, i);
        gethdr := true
    end
end;
```

gethdr uses getword, which we wrote for include; equal, which we wrote for compare; and ctoi, from Chapter 2. Rather than inventing new routines for the same job each time, we are accumulating a library of useful functions.

makehdr and gethdr are independent of the specific header chosen; if you don't care for -h-, one string in initarch is all that need be changed to install a new one.

fskip uses the size returned by gethdr to skip over the archived file; if all is consistent, this should leave the file positioned at a new header for the next call of gethdr. In a congenial system fskip will be a primitive that skips without reading the intervening data. For use in hostile environments, here is a version that reads the right number of characters:

```
{ fskip -- skip n characters on file fd }
procedure fskip (fd : filedesc; n : integer);
var
    c : character;
    i : integer;
begin
    for i := 1 to n do
        if (getcf(c, fd) = ENDFILE) then
            error('archive: end of file in fskip')
end;
```

filearg tests whether the file name from the archive matches any of the file names in the argument list, using equal to do the string comparison. If there are no file arguments, filearg also considers that to be a match.

```
{ filearg -- check if name matches argument list }
function filearg (var name : string) : boolean;
var
    i : integer;
    found : boolean;
begin
    if (nfiles <= 0) then
        filearg := true
    else begin
        found := false;
        i := 1;
        while (not found) and (i <= nfiles) do begin
            if (equal(name, fname[i])) then begin
                fstat[i] := true;
                found := true
            end;
            i := i + 1
        end;
        filearg := found
    end
end;
```

fstat[i] records whether the ith named file argument has ever been "found." Initially false for all arguments, the corresponding position is set to true if filearg finds a match. This list is used by notfound to print names which were arguments but not in the archive.

```
{ notfound -- print "not found" warning }
procedure notfound;
var
    i : integer;
begin
    for i := 1 to nfiles do
        if (fstat[i] = false) then begin
            putstr(fname[i], STDERR);
            message(': not in archive');
            errcount := errcount + 1
        end
end;
```

It also sets the error count, but that isn't used by table, since it hardly matters when we are not attempting to alter the archive.

A point of style: in filearg and other routines, we tested whether nfiles was equal to *or less than* zero. But from reading the code, we *know* that nfiles can never become negative, so why bother?

This is what is known as "defensive programming." It costs next to nothing in source text or execution time, yet it reduces the chance of the program going wild should an important control variable somehow be damaged. You can't print out error messages everywhere, but you can and should take out insurance whenever possible.

There is a similar situation in `fskip`: even though the archive header contains a count that is surely right, the loop tests each character to make sure it isn't `ENDFILE`; if it is, the count is wrong.

It is much easier to debug a program if the output is not voluminous and if storage overwrites do not occur as a side effect of the original bug. The way to ensure saner behavior is to do as we did. Write your tests so they steer crazy situations back in a safe direction. Use the last `else` of a chain of `else-if`'s to catch conditions that should "never" occur, but just might. Never check for equality if it doesn't hurt to check for "greater than or equal to" or for "less than or equal to." Don't let loops repeat when a variable is out of its expected range. Don't make your program a sucker for bugs.

The next step in the incremental construction is *extracting* — to get the information back out of the archive once we put it in. The logic is clear enough:

```
open archive
for each file in archive
    if (it's to be extracted)
        create file
        copy from archive to file
warn about any that couldn't be extracted
```

We also allow archive contents to be collected on the standard output instead of in files. The -p command lists members, or extracts them with different names from those they were stored with. For example,

```
archive -p arch file1 >file2
```

extracts `file1` into `file2`. Of course to permit this usage, the program must avoid verbiage like

```
successful extraction
1 files extracted
contents of file1:
```

This is good practice for a tool-using environment, where gratuitous comments interfere with the smooth interconnection of programs, and good design for people, who soon get weary of programs that talk too much.

```
{ extract -- extract files from archive }
procedure extract (var aname: string; cmd : character);
var
    ename, inline : string;
    afd, efd : filedesc;
    size : integer;
begin
    afd := mustopen(aname, IOREAD);
    if (cmd = ord('p')) then
        efd := STDOUT
    else         { cmd is 'x' }
        efd := IOERROR;
    while (gethdr(afd, inline, ename, size)) do
        if (not filearg(ename)) then
            fskip(afd, size)
        else begin
            if (efd <> STDOUT) then
                efd := create(ename, IOWRITE);
            if (efd = IOERROR) then begin
                putstr(ename, STDERR);
                message(': can''t create');
                errcount := errcount + 1;
                fskip(afd, size)
            end
            else begin
                acopy(afd, efd, size);
                if (efd <> STDOUT) then
                    close(efd)
            end
        end;
    notfound
end;
```

Again, most of the complexity is in error detection and recovery, not in the operation itself.

acopy copies a member of an archive onto a file, using the size information from the header, instead of looking for the next header. (The test for ENDFILE is another safety measure.) That way it can be used to copy any kind of information at all — it is independent of the content of the archived files.

```
{ acopy -- copy n characters from fdi to fdo }
procedure acopy (fdi, fdo : filedesc; n : integer);
var
    c : character;
    i : integer;
begin
    for i := 1 to n do
        if (getcf(c, fdi) = ENDFILE) then
            error('archive: end of file in acopy')
        else
            putcf(c, fdo)
end;
```

Deleting is identical to updating except that no file replaces a deleted file; we can use `replace` for both the -u and -d commands.

```
{ delete -- delete files from archive }
procedure delete (var aname : string);
var
    afd, tfd : filedesc;
begin
    if (nfiles <= 0) then    { protect innocents }
        error('archive: -d requires explicit file names');
    afd := mustopen(aname, IOREAD);
    tfd := mustcreate(archtemp, IOWRITE);
    replace(afd, tfd, ord('d'));
    notfound;
    close(afd);
    close(tfd);
    if (errcount = 0) then
        fmove(archtemp, aname)
    else
        message('fatal errors - archive not altered');
    remove(archtemp)
end;
```

We have made the command

```
archive -d archname
```

illegal — it does *not* delete all the files from the archive. If you really want to do that, you have to remove them explicitly. It is a small refinement, but it makes the program safer.

Here is `replace`.

```
{ replace -- replace or delete files }
procedure replace (afd, tfd : filedesc; cmd : integer);
var
    inline, uname : string;
    size : integer;
begin
    while (gethdr(afd, inline, uname, size)) do
        if (filearg(uname)) then begin
            if (cmd = ord('u')) then      { add new one }
                addfile(uname, tfd);
            fskip(afd, size)     { discard old one }
        end
        else begin
            putstr(inline, tfd);
            acopy(afd, tfd, size)
        end
end;
```

replace uses addfile to copy the new version of a file to the temporary,
fskip to skip over the archived version, and acopy to copy members that are
unchanged.

Finally we can show the entire main procedure for archive:

```
{ archive -- file maintainer }
procedure archive;
const
    MAXFILES = 100; { or whatever }
var
    aname : string;        { archive name }
    cmd : string;          { command type }
    fname : array [1..MAXFILES] of string;  { filename args }
    fstat : array [1..MAXFILES] of boolean; { true=in archive }
    nfiles : integer;    { number of filename arguments }
    errcount : integer; { number of errors }
    archtemp : string;   { temp file name 'artemp' }
    archhdr : string;    { header string '-h-' }
#include "archproc.p"
begin
    initarch;
    if (not getarg(1, cmd, MAXSTR))
      or (not getarg(2, aname, MAXSTR)) then
        help;
    getfns;
    if (length(cmd) <> 2) or (cmd[1] <> ord('-')) then
        help
    else if (cmd[2] = ord('c')) or (cmd[2] = ord('u')) then
        update(aname, cmd[2])
    else if (cmd[2] = ord('t')) then
        table(aname)
    else if (cmd[2] = ord('x')) or (cmd[2] = ord('p')) then
        extract(aname, cmd[2])
    else if (cmd[2] = ord('d')) then
        delete(aname)
    else
        help
end;
```

Variables are initialized by `initarch`:

```
{ initarch -- initialize variables for archive }
procedure initarch;
begin
    { setstring(archtemp, 'artemp'); }
        archtemp[1] := ord('a');
        archtemp[2] := ord('r');
        archtemp[3] := ord('t');
        archtemp[4] := ord('e');
        archtemp[5] := ord('m');
        archtemp[6] := ord('p');
        archtemp[7] := ENDSTR;
    { setstring(archhdr, '-h-'); }
        archhdr[1] := ord('-');
        archhdr[2] := ord('h');
        archhdr[3] := ord('-');
        archhdr[4] := ENDSTR;
end;
```

The file `archproc.p` simply includes all of the procedures and functions used by `archive`, in the proper order. It's not very interesting, but here it is:

```
{ archproc -- include procedures for archive }
#include "getword.p"
#include "gethdr.p"
#include "filearg.p"
#include "fskip.p"
#include "fmove.p"
#include "acopy.p"
#include "notfound.p"
#include "addfile.p"
#include "replace.p"
#include "help.p"
#include "getfns.p"
#include "update.p"
#include "table.p"
#include "extract.p"
#include "delete.p"
#include "initarch.p"
```

By now it may have struck you that about half the code in `archive` is concerned with error-checking. Many programs can afford to be somewhat cavalier about protecting users from the operating system and their own innocence, because even if the program is badly used, the results aren't likely to be calamitous. But error handling is particularly important for a program like `archive`, because it *changes* files rather than simply making new ones. It overwrites existing files with supposedly correct new contents, so it had better be cautious. For example, it may seem paranoid to abort an entire updating operation merely because one of the files couldn't be accessed. But safety first! It's better to have to run it again than to risk destroying an archive.

3.10 Program Structure

At this point you may well be lost, not because `archive` is a complicated program but because there are an awful lot of pieces. Many of the pieces are old friends, however. These include the file maintenance primitives `open`, `create`, `close` and `remove`; the input and output primitives `getline`, `getarg` and `putstr`; the diagnostic printers `error` and `message`; and utilities like `ctoi`, `itoc`, `length`, `scopy`, `equal` and `getword`. You should learn to think of these low level assistants as *language extensions,* facilities that help you express common operations succinctly, and without distracting you from the real task at hand.

The remaining complexity can be grasped by writing out the *hierarchy* of procedures written specifically for `archive`. This tells you how the program is organized by showing what routines call on what others to do the job. It turns out that the hierarchical structure of a program changes much less from its earliest design than does the code, so a program hierarchy is a useful document to supplement the actual program listing — unlike flowcharts, which merely echo the code and quickly get out of phase with it as changes are made. Some people even draw "structure charts" showing the hierarchy of calls and the arguments passed and returned on each call.

For `archive` we can write the hierarchy as

```
archive
    initarch
    help
    getfns
    update
        replace
            gethdr, filearg, fskip, addfile, acopy
        addfile
            makehdr, fcopy
        fmove
    table
        gethdr, filearg, fskip, notfound, tprint
    extract
        gethdr, filearg, fskip, notfound, acopy
    delete
        replace, notfound, fmove
```

This says that `archive` makes calls on `initarch`, `help`, `getfns`, `update`, `table`, `extract` and `delete` (in addition to various low level routines) to do its job. `update` in turn calls `replace`, `addfile`, and `fmove`; `replace` and `addfile` call still other routines; and so on. We list some of the sets horizontally, separated by commas, instead of vertically, to save space. We also don't bother to show an expansion more than once (note the instance of `replace` in the last line), for much the same reason that we leave out all the low level routines: it just adds clutter. We will frequently present hierarchies for the larger programs, to help you keep track of the organization.

The hierarchy reveals several things. First, the overall structure of `archive` is just a multi-way branch, making a call on one of the four cases `update`, `table`, `extract` or `delete`. Each case is expanded in terms of a handful of *action* routines. `gethdr`, `filearg`, etc., play a role similar to `open`, `getline`, and the other primitives — they permit the basic functions that must be performed to be expressed at a more abstract (and readable) level, as well as insulating `archive` from low level implementation decisions. At each level the lower routines are used as building blocks that perform some function, with relatively little dependence on *how* they perform it.

Notice that no routine has more than a handful of immediate subordinates. It is a good rule of thumb that a person can't properly keep track of more than half a dozen things at a time, so this hierarchy gives some reassurance that no part of the design will be too difficult to grasp. Finally, it is worth observing that operations as diverse as `update`, `table`, and `delete` make use of essentially the same action routines in different sequences. This is the reward of orderly design, that common operations can be identified and singled out as basic actions. Programs built this way are easier to get right and to maintain, because the strategy for each case (`update`, `table`, etc.) and the details of each action (`gethdr`, `filearg`, etc.) can be dealt with separately.

Exercise 3-18. How do you represent the hierarchy of a program that contains a recursive procedure, i.e., one that calls itself? How about a program with mutual recursion, e.g. A calls B which in turn calls A? What does each of these practices do to a structure chart? Can you think of a better way to document the structure of a highly recursive program with multiply-used low level functions? □

Exercise 3-19. Now that you have seen `archive` with a distributed directory, design and implement a version with the directory at the beginning. Compare the advantages and disadvantages. Observations about "efficiency" should be supported by empirical studies of the operations people really perform on an archive. □

Exercise 3-20. `archive` could be simpler and faster if the operating system provided certain primitive operations, such as renaming the temporary instead of copying, knowing how big a file is without having to read it, moving to an arbitrary point in a file without reading intervening material, and selectively overwriting parts of a file. Consider these and other primitives that might be useful. Do they exist in the operating system you use? Could they? How do such primitives affect the directory-at-the-front version? □

Exercise 3-21. In most systems, an archive program saves space because it collects small files into one big one; this eliminates the breakage or fragmentation that normally comes from putting each file into an integral number of blocks or tracks on some secondary storage device. Theoretically, what is this saving? Measure and see how well the theoretical prediction is observed in practice. □

Exercise 3-22. `archive` makes no comment about

```
archive -u arch
```

Should it? If you could find out the date and time a file was last changed, what would be a useful interpretation for this command? Should there be separate commands for creating a new archive and updating an existing one? □

Exercise 3-23. If you work in an interactive environment, add a "verbose" option, so `archive` will print out messages about what it is doing as it runs, and perhaps offer you the choice on each file of having the command operate or not. □

Exercise 3-24. How can you add a file `f` to an archive that already contains an `f`? Should multiple occurrences be allowed in an archive? If you concatenate two archives with `concat`, is the result a valid archive? □

Exercise 3-25. `archive` provides no way to specify the position of a file added to an archive. Does it need one? What syntax would you use? Implement it. □

Exercise 3-26. Our archive files are always made as small as possible, by recreating them when they change. Some systems provide programs rather like `archive` that don't reclaim space unless explicitly requested. Discuss the merits and demerits of such an organization. □

Exercise 3-27. What happens if two people run `archive` in the same part of a file system at the same time? How would you remedy the situation? □

3.11 Summary

This chapter has discussed how programs interface to their environment, particularly how they access file information. Few systems are regular and systematic in the interface they present, and of course there are great differences between systems. We have tried to write the discussion and the programs in terms of a handful of primitive operations that are likely to exist or at least be implementable on most operating systems. Describing system interactions exclusively with such primitives is the most effective approach we know for coping with the bewildering complexity of typical operating systems.

The file system primitives we use are:

`open`   Connect the external name of an information stream (a "file") to an internal name which is then usable by the program. Position the file at the beginning. Opening a fresh instance of an already open file should be permissible.

`create`   Create a new file, given its external name, from within a running program. If the file already exists, the old version should be removed or truncated and overwritten. `create` is a crucial primitive, but the least likely to be available. Even some major operating systems do not provide it.

`close`   Break the connection made by `open` or `create` and free the file descriptor for re-use. Mark the end of the file if necessary, so that subsequent reads will find an `ENDFILE` at the proper point.

`remove`   Remove a file from the file system.

We assume that when a program is started by our standard environment it already has the three files `STDIN`, `STDOUT` and `STDERR` open and ready to go. We presume that when a program terminates for any reason, any open files are closed gracefully. We have also assumed that a file is made the right size by the system — if you write more information on it, it gets bigger automatically. It seems intuitively obvious that a file should be as big as it is (and no bigger), and that it should get bigger as you put more into it, but on all too many systems you have to arrange this yourself, clumsily.

One mark of a good operating system is that all of these operations are available, uniform, easy to use, and applicable without major exception to all files from all programs. You might find it an enlightening experience to read some of the manuals for your system and see how well it does by these criteria.

Bibliographic Notes

The problem of file comparison has not been fully solved, but various forms of it are attacked by algorithms that compute a minimum set of changes necessary to convert one n-line file into another, in time $n^2\log n$ worst case, but typically much better, often linear in the file size. The basic procedure itself is not too difficult, but it requires considerable help from the local operating system in order to handle lines of *a priori* unknown length without wasting great amounts of storage. For more information, see "A fast algorithm for computing longest common subsequences," by J. W. Hunt and T. G. Szymanski, *CACM,* May, 1977. A discussion of pragmatic issues using this algorithm can be found in M. D. McIlroy and J. W. Hunt, "An algorithm for differential file comparison," Bell Labs Computing Science Technical Report 41, 1976.

Although there is a substantial literature on the implementation of file systems, relatively little is concerned with the programmer interface. The model for most of our I/O primitives has been the Unix operating system, which provides an exceptionally clean set. See "The Unix time-sharing system," by K. L. Thompson and D. M. Ritchie, *CACM,* July, 1974, reprinted with related papers in *The Bell System Technical Journal,* July, 1978. The paper "A Portable File Directory System," by D. R. Hanson, *Software Practice and Experience,* August, 1980, discusses how to provide a similar environment on any system. "A Virtual Operating System," by D. E. Hall, D. K. Scherrer and J. S. Sventek, *CACM,* September, 1980, describes how pipes and file redirection can be implemented on a variety of systems.

Structure charts are described in W. P. Stevens, G. J. Myers and L. L. Constantine, "Structured design," *IBM Systems Journal,* April, 1974.

Sorting is an everyday programming task, and often a building block in larger processes. In this chapter we will tackle sorting, but we will be more concerned with the human interface of a sort program than with presenting some "best possible" sorting algorithm. If a sorting program is so poorly packaged that people feel compelled to write their own instead of figuring out how to use it, then the quality of its sorting algorithm is surely irrelevant. But if the packaging is good, if users perceive sorting as a convenient *tool,* then it will be used, the algorithm can be improved as needed, and *all* users will benefit.

4.1 Bubble Sort

Every programmer is familiar with some variant of the interchange sort. For example the *bubble sort* sorts the first n elements of an array of integers (of type intarray) into ascending order like this:

```
{ bubble -- bubble sort v[1] ... v[n] increasing }
procedure bubble (var v : intarray; n : integer);
var
    i, j, k : integer;
begin
    for i := n downto 2 do
        for j := 1 to i-1 do
            if (v[j] > v[j+1]) then begin    { compare }
                k := v[j];   { exchange }
                v[j] := v[j+1];
                v[j+1] := k
            end
end;
```

The inner loop rearranges out-of-order adjacent elements on each pass; by the end of the pass, the largest element has been "bubbled" to the end, that is, to v[i]. The outer loop repeats the process, each time decreasing the current array limit i by one.

The main advantage of the bubble sort is its simplicity. Its drawback, a serious one, is that it gets very slow very fast as the number of elements to be sorted gets large. The *time complexity* of bubble sorting (and similar sorts) is n^2. That is, the time required to sort varies as the square of the number of items to be sorted: twice as big takes four times as long. How large is too large? That depends on the alternative being considered, and on how often the data is to be sorted, but something between ten and fifty items might be a reasonable limit, above which the bubble sort is better replaced by a more sophisticated algorithm.

In real life, by the way, you would certainly name the routine `sort`, not `bubble`, so you could change the algorithm without upsetting users. We use `bubble` here because we want a unique name for each program.

4.2 Shell Sort

In a sense, the Shell sort is the next step up in complexity from the bubble sort; we present it because it is similar in spirit, compact, but much faster for large arrays. The time complexity of the Shell sort is approximately $n^{1.5}$.

The basic idea of the Shell sort is that in the early stages far-apart elements are compared, instead of adjacent ones. This tends to eliminate large amounts of disorder quickly, so later stages have less work to do. Gradually the interval between compared elements is decreased, until it reaches one, at which point it effectively becomes an adjacent interchange method.

```
{ shell -- Shell sort v[1]...v[n] increasing }
procedure shell (var v : intarray; n : integer);
var
    gap, i, j, jg, k : integer;
begin
    gap := n div 2;
    while (gap > 0) do begin
        for i := gap+1 to n do begin
            j := i - gap;
            while (j > 0) do begin
                jg := j + gap;
                if (v[j] <= v[jg]) then      { compare }
                    j := 0  { force loop termination }
                else begin
                    k := v[j];  { exchange }
                    v[j] := v[jg];
                    v[jg] := k
                end;
                j := j - gap
            end
        end;
        gap := gap div 2
    end
end;
```

The outermost loop controls the gap between compared elements. Initially n/2, it shrinks by a factor of two each pass until it becomes zero. The middle loop compares elements separated by `gap`; the innermost loop reverses any that are out of order. Since `gap` is eventually reduced to one, eventually all elements are ordered correctly.

A word on modularity. Many sorting procedures have three distinct parts. A *comparison* operation decides what the order of two elements is. An *exchange* operation interchanges two out-of-order elements. Finally, a *sorting algorithm* decides what comparisons and exchanges must be made. Often the only thing that need change between two sorting procedures is the algorithm, so a program should be carefully organized to take this into account. If the three aspects are clearly separated, each may be individually improved without affecting the others.

Exercise 4-1. How would you test a sorting program? What are the obvious boundary conditions that must be checked to ensure correct operation? What programs would you write to help in your verification? What programs have we already written that help? □

Exercise 4-2. Compare the bubble sort and the Shell sort experimentally. Where is the crossover point at which the Shell sort becomes better on your machine and compiler? □

Exercise 4-3. In our version of the Shell sort, when two out-of-order elements are found they are immediately exchanged. If an element is small relative to the other elements at the current gap, however, several unnecessary exchanges may be performed. Redistribute the exchange so the element moving toward the beginning of the array is held in a temporary location until its correct position has been found. Measure this version to decide if the increase in speed outweighs the loss of clarity in the algorithm. □

Exercise 4-4. The Shell sort has been observed to run somewhat faster when the value of `gap` is always odd. Modify `shell` accordingly and experiment to see how large the effect is. □

4.3 Sorting Text

Since many of the tools we discuss in this book are for manipulating text, it is worth adapting our sorting procedure for this kind of operation too. One especially useful form is a program that sorts a text file line by line into increasing lexicographic order. As we shall soon see, this operation is useful in its own right, and also as a part of other processes.

There are two major considerations in the design — convenience and efficiency. `sort` should be dead easy to use, requiring no setup at all for common sorting tasks. At the same time it should be reasonably effective (i.e., cheap) on both small files and on moderately big ones. `sort` is not intended to replace a carefully tailored sort for a repeated production application, but it should be a tool that is convenient and economical over a wide spectrum of input file sizes — one which will encourage a casual user to select it as a matter of course. The first draft will be a program that sorts a set of lines that fits into memory all at once. Later we will expand it to handle files too big to be stored completely in memory.

We will write the sorting program to read its standard input and write its standard output, so it can be used as a filter. Of course sort can't produce any output until all of the input has been read (why?), so calling it a filter may seem to be stretching a point, but that is not important. What is important is that as far as the user is concerned, the program *looks like* a filter, so it can be used in a pipeline.

The procedures presented earlier in this chapter sorted arrays of integers; here we want to treat lines of text. Unfortunately lines are not all of the same length. Although we have been able so far to get away with a fixed size for all lines, this is just not realistic for sorting, where running time will be strongly dependent on how many lines fit in memory at one time. We need a data representation that will cope efficiently and conveniently with variable length lines.

One solution is to refer to the lines *indirectly,* by pointers. It is difficult, however, to arrange for pointers to arbitrary-length lines; furthermore, there is no way to detect when we have run out of storage if we use the standard procedure new to allocate space for lines. Instead we will use indices into an array as pointer equivalents. A big array linebuf of characters holds the lines to be sorted, packed end to end. A second array, linepos, contains indices that tell where the corresponding lines begin in linebuf. That is, linepos[i] is the position in linebuf of the beginning of the ith line. When an exchange is called for, the indices are exchanged, not the text lines themselves. This eliminates the twin problems of complicated storage management and high overhead that would be part of moving the lines themselves. The figure below shows how the positions and text for the sentences of this paragraph would look before sorting.

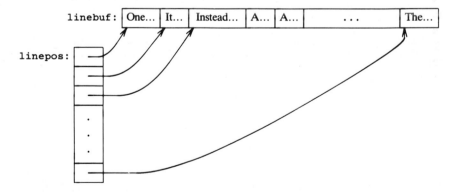

The in-memory sort thus reads lines into a convenient data structure, sorts them (rearranging only the positions in linepos), then prints them.

```
    { sort -- sort text lines in memory }
    procedure inmemsort;
    const
        MAXCHARS = 10000;    { maximum # of text characters }
        MAXLINES = 300;      { maximum # of lines }
    type
        charbuf = array [1..MAXCHARS] of character;
        charpos = 1..MAXCHARS;
        posbuf = array [1..MAXLINES] of charpos;
        pos = 0..MAXLINES;
    var
        linebuf : charbuf;
        linepos : posbuf;
        nlines : pos;
    #include "gtext.p"
    #include "shell.p"
    #include "ptext.p"
    begin
        if (gtext(linepos, nlines, linebuf, STDIN)) then begin
            shell(linepos, nlines, linebuf);
            ptext(linepos, nlines, linebuf, STDOUT)
        end
        else
            error('sort: input too big to sort')
    end;
```

sort calls a modified version of shell, which we will show in a moment, that moves the indices in linepos, not the lines themselves. gtext reads the lines and sets up the indices; ptext uses them to output the lines in sorted order.

gtext stops reading when it cannot guarantee enough space for another line. It returns true if end of file was encountered during input, which is used here only to provide some error checking. linepos[i] is set to the position in linebuf of the first character of the ith line. MAXSTR is the length of the longest line we are willing to deal with, MAXCHARS is the maximum space for characters, and MAXLINES the maximum number of lines.

```
{ gtext -- get text lines into linebuf }
function gtext (var linepos : posbuf; var nlines : pos;
        var linebuf : charbuf; infile : filedesc) : boolean;
var
    i, len, nextpos : integer;
    temp : string;
    done : boolean;
begin
    nlines := 0;
    nextpos := 1;
    repeat
        done := (getline(temp, infile, MAXSTR) = false);
        if (not done) then begin
            nlines := nlines + 1;
            linepos[nlines] := nextpos;
            len := length(temp);
            for i := 1 to len do
                linebuf[nextpos+i-1] := temp[i];
            linebuf[nextpos+len] := ENDSTR;
            nextpos := nextpos + len + 1  { 1 for ENDSTR }
        end
    until (done) or (nextpos >= MAXCHARS-MAXSTR)
            or (nlines >= MAXLINES);
    gtext := done
end;

{ ptext -- output text lines from linebuf }
procedure ptext (var linepos : posbuf; nlines : integer;
        var linebuf : charbuf; outfile : filedesc);
var
    i, j : integer;
begin
    for i := 1 to nlines do begin
        j := linepos[i];
        while (linebuf[j] <> ENDSTR) do begin
            putcf(linebuf[j], outfile);
            j := j + 1
        end
    end
end;
```

Of course we can write and test gtext and ptext independently of whatever sorting procedure we use. In fact there need not even be a sort during testing: a dummy shell that returns without doing anything is enough for verifying that gtext indeed builds arrays that ptext can interpret properly. It is hard to cope with a single routine of tightly interwoven code. Incremental construction and testing make it easy to test a program whose pieces implement separate functions and interact only through clear, well-defined interfaces.

Our sort must also be modified to treat comparison and exchange as procedures, called cmp and exchange. (We use cmp instead of compare to avoid a name used in Chapter 3.) Here is the Shell sort.

```
{ shell -- ascending Shell sort for lines }
procedure shell (var linepos : posbuf; nlines : integer;
        var linebuf : charbuf);
var
    gap, i, j, jg : integer;
#include "cmp.p"
#include "exchange.p"
begin
    gap := nlines div 2;
    while (gap > 0) do begin
        for i := gap+1 to nlines do begin
            j := i - gap;
            while (j > 0) do begin
                jg := j + gap;
                if (cmp(linepos[j],linepos[jg],linebuf)<=0) then
                    j := 0  { force loop termination }
                else
                    exchange(linepos[j], linepos[jg]);
                j := j - gap
            end
        end;
        gap := gap div 2
    end
end;
```

The operator div yields the integer quotient of its operands.

The exchange operation is the easier part: exchange only needs to exchange the two line positions.

```
{ exchange -- exchange linebuf[lp1] with linebuf[lp2] }
procedure exchange (var lp1, lp2 : charpos);
var
    temp : charpos;
begin
    temp := lp1;
    lp1 := lp2;
    lp2 := temp
end;
```

cmp returns a negative value if its first argument is less than its second, zero if its arguments are equal, and a positive value if the first is greater than the second.

How do we handle comparisons? The main difficulty is the perennial problem of the character set being used. Pascal guarantees that digits compare among themselves the way we expect, and that letters do too, but may be interspersed with other funny characters. It says nothing, however, about how digits compare with letters, or punctuation with anything else. The whole topic is a can of worms!

One solution is to provide a two-argument routine lexorder, which returns the lexical ordering that holds between any pair of characters:

```
function lexorder (c1, c2 : character) : integer;
```

returns a negative value if c1<c2, zero if c1=c2, and positive if c1>c2. cmp could then call lexorder when it needs to know the relationship between two characters. Of course it typically only has to call lexorder once per call of cmp (why?), so this organization is not as expensive as you might think at first.

A second solution, which we will adopt, assumes that the character set is well-behaved, so that letters, digits and punctuation all sort into a sensible order. This is true of ASCII and EBCDIC, for instance, even though they sort somewhat differently.

In some circumstances, more effort may be needed. Each character can be mapped into its correct place in the ordering immediately upon input. Comparisons may then be made directly. The characters are mapped back into external representation before output. This is a compromise between efficiency and portability, but if the character set is truly disorderly, it's the cheapest organization. It's better to map the characters once on input and once on output rather than every time they must be compared.

Here is a version of cmp which is appropriate if letters and numbers each sort in increasing order.

```
        { cmp -- compare linebuf[i] with linebuf[j] }
        function cmp (i, j : charpos; var linebuf : charbuf)
                : integer;
        begin
            while (linebuf[i] = linebuf[j])
              and (linebuf[i] <> ENDSTR) do begin
                i := i + 1;
                j := j + 1
            end;
            if (linebuf[i] = linebuf[j]) then
                cmp := 0
            else if (linebuf[i] = ENDSTR) then   { 1st is shorter }
                cmp := -1
            else if (linebuf[j] = ENDSTR) then   { 2nd is shorter }
                cmp := +1
            else if (linebuf[i] < linebuf[j]) then
                cmp := -1
            else
                cmp := +1
        end;
```

cmp makes no assumptions about the value of ENDSTR. It could be shorter and faster if ENDSTR were guaranteed to be less than any character.

The procedure organization in sort is such that a knowledgeable user can readily provide private versions of cmp and exchange for special applications, while still deriving the benefit of whatever sophistication has gone into the sorting algorithm.

Exercise 4-5. The sorting program has a fair amount of overhead in the inner loop. Experiment with moving the comparison and exchange into shell. How much improvement does this make? Make some reasonable assumptions about how often sort will be used and how big the files will be, then decide if it should be changed. □

Exercise 4-6. Add an option to sort to allow the direction of sorting to be reversed:

        sort -r

sorts into decreasing order instead of ascending. Where should the direction-changing code go — in cmp, in shell, in ptext, or somewhere else? □

4.4 Quicksort

One of the best sorting algorithms known is *quicksort*, invented by C. A. R. Hoare. Although in the worst case its running time can be proportional to n^2, quicksort can be arranged so the worst case rarely occurs, and its average running time is $n\log n$.

Quicksort is best described as a recursive procedure. The essential idea is to partition the original set to be sorted by rearranging it into two groups — all those elements less than some arbitrary value chosen from the set, and all those greater than or equal to the value. Then the same partitioning process is applied to the two subsets in turn until each subset contains only one element. When all subsets have been partitioned, the original set is sorted.

```
procedure quick(v, i, j)
    if (i < j)
        partition the elements v[i] ... v[j] so that
          v[i], v[i+1] ... v[k-1] <= v[k] <= v[k+1] ... v[j]
            where i <= k <= j
        quick(v, i, k-1)
        quick(v, k+1, j)
```

To sort an array v, just say

```
quick(v, 1, n)
```

and stand well back. You should go through a few small test cases by hand to be sure you understand the basic flow of control, before reading on into the details.

The heart of the algorithm is "partition the elements so that ... ." The recursive algorithm does not make any copies of the original array v; all work is done by passing indices to indicate what range of v is to be rearranged at a particular step. This means that the only extra storage needed by quicksort is space for the stack of array limits describing subsets not yet partitioned. It is easy to show that if at each stage quicksort deals with the shorter subset before the longer, the stack never gets deeper than $\log_2 n$. Even for n equal to a million, $\log_2 n$ is only 20, so this extra space requirement is insignificant.

Recursive algorithms are sometimes less efficient than equivalent iterative ones, often because of procedure call overhead, but for quicksort it's not a significant effect — the recursion is not in the innermost loop. Some of the exercises deal with efficiency questions once the basic algorithm is in hand.

Partitioning is the important step. Suppose the current limits in the array are `lo` and `hi`. We select a "pivot" element `pivline` arbitrarily — the last element in the set, `v[hi]` — and rearrange all lines with respect to the pivot value. The elements are rearranged entirely within the subset of v between `lo` and `hi`.

```
i := lo
j := hi
pivline := last line, i.e., line[hi]
repeat
    increase i until i >= j or line[i] > pivline
    decrease j until j <= i or line[j] < pivline
    { at this point, either i and j have met }
    { or we have an out-of-order pair }
    if (i < j)  { exchange out-of-order pair }
        exchange line[i] and line[j]
until (i >= j)
{ move the pivot element pivline to the 'middle' }
exchange line[i] and line[hi]
```

We can now put the pieces together for the final version of quicksort, procedure `quick`:

```
{ quick -- quicksort for lines }
procedure quick (var linepos : posbuf; nlines : pos;
        var linebuf : charbuf);
#include "rquick.p"
begin
    rquick(1, nlines)
end;
```

The real work is done in `rquick`:

```
{ rquick -- recursive quicksort }
procedure rquick (lo, hi: integer);
var
    i, j : integer;
    pivline : charpos;
begin
    if (lo < hi) then begin
        i := lo;
        j := hi;
        pivline := linepos[j];   { pivot line }
        repeat
            while (i < j)
              and (cmp(linepos[i],pivline,linebuf) <= 0) do
                i := i + 1;
            while (j > i)
              and (cmp(linepos[j],pivline,linebuf) >= 0) do
                j := j - 1;
            if (i < j) then       { out of order pair }
                exchange(linepos[i], linepos[j])
        until (i >= j);
        exchange(linepos[i], linepos[hi]); { move pivot to i }
        if (i - lo < hi - i) then begin
            rquick(lo, i-1);
            rquick(i+1, hi)
        end
        else begin
            rquick(i+1, hi);
            rquick(lo, i-1)
        end
    end
end;
```

Like most sorting algorithms, quicksort has many variations. We can only suggest a few here; the bibliography at the end of the chapter indicates others.

As presented, quick does not use the fact that there may be several elements all equal to the pivot. If all such elements are brought together at one partitioning, no further partitions need involve them. The "fat pivot" algorithm returns two values k1 and k2 from the partitioning, such that

$$v[lo] \; ... \; v[k1-1] < v[k1] = \; ... \; = v[k2] < v[k2+1] \; ... \; v[hi]$$

and successive partitions are done on the subsets

$$lo \; ... \; k1-1 \quad and \quad k2+1 \; ... \; hi$$

This organization is faster for sorting data like word lists, which frequently contain many duplicate entries.

Exercise 4-7. Experiment with a fat pivot algorithm. How much faster is it on files with significant duplication? How much slower is it than a regular quicksort on files with little or no duplication? □

Exercise 4-8. Write a non-recursive version of quicksort and contrast its speed with the recursive one. ☐

Exercise 4-9. If an array is already sorted in either order, pivoting on the end element is a bad thing to do: it converts the algorithm into an n^2 procedure. (Why?) One solution is to pivot on the middle element of a set instead. More complicated but more effective is to pivot on the median of three or more elements. Investigate these variations. ☐

Exercise 4-10. Our quicksort may make more comparisons and exchanges than are absolutely necessary. Find a version that cuts down on the number of comparisons between actual lines, even at the expense of doing more of other bookkeeping operations, and see how much difference this makes. ☐

Exercise 4-11. When the number of elements in a partition is small, it may be faster to sort them with a bubble sort because it has lower overhead. Experiment to see how large the effect is. ☐

4.5 Sorting Big Files

"Big" means more data than will fit in memory all at once; this is where life gets complicated. This kind of sorting is often called *external* sorting, because some of the data has to reside on temporary intermediate files. What we did in the previous section is by contrast *internal* sorting.

As with internal sorting, there is an astonishing variety of external sorting methods to choose from. The central idea of most is simple: chunks of the input (as big as possible) are sorted internally and copied onto intermediate files; each chunk is called a run. When the entire input has been split into sorted runs, the runs are merged, typically onto further intermediate files. Eventually all the data winds up merged on one file; this final run is the sorted output.

Not all operating systems let you create an arbitrary number of files, which is implied by this approach, so it may be necessary to add the complexity of managing a limited number of intermediates. Even if you can have lots of intermediate files, however, merging from a large number of sources has to be properly organized or it becomes too slow. (Consider the extreme case: if each file contains only one line of the original input, how long would merging take, as a function of the number of lines?)

One of the clearest sorting procedures is to place each run on a separate file, until the input is exhausted. Then the first *m* files are merged onto a new file, and the *m* files removed. (*m* is a parameter, typically between 3 and 7, called the *merge order*). This process is repeated with the next *m* files until there is only one file left, which is the sorted output. This procedure never has to deal with more than *m* merge files plus one output file at a time.

The main routine of the next version of sort implements this strategy. Most of it is concerned with creating, opening, closing and removing files at the right times.

```
{ sort -- external sort of text lines }
procedure sort;
const
    MAXCHARS = 10000;    { maximum # of text characters }
    MAXLINES = 300;      { maximum # of lines }
    MERGEORDER = 5;
type
    charpos = 1..MAXCHARS;
    charbuf = array [1..MAXCHARS] of character;
    posbuf = array [1..MAXLINES] of charpos;
    pos = 0..MAXLINES;
    fdbuf = array [1..MERGEORDER] of filedesc;
var
    linebuf : charbuf;
    linepos : posbuf;
    nlines : pos;
    infile : fdbuf;
    outfile : filedesc;
    high, low, lim : integer;
    done : boolean;
    name : string;
#include "sortproc.p"
begin
    high := 0;
    repeat   { initial formation of runs }
        done := gtext(linepos, nlines, linebuf, STDIN);
        quick(linepos, nlines, linebuf);
        high := high + 1;
        outfile := makefile(high);
        ptext(linepos, nlines, linebuf, outfile);
        close(outfile)
    until (done);
    low := 1;
    while (low < high) do begin { merge runs }
        lim := min(low+MERGEORDER-1, high);
        gopen(infile, low, lim);
        high := high + 1;
        outfile := makefile(high);
        merge(infile, lim-low+1, outfile);
        close(outfile);
        gremove(infile, low, lim);
        low := low + MERGEORDER
    end;
    gname(high, name);   { final cleanup }
    outfile := open(name, IOREAD);
    fcopy(outfile, STDOUT);
    close(outfile);
    remove(name)
end;
```

The merge phase of sort uses two indices, low and high, to indicate the range of files still active. high is incremented by 1, MERGEORDER files starting at low are merged onto file high, then low is incremented by MERGEORDER. When low catches up to high, the merging is finished, so the single run on the last file is copied onto the final output.

We have already seen gtext, ptext, and quick earlier in this chapter, and fcopy, which copies one file to another, is from Chapter 3. sortproc includes all the procedures needed by sort:

```
{ sortproc -- procedures for sort }
#include "cmp.p"
#include "exchange.p"
#include "gtext.p"
#include "ptext.p"
#include "quick.p"
#include "gname.p"
#include "makefile.p"
#include "gopen.p"
#include "merge.p"
#include "gremove.p"
```

Within the main routine, files are referred to by a number corresponding to their order of creation. makefile creates a new temporary file for a given number, using gname to convert the number into a unique, systematic name.

```
{ makefile -- make new file for number n }
function makefile (n : integer) : filedesc;
var
    name : string;
begin
    gname(n, name);
    makefile := mustcreate(name, IOWRITE)
end;
```

gname copies a standard prefix (stemp) into name, then appends n as a character string. Thus the temporary files used by sort are called stemp1, stemp2, and so on.

```
{ gname -- generate unique name for file id n }
procedure gname (n : integer; var name : string);
var
    junk : integer;
begin
    { setstring(name, 'stemp'); }
        name[1] := ord('s');
        name[2] := ord('t');
        name[3] := ord('e');
        name[4] := ord('m');
        name[5] := ord('p');
        name[6] := ENDSTR;
    junk := itoc(n, name, length(name)+1)
end;
```

gopen and gremove open and remove consecutively numbered sets of files. They both regenerate the file names rather than carry them around.

```
{ gopen -- open group of files f1 ... f2 }
procedure gopen (var infile : fdbuf; f1, f2 : integer);
var
    name : string;
    i : 1..MERGEORDER;
begin
    for i := 1 to f2-f1+1 do begin
        gname(f1+i-1, name);
        infile[i] := mustopen(name, IOREAD)
    end
end;


{ gremove -- remove group of files f1 ... f2 }
procedure gremove (var infile : fdbuf; f1, f2 : integer);
var
    name : string;
    i : 1..MERGEORDER;
begin
    for i := 1 to f2-f1+1 do begin
        close(infile[i]);
        gname(f1+i-1, name);
        remove(name)
    end
end;
```

At any given time there are no more than MERGEORDER input files and one output file open, although there may be other temporary files created but not open. sort assumes that files can be created dynamically and made as large as necessary while the input is being read, although on some systems you may in fact have to specify size limits for these files. In any case, it is critically important that the files come and go without the knowledge of the user. Few things

put people off so fast as having to provide a collection of scratch files with myst-
ical parameters for what should be a simple process.

merge is now the only unspecified code. In principle its task is easy. Since
the input files are sorted, the first line on each file is the smallest. merge
selects the smallest of these, which is necessarily the smallest line in the entire
group, and copies it to the output. The next line from that file replaces the line
that went out, and a fresh smallest one is identified. When ENDFILE is
encountered on a file, the corresponding run is finished. When the run on each
file is finished, merge is done.

The main question is how to efficiently select the smallest line each time.
The obvious method, linearly searching the MERGEORDER lines currently available, is acceptable if MERGEORDER is small, but we can do better with a better
algorithm and data structure.

One of the best is to arrange the lines as a *heap*. A heap has two desirable
properties: its smallest entry can be found immediately, and a new element can
be put into the proper position in a heap in a time that grows only logarithmi-
cally with the heap size. You can imagine a heap as a binary tree (that is, each
element has at most two descendants) in which each element is less than or
equal to its children. From a programming standpoint, it is easier to represent
a heap as an array h such that the children of element k are stored at positions
2k and 2k+1. Then h[1] is less than or equal to h[2] and h[3]; h[2] is
less than or equal to h[4] and h[5], and in general, h[k] is less than or
equal to h[2k] and h[2k+1]. h[1] is the smallest thing in the heap.

With a heap, the merging process is as follows.

```
read one line from each file
form a heap
while (there's still input)
    output smallest line, heap[1]
    get a new line into heap[1] from same file
    reheap: move new line into its proper place in the heap
```

The smallest line is in the first position. That element is output, a new one is
read in to take its place from the file whose line was just output (why?), and
the new element is moved to its proper place in the heap ("reheaping"). The
initial heap can be formed by using quick to sort the lines, since a sorted array
is a heap (why?) although the converse is not true (why?). True, sorting does a
bit more work than necessary, but the difference will be imperceptible. Why
write extra code?

```
{ merge -- merge infile[1] ... infile[nf] onto outfile }
procedure merge (var infile : fdbuf; nf : integer;
        outfile : filedesc);
var
    i, j : integer;
    lbp : charpos;
    temp : string;
#include "reheap.p"
#include "sccopy.p"
#include "cscopy.p"
begin
    j := 0;
    for i := 1 to nf do { get one line from each file }
        if (getline(temp, infile[i], MAXSTR)) then begin
            lbp := (i-1)*MAXSTR + 1; { room for longest }
            sccopy(temp, linebuf, lbp);
            linepos[i] := lbp;
            j := j + 1
        end;
    nf := j;
    quick(linepos, nf, linebuf);      { make initial heap }
    while (nf > 0) do begin
        lbp := linepos[1];   { lowest line }
        cscopy(linebuf, lbp, temp);
        putstr(temp, outfile);
        i := lbp div MAXSTR + 1;     { compute file index }
        if (getline(temp, infile[i], MAXSTR)) then
            sccopy(temp, linebuf, lbp)
        else begin   { one less input file }
            linepos[1] := linepos[nf];
            nf := nf - 1
        end;
        reheap(linepos, nf, linebuf)
    end
end;
```

To avoid complicated storage management, merge reserves space for the longest possible line in each slot. This makes it easy to decide which file is associated with a particular line, by dividing the line origin by the maximum line size.

merge also calls upon two general-purpose string copying routines that are useful for manipulating the variable-length lines used in sort. sccopy copies a string into a charbuf; cscopy does the opposite.

```
{ sccopy -- copy string s to cb[i]... }
procedure sccopy (var s : string; var cb : charbuf;
        i : charpos);
var
    j : integer;
begin
    j := 1;
    while (s[j] <> ENDSTR) do begin
        cb[i] := s[j];
        j := j + 1;
        i := i + 1
    end;
    cb[i] := ENDSTR
end;

{ cscopy -- copy cb[i]... to string s }
procedure cscopy (var cb : charbuf; i : charpos;
        var s : string);
var
    j : integer;
begin
    j := 1;
    while (cb[i] <> ENDSTR) do begin
        s[j] := cb[i];
        i := i + 1;
        j := j + 1
    end;
    s[j] := ENDSTR
end;
```

Reheaping compares the top element to its children. If the element is less than or equal to both, it is in its proper position and the job is done. If not, then the element is exchanged with the smaller of its children, and the process repeated at the next level of the tree, i.e., by comparing the element with its children in its new position. Eventually the element percolates through the tree to the place where it belongs.

It is easy to show that the reheaping time is proportional to log(MERGEORDER), while a linear search naturally takes time linearly proportional to MERGEORDER. The heap procedure is only a few more lines of code than the linear version and should be faster for typical values of MERGEORDER.

```
{ reheap -- put linebuf[linepos[1]] in proper place in heap }
procedure reheap (var linepos : posbuf; nf : pos;
        var linebuf : charbuf);
var
    i, j : integer;
begin
    i := 1;
    j := 2 * i;
    while (j <= nf) do begin
        if (j < nf) then    { find smaller child }
            if (cmp(linepos[j],linepos[j+1],linebuf)>0) then
                j := j + 1;
        if (cmp(linepos[i], linepos[j], linebuf)<=0) then
            i := nf { proper position found; terminate loop }
        else
            exchange(linepos[i], linepos[j]);    { percolate }
        i := j;
        j := 2 * i
    end
end;
```

Notice that `quick`, `merge` and `reheap` all work properly if called with no data items. This is because all of the loops in the code test at the top instead of the bottom. It is a good omen for the overall reliability of a program when its boundaries are reliable without special attention.

You should also glance back over the organization of `sort` and observe the way in which it is broken into modules. The sort, the merge, the compare, the input and the output can each be replaced separately without upsetting the rest of the program.

We are now in a position to specify the manual page for `sort`:

PROGRAM
    sort   sort text lines
USAGE
    sort
FUNCTION
    sort sorts its input into ascending lexicographic order. Two lines are in order if they are identical or if the leftmost character position in which they differ contains characters which are in order, using the internal numeric representation of the characters. If a line is a proper prefix of another line, it precedes that line in sort order.
    sort writes intermediate data to files named stemp#, where # is a small decimal digit string; these filenames should be avoided.
EXAMPLE
    To print the sorted output of a program:
        program | sort | print

Exercise 4-12. How much intermediate file space is needed all at once to sort input containing n characters? □

4.6 Improvements

Once the basic version works, we can make `sort` faster and we can make it do more things. Since this is a book about tools, not algorithms, we are more interested in functional enhancements, but let us first mention some efficiency considerations.

We measured `sort` on several different inputs. We set limits of 10,000 characters in `linebuf` and 300 lines in `linepos`. For the first three tests, the merge order was 3.

The first test was 298 lines (6640 characters) of Pascal source code, which all fits in memory, so only one temporary file was created. This took 4.7 seconds (on a VAX 11/780), of which input was 39.6 percent, output 30.6 percent, `cmp` 10.8 percent, `rquick` 4.9 percent, `ptext` 3.8 percent, `fcopy` 3.5 percent, and `gtext` 2.1 percent.

The second test was 890 lines (19,240 characters) of Pascal. This was sorted into three initial runs, then merged in a single pass. Run time was 19.3 seconds, with input 36.5 percent, output 34.1 percent, `cmp` 10.1 percent, `rquick` 2.6 percent, `scopy` and `cscopy` together 4.5 percent, `gtext` and `ptext` 3.7 percent, `fcopy` 1.8 percent, `reheap` 1.1 percent, and `merge` 0.6 percent.

The third test was a text file of 2170 lines and 53,000 characters, which required 71 seconds to sort. It created eight initial runs, merged these onto three more, then merged those onto a final one. Again, input dominated, with 42.8 percent, output 32.9 percent, `cmp` 7.5 percent (smaller this time), `sccopy` and `cscopy` each 3.2 percent, and so on.

The final test was to repeat the third test with the merge order set to 5. This created eight initial runs, then merged them onto two more which were merged. This took 63 seconds, somewhat less. Input was 40.4 percent, output 32.9 percent, `cmp` 9.7 percent. Merging and reheaping was less than 2 percent.

The input times are inflated on this system since input buffer sizes are small, so these times could be improved somewhat. Nevertheless, for any likely improvement, I/O will still dominate. Since you can't avoid copying the data in and out, you have to find an algorithm that reduces *intermediate* I/O.

Exercise 4-13. When there are at most MERGEORDER intermediate files left, one complete pass over the data can be avoided by merging directly onto the final output file instead of onto an intermediate file. And as a special case, if the original input fits entirely into memory, there is no need for any merging or any intermediate files. Modify `sort` to handle these situations efficiently. According to the measurements above, how much faster will these changes make `sort`? □

The running time of `sort` is strongly affected by the number of passes made over the input data, which in turn depends on the length of the runs created in the initial pass. You can always get longer runs with more memory, but you can't always get more memory.

A particularly elegant way to create long initial runs is "replacement selection." A memory-load is sorted as before. But then, as `ptext` outputs a line, a fresh line is immediately read in to replace it. If this fresh line is greater than or equal to the line that it replaced it can form part of the run that is currently going out! If it's smaller, it can't go out in this run and must be held until the next one.

The payoff from this organization is significant. For files with random contents, it turns out that the expected run length is twice the memory size, so we can save one full pass over the data. And of course the effect is even stronger on files that are already partly sorted.

Replacement selection needs careful storage management if the lines are not all the same length. It also requires an algorithm for quickly finding the right position for a replacement among the already-sorted elements in memory. It is too slow to search through all the current lines to find the right place. The solution is to use a data structure like a heap, where the right position can be found in logarithmic time instead of linear. We will not go into this here; the topic is discussed in considerable detail in Knuth's *The Art of Computer Programming; Volume 3: Sorting and Searching*.

What can you do if your system won't let you create a lot of files? One method of getting by with a few files is the "balanced two-way merge." Suppose you are allowed four intermediates. During the first phase runs are placed alternately on files 1 and 2 until the input is exhausted. Then the runs on files 1 and 2 are merged, with the output runs (half as many, each twice as big) going alternately onto files 3 and 4. Then the runs on 3 and 4 are merged back onto 1 and 2, making runs of length four times the original. The process continues until all the data is merged onto one completely sorted file which can then be copied to the output. Since the length of the runs is doubled on each pass and the number of runs cut by a factor of two, there are $\lceil \log_2 r \rceil$ passes made, where r is the number of runs created in the initial phase.

The balanced two-way merge can be generalized to any number (3 or more) of intermediate files. The available files are divided into two groups as nearly equally as possible and merging is done back and forth between the two groups.

Exercise 4-14. Implement a balanced two-way merge sort. The main complication you will have to worry about is keeping track of the end of each run on each file. Compare the complexity and the running time of the balanced merge program with `sort`. □

Exercise 4-15. By default, `sort` reads from the standard input. Modify `sort` so that if it is called with filename arguments, it will instead take its input from the named files:

>   sort *file1 file2* ...

will sort the data on the files named. Reading either from a set of named files, or from the standard input if none are named, is an exceedingly useful design for many programs; you should always consider it. □

Exercise 4-16. Add an option to let the output file be specified by name, instead of just the standard output. Ensure that the output can be the same as one of the inputs. Do you want the final merge done directly onto it? □

Exercise 4-17. Add an option -m to merge already-sorted files:

    `sort -m` *file1 file2* ...

merges the data (presumed sorted) on the files onto the standard output. The command

    `sort -m`

without file names is silly. Does your version do something intelligent anyway? □

Exercise 4-18. Provide a `sort` option -r to reverse the direction of sorting. If you did the earlier exercise on this topic, did you have to change your decision about where to put the direction-changing code? □

Exercise 4-19. Add a -d option so `sort` sorts by dictionary order: upper and lower case letters should sort together, so that 'a' and 'A' appear together, not separated by an entire case of the alphabet. Is it sufficient to define `a<A<b<B`...? Should dictionary order be the default behavior? What should be done about special characters like periods, commas, and so on? What about digits? □

Exercise 4-20. Add the -n option: an initial numeric string with optional sign is sorted by arithmetic value while the rest of the line is sorted normally. All-numeric lines are a special case of this kind of input. Does your routine work regardless of the size of the numbers? Does the -n option work in conjunction with -r? □

Exercise 4-21. Add options so sorting can be done on fields within lines. You will need a way to specify the beginning and end of each field, and you will probably also want to allow fields to be independently numeric, dictionary order, reversed, etc. The challenge here is not so much the bookkeeping needed to make the program work as it is designing the options so they are easy for users to specify. Remember that specifying a field by character position is hard to do, particularly if the input doesn't come in neat columns. □

By now you are near the complexity provided by some commercial sort packages, but at least you got there in modest increments, and you always had a useful tool at each step. By default, though, `sort` still puts text lines into order, taking its input from the standard input and writing on the standard output. It is still an easy-to-use service for people who just want to sort text. The most frequent and easy operations should be easy to remember and to specify; you shouldn't *always* need a reference manual.

Exercise 4-22. Some systems provide a powerful but complicated *sort generator* that creates efficient sorts for big production jobs. If your system has one of these, design and implement a language that makes it easier for casual users to create the sorting process they want. □

4.7 Separation of Function: unique

One common reason for sorting is to bring together all occurrences of a particular item so they can be treated as a group. Sometimes this is done just to discard all but one occurrence in a group, for instance to make a list of all the words in a document. It's certainly easy to add an option to `sort` which discards multiple occurrences of an input line. (Where should this code be inserted?) But should this code be part of `sort` at all?

This question touches on an area of fundamental importance in designing good tools — proper separation of function. What should be included in a program? What should be a separate program? It happens to be more efficient to put this particular function into the sort program — we can save a pass over the data. More important, the decision whether two lines are the same depends on the comparison function being used, which is of course determined by the sorting options specified. If sorting and casting out duplicates are combined, we are assured that the comparison is done consistently and efficiently.

Why should there be two separate programs when a single slightly more complicated one will do? One good reason is that someone might want one function without the other. By separating the function of stripping duplicates from that of sorting, we can do things that are not possible when they are combined. You might really like to know which lines are *not* duplicated, or which lines *are* duplicated, or you might like to *count* adjacent duplicates. If sorting, duplicate-stripping and counting are all combined, the sort program is more complicated; and of course it's conceivable that you don't want the input sorted before you strip the duplicates!

Combining functions too early is a mistake. In its early stages, at least, a program should implement a single function. Sure, it may eventually have lots of options, but the things it does should be closely related. Then when users come along with new ways to combine programs, you will not have precluded some useful operation by your assumptions about what they are likely to do. Our own experience is instructive here. For years, sorting and duplicate stripping were separate programs. Finally efficiency began to be a major factor, and they were integrated: an option was added to `sort` which specifies the stripping of adjacent duplicates (although of course the old duplicate-stripper remained available and often used). But no one knew at the start that this was a good combination. The lesson: keep functions separate until you know *how* to combine them.

Here is `unique`, for stripping adjacent duplicates. It is most often used with `sort`, but is sufficiently useful in its own right to be worth a separate program.

```
{ unique -- remove adjacent duplicate lines }
procedure unique;
var
    buf : array [0..1] of string;
    cur : 0..1;
begin
    cur := 1;
    buf[1-cur][1] := ENDSTR;
    while (getline(buf[cur], STDIN, MAXSTR)) do
        if (not equal(buf[cur], buf[1-cur])) then begin
            putstr(buf[cur], STDOUT);
            cur := 1 - cur
        end
end;
```

Note that we use the same sort of trickery, treating indices as pointers, as in sort.

PROGRAM
   unique   delete adjacent duplicate lines
USAGE
   unique
FUNCTION
   unique writes to its output only the first line from each group of adjacent identical input lines. It is most useful for text that has been sorted to bring identical lines together; in this case it passes through only unique instances of input lines.
EXAMPLE
   To eliminate duplicate lines in the output of a program:
      program ¦ sort ¦ unique

Exercise 4-23. What are boundaries that should be tested to be confident that unique works correctly? □

Exercise 4-24. Our version of unique uses a variable to distinguish which buffer holds the current input line. Rewrite it so that the flow of control makes this distinction. Rewrite it to simply copy a line from one buffer into the other whenever a comparison fails. Which of the three versions do you prefer? □

Exercise 4-25. Add the option -n to unique, to prefix each line with the number of occurrences of the line in the original input. The command

```
unique -n
```

with the input

```
        a
        a
        b
```

produces

```
2    a
1    b
```

Is it better if the count precedes or follows the line? Add an option to print only one instance of only the replicated lines. ☐

Exercise 4-26. Combine `translit`, `sort`, and `unique` (with the -n option) into a pipeline that produces a word frequency list for a document, sorted into order of decreasing frequency. What happens to empty input lines? ☐

Exercise 4-27. Combine `translit`, `sort` (with the -d option) and `unique` into a pipeline that checks a program for occurrences of names in both upper and lower case, like `SIZE` and `size`. ☐

Exercise 4-28. Write the program `common`, for comparing lines in two sorted text files.

>   common *file1 file2*

produces a three-column output: lines which appear only in *file1*, lines only in *file2*, and lines in both files. `common` allows the optional arguments -1, -2, and -3, which specify the printing of only the corresponding column. Thus

>   common -3 *file1 file2*

prints only the lines common to both files, and

>   common -1 *file1 file2*

prints lines which are in the first file but not in the second. If there is only one file argument, *file2* refers to the standard input. ☐

What good is `common`? Suppose we have available a dictionary of English. Then consider this pipeline:

```
concat file1 file2 file3 ... !
    translit A-Z a-z !
        translit ^a-z @n !
            sort !
                unique !
                    common -2 dictionary
```

This collects a set of files together (`concat`), converts them to a single case (`translit`), discards punctuation and spaces and puts each word on a line by itself (`translit`), sorts them (`sort`), casts out duplicates (`unique`), and then selects those words which appear in the original files but not in the dictionary (`common`).

What's a word that appears in a document but not in a dictionary? Right — it's a plausible contender for being a spelling mistake. This pipeline is a first draft of a program for finding spelling mistakes. It won't do a perfect job by any means, but on the other hand it can be made out of spare parts in a few minutes, and it forms an excellent base for a more sophisticated process.

Exercise 4-29. What improvements would you make to the spelling-mistake finder? What experiments would you perform before undertaking "improvements"? ☐

Exercise 4-30. The output from the spelling mistake finder often consists mostly of technical jargon like `byte` and `translit`, and proper names like Knuth and Wirth. Once you have eliminated the true errors from this output, you now have a *glossary* of special words for a document. How would you modify the pipeline to eliminate glossary words from subsequent checks for spelling errors? □

4.8 Permuted Index

Once a flexible sorting program is available, other programs can use it as a component. In this section we will describe one such application, a program for creating a *permuted index* (often called a *keyword-in-context* or "KWIC" index). A permuted index lists each word (or some similar useful token) in its original context, but sorted by word and rearranged so the keywords line up. For example, this sentence would produce this output:

```
output:                        For  example, this sentence would produce this
            this output:            For example, this sentence would produce
       sentence would produce this  output:                        For example, this
       example, this sentence would  produce this output:                        For
               For example, this  sentence would produce this output:
         this sentence would produce  this output:                        For example,
                  For example,  this sentence would produce this output:
       For example, this sentence  would produce this output:
```

One program organization is like this.

```
for each input line
    for each token in the line
        rotate line so token is at front
        output onto temporary file
sort temporary file
for each line in temporary file
    re-rotate first token to center
    print line
```

This process can be viewed as a pipeline of three independent programs:

```
create rotations | sort | unrotate and print
```

but how it should be implemented on any particular system depends on what mechanisms are available. The advantage of a pipeline is that we already have `sort` nicely packaged, and the other two pieces are easy.

A second way to write `kwic` is to invoke `sort` as a self-contained program *from within* a program that does the rotating and unrotating with normal procedure calls. This method assumes that the operating system provides a way to run any program from within a running program, and regain control when it is done. We can indicate the structure as

```
do rotations onto temp1
run("sort <temp1 >temp2")
unrotate from temp2
remove temp1 and temp2
```

sort remains a black box, yet the overall process is effectively confined to one program.

However the program is eventually organized, it is important to observe that the original *design* should always be like this. We want to keep the pieces of the solution as uncoupled as possible, no matter what, so we pretend from the start that the most restrictive implementation possible (such as a pipeline) will be the one chosen. That way, we are less likely to let our guard down and admit sneak paths for communication between modules. Decisions about actual packaging should be made as late as possible, to maximize alternatives.

We leave the particular organization up to you, and show the routines for rotating and unrotating, written for use in a pipeline. Here is the driver for the rotation part.

```
{ kwic -- make keyword in context index }
procedure kwic;
const
    FOLD = DOLLAR;
var
    buf : string;
#include "putrot.p"
begin
    while (getline(buf, STDIN, MAXSTR)) do
        putrot(buf)
end;
```

The work is done in `putrot`, which finds the keywords in each line. A keyword is a string of letters or digits, but excludes punctuation like parentheses, commas and so on. These must be excluded so that words which appear adjacent to them will be properly lined up in columns when the output is printed. `putrot` finds the beginning of each token, that is, the first alphanumeric character, and calls `rotate` to output a line with that character rotated to the front.

```
{ putrot -- create lines with keyword at front }
procedure putrot (var buf : string);
var
    i : integer;
#include "rotate.p"
begin
    i := 1;
    while (buf[i] <> NEWLINE) and (buf[i] <> ENDSTR) do begin
        if (isalphanum(buf[i])) then begin
            rotate(buf, i); { token starts at "i" }
            repeat
                i := i + 1
            until (not isalphanum(buf[i]))
        end;
        i := i + 1
    end
end;


{ rotate -- output rotated line }
procedure rotate (var buf : string; n : integer);
var
    i : integer;
begin
    i := n;
    while (buf[i] <> NEWLINE) and (buf[i] <> ENDSTR) do begin
        putc(buf[i]);
        i := i + 1
    end;
    putc(FOLD);
    for i := 1 to n-1 do
        putc(buf[i]);
    putc(NEWLINE)
end;
```

rotate marks the end of the original line (the place where the line has been folded) by adding a FOLD character — some character unlikely to occur in normal text. FOLD will be used by the unrotating program to position the permuted lines correctly. Thus if we use $ as the fold character, the input line

```
now is the time
```

will yield the four output lines

```
now is the time$
is the time$now
the time$now is
time$now is the
```

We wrote isalphanum for Chapter 2.

PROGRAM
   `kwic`   produce lines for KWIC index
USAGE
   `kwic`
FUNCTION
   `kwic` writes one or more "folded" versions of each input line to its output. A line is "folded" at the beginning of each alphanumeric string within the line by writing from that string through the end of the line, followed by the fold character `$`, followed by the beginning of the line.

   `kwic` is used with `sort` and `unrotate` to produce a KeyWord In Context, or KWIC, index.
EXAMPLE
```
     kwic
     This is a test.
     This is a test.$
     is a test.$This
     a test.$This is
     test.$This is a
```
Normal usage is
```
     kwic <document | sort | unrotate
```

The other end of the pipeline is `unrotate`, which unrotates and prints the rotated lines, lined up on column `MIDDLE`. It copies the second half of the line, beginning at position `MIDDLE-1` and working backwards, wrapping around at the beginning if necessary. It then copies the first half of the line, working forward from `MIDDLE+1`. Finally it deletes trailing blanks.

```
{ unrotate -- unrotate lines rotated by kwic }
procedure unrotate;
const
    MAXOUT = 80;
    MIDDLE = 40;
    FOLD = DOLLAR;
var
    inbuf, outbuf : string;
    i, j, f : integer;
begin
    while (getline(inbuf, STDIN, MAXSTR)) do begin
        for i := 1 to MAXOUT-1 do
            outbuf[i] := BLANK;
        f := index(inbuf, FOLD);
        j := MIDDLE - 1;
        for i := length(inbuf)-1 downto f+1 do begin
            outbuf[j] := inbuf[i];
            j := j - 1;
            if (j <= 0) then
                j := MAXOUT - 1
        end;
        j := MIDDLE + 1;
        for i := 1 to f-1 do begin
            outbuf[j] := inbuf[i];
            j := j mod (MAXOUT-1) + 1
        end;
        for j := 1 to MAXOUT-1 do
            if (outbuf[j] <> BLANK) then
                i := j;
        outbuf[i+1] := ENDSTR;
        putstr(outbuf, STDOUT);
        putc(NEWLINE)
    end
end;
```

index is from Chapter 2; it returns the index of a character in a string.
unrotate stays sane even on input that has no FOLD character, because
index returns zero when it finds no match. This is another example of defensive programming — writing the program so it can cope with small disasters.
Of course disasters come in many sizes, and you should avoid paranoia, but in
this specific instance the insurance is cheap.

PROGRAM
    `unrotate`   format lines for KWIC index
USAGE
    `unrotate`
FUNCTION
    `unrotate` reads its input a line at a time and writes an "unfolded" version to its output. A line is "folded" if it contains within it an instance of the fold character `$`; "unfolding" involves writing from the end of the line down to but not including the fold character, starting in column 39 of the output line, wrapping characters that would thus appear before column 1 around to the end of the line, then writing the remainder of the line starting at column 41 and wrapping around at column 80 if necessary.
    `unrotate` is used with `kwic` and `sort` to produce a KeyWord In Context, or KWIC, index.
EXAMPLE

```
    unrotate
    a test.$This is
    is a test.$This
    test.$This is a
    This is a test.$
    <ENDFILE>
                    This is  a test.
                    This  is a test.
               This is a  test.
          test.      This is a
```

Exercise 4-31. `kwic` and `unrotate` don't properly handle text containing tabs or backspaces. They also ignore the possibility that the text contains FOLD characters. Fix them. □

Exercise 4-32. Modify `kwic` so it will not split a word on output. □

Exercise 4-33. You will quickly find that you don't want words like *a, the, and, of,* and so on in your index. Conversely you might want lists that contain *only* certain words. Add the capability to specify either an "omit" file (words that are not to be indexed) or an "include" file (words to be indexed). Chapter 8 discusses some table handling procedures. □

Exercise 4-34. Modify `kwic` to handle multiple files as an alternative to the standard input, just as `print` does. In a large document consisting of several input files, it is useful to know precisely where in the input a particular line was found. Add an option `-t` to tag output lines with some identification of their source position, like file name and line number. Should this be the default mode? □

Exercise 4-35. One use we have made of our `kwic` program is as a quick (and dirty) way to check that all variables in our Pascal programs were used as well as declared. This still requires manual effort, however, and so is not as good a solution as it could be. If your compiler doesn't do it for you, build a program that checks your programs to see that there are no unused variables. □

Exercise 4-36. Build a program that forms a cross-reference listing of a document (the document often, though not always, being a program). That is, for each token, list the numbers of all lines that contain that token. □

Bibliographic Notes

The standard reference on internal and external sorting is D. E. Knuth's *The Art of Computer Programming; Volume 3: Sorting and Searching* (Addison-Wesley, 1973). This contains precise descriptions and detailed analyses of a wide variety of sorting methods. Another source for internal sorting methods is R. P. Rich, *Internal Sorting Methods Illustrated With PL/I Programs* (Prentice-Hall, 1972), which contains actual PL/I programs, and extensive run time and space measurements.

Our quicksort was contributed by M. D. McIlroy. Other variants of quicksort are discussed in an article by R. Loeser, "Some performance tests of quicksort and descendants," *CACM,* March, 1974. This article contains Fortran programs for all of the procedures.

A paper by D. L. Parnas, "On the criteria to be used in decomposing systems into modules" (*CACM*, December, 1972), discusses how to modularize a permuted index program. Compare his organization with ours.

The pipeline for catching spelling mistakes was conceived by S. C. Johnson. "Computer Programs for Detecting and Correcting Spelling Errors," by J. L. Peterson (*CACM*, December, 1980) reviews the subject.

Remember the `time` finder we discussed in the Introduction? That job needed a program to look for the word `time` anywhere in an input line and print all such lines found.

But no one wants a program that will only find a particular Pascal identifier, nor one limited to looking at Pascal programs, nor even one restricted to looking at programs. `time` is a specific *text pattern*; we want a program `find` that accepts the pattern to be looked for as an argument, so we can say

        find *pattern*

to print each input line that contains an occurrence of the specified pattern. For instance, to find instances of `time`, we just say

        find time

Some people might argue that what is really needed here is a text editor that can search for text patterns. Indeed we do want such an editor, and in the next chapter we will build one. But we still want `find` besides. The reason is that an editor is *too* general for some purposes. We have to invoke the editor, tell it one at a time which files we wish to process, then repeat the search command for each file. There is simply too much setup. `find`, on the other hand, does exactly what is wanted, and it does so with a minimum of fuss.

Hardly a working day goes by that we do not make extensive use of `find`. The most obvious application is to answer questions like "When did we first mention the `create` primitive?" or "Where are all the references to that variable?" But it is also a filter to *select* from more voluminous output, as in a pipeline like

        program ¦ find error

to print only messages containing the word "error." (This is much harder with a text editor.)

We even use `find` to improve our writing style. You may have noticed that the word "simple" and its derivatives occur frequently in the book. This is understandable, for simplicity in programs is a virtue. But overuse robs the word of force, so periodically we scanned through the text with

```
find simpl
```

(which also catches "simply" and "simplicity"), then replaced some occurrences by appropriate synonyms. We even counted them a couple of times, with

```
find simpl | linecount
```

5.1 Text Patterns

There is no point to making `find` capable of recognizing all conceivable text patterns. We could be perverse, for instance, and insist on a program that could look for *all* legal ways of writing the identifier `time` in Pascal — with mixed upper or lower case, perhaps. We could further insist that *only* instances of the identifier `time` be printed — omitting lines with character strings that contain the string `time` in comments or in longer variable names. But by the time we are able to handle something as tricky as

```
stime[i] := 'time'; { time recorded }
```

we have written most of the parser for a Pascal compiler!

Our `find` program will not handle all these pathological cases, to be sure, but how often do they occur? So long as *all* the lines you want to see are printed, it doesn't hurt much if a few extra also appear. And if you don't plan to be perfectly precise, you may as well draw the line at a reasonable place. We accept a few shortcomings in any one application in trade for a much broader spectrum of uses. Most users of a tool are willing to meet you halfway; if you do ninety percent of the job, they will be ecstatic.

We will confine ourselves to a notation that has been used in a number of conversational text editors and other pattern matching programs. For all its economy, the notation is surprisingly versatile. We will suggest some useful extensions as exercises.

A text pattern can be a single character, like the letter `t`, or a more elaborate construct built up from simple things, like the string `time`. To build arbitrary text patterns, you need remember only a handful of rules.

Any literal character, like `t`, is a text pattern that matches that same character in the text being scanned. A sequence of literal characters, like `123` or `time`, is a pattern that matches any occurrence of that sequence of characters in a line of input.

A pattern is said to *match* part of a text line if the text line contains an occurrence of the pattern. For example, the pattern `aa` matches the line `aabc` once at position 1, the line `aabcaabc` in two places, and the line `aaaaaa` in five (overlapping) places. Matching is done on a line-by-line basis: no pattern can match across a line boundary. Text patterns may be *concatenated*: a text pattern followed by another text pattern forms a new text pattern that matches anything matched by the first, followed immediately by anything matched by the second. A sequence of literal characters is an example of concatenated patterns.

Although it is an easy task to write a program that looks only for literal strings of characters (and it is a useful first step), you will soon find it restrictive. Accordingly, we will add some more capabilities to find — the ability to search for patterns that match classes of characters, that match patterns only at particular positions on a line, or that match text of indefinite length.

To be able to express these more general patterns, we need to preempt some characters to represent other types of text patterns, or to delimit them. For example, we will use the character ? as a text pattern that matches *any* single character except a newline. The pattern x?y matches x+y, xay, x?y and similar strings.

The ? and other reserved characters are often called *metacharacters*. We try to choose characters which will not appear with high frequency in normal text, but still there are occasions when we want to look for a literal occurrence of a metacharacter. Thus the special meaning of any metacharacter can be turned off by preceding it with the *escape character* @, as in the character translator translit of Chapter 2. Thus @? matches a literal question mark, and @@ matches a literal at-sign.

The metacharacter [signals that the characters following, up to the next], form a *character class*, that is, a text pattern that matches any single character from the bracketed list. Character classes use the same notation that was used to specify from strings in translit: [aA] matches a or A, [a-z] matches any lower case letter, [^a] matches any character *except* an a, and so forth. The one difference is that, for convenience, we will say that negated character classes, such as the last example, will never match a newline. The escape convention can also be used inside character classes if the character class is to contain ^ or - or @ or].

Two other metacharacters do not match literal characters but rather match positions on the input line. % matches the *beginning* of a line: %end is a pattern that matches end *only* if it occurs as the first three characters of an input line. Analogously, $ matches the *end* of a line: end$ matches end only if it is the last thing on a line, before the newline. Of course these can work together: %end$ matches a line that contains *only* end, and %$ matches only empty lines (lines containing only a newline).

Any of the text patterns above that match a single character (everything but % and $) can be followed by the character * to make a text pattern which matches *zero or more* successive occurrences of the single character pattern. The resulting pattern is called a *closure*. For example, x* matches zero or more x's; xx* matches *one* or more x's; [a-z]* matches any string of zero or more lower case letters.

Since a closure matches zero or more instances of the pattern, which do we pick if there's a choice? find itself only needs to know whether at least one match occurs in a line, but later we will want to use the matched substring. It turns out to be convenient if find matches the longest possible string even when a null-string match would be equally valid. Thus [a-zA-Z]* matches an entire word (which may be a null string), [a-zA-Z][a-zA-Z]* matches an entire word (one or more letters but not a null string), and ?* matches a whole line (which may be a null string). Any ambiguity in deciding which part of a line matches a pattern will be resolved by choosing the match beginning with the *leftmost* character, then choosing the *longest* possible match at that point. So [a-zA-Z][a-zA-Z0-9]* matches the leftmost Pascal identifier on a line, (?*) matches anything between parentheses (not necessarily balanced), and ??* matches an entire line of one or more characters but not a line containing only a newline.

Finally, no pattern will match across a line boundary. This is often most natural and useful, and it prevents an unwise ?* from eating up an entire input.

Technically, our text patterns are a subclass of the class of patterns called *regular expressions,* which have been extensively studied. General regular expressions typically include a way to specify alternates and the ability to parenthesize patterns, so that for example x(a|bc)y matches either xay or xbcy. (The parentheses and bar become metacharacters.) These more general patterns add power at the price of complexity. For our purposes the complexity outweighs the power, but we will discuss some of the issues involved as we proceed.

Exercise 5-1. Write a text pattern that matches only those words that contain the six vowels **aeiouy** in order, like **abstemiou**sly or **facetiou**sly. Write a text pattern that matches the words that can be made with the letters you can create by holding a pocket calculator upside down. (The letters are usually BEhILOS, from the digits 8341705.) □

Exercise 5-2. Write text patterns that match PL/I identifiers, Cobol identifiers, Basic identifiers, identifiers accepted by your local assembly language. How would you use translit, sort, unique, and find to list all identifiers and keywords used in a program? Is there any easy way to eliminate the keywords? (Hint: look at the programs for checking spelling mistakes, in Chapter 4.) Is it worth it? □

Exercise 5-3. Most languages actually insist that identifiers have some maximum length; many implementations of Pascal use only the first eight characters of an identifier. Given text patterns as defined above, can you write one that matches Pascal identifiers of at most eight characters? □

Exercise 5-4. Can you use find to remove all the blank lines from text? To remove all comment cards from a Fortran program? To remove all comments from a Pascal program? □

Exercise 5-5. Do any of the following patterns make sense, according to the definitions given above? If not, why not? If so, what do they mean?

```
a**
aa*
a%b$c
%*a
[^ @t]*[ @t]
%$
%
*
@@t
```

□

5.2 Implementation

Now that we know the sort of patterns we want to look for, we can start lay-
ing out the program. Without going into any detail, we can foresee the need
for an array pat to hold the pattern, and a main routine like this:

```
{ find -- find patterns in text }
procedure find;
#include "findcons.p"
var
    arg, lin, pat : string;
#include "getpat.p"
#include "match.p"
begin
    if (not getarg(1, arg, MAXSTR)) then
        error('usage: find pattern');
    if (not getpat(arg, pat)) then
        error('find: illegal pattern');
    while (getline(lin, STDIN, MAXSTR)) do
        if (match(lin, pat)) then
            putstr(lin, STDOUT)
end;
```

getpat uses the argument to put the scan pattern into pat. match looks
for an occurrence of the pattern anywhere in the input line lin and returns a
true or false answer.

Often it is possible not only to write code without knowing entirely where
you're going, but also to test it. That's what we did with find. By using
dummy versions of getpat and match, we were able to verify that lines of
text are properly read and written — which means that ENDFILE is detected at
the correct time and that the internal representation in lin is consistently
treated, at least by getline and putstr. A minor variation of getpat exer-
cised the error message. And a trivial match, which could detect only a leading 'x', verified that lines could be printed selectively.

All this may seem pretty elementary, but it's surprising how many bugs are
caught early this way. In large software projects the majority of bugs arise

because the pieces of the system do not go together as they were expected to, despite detailed interface specifications known to everyone from the start. And many other bugs survive elaborate checks on individual routines, surfacing only when the routine first interacts with the rest of the code.

It seems only natural, then, to test at the highest, most integrated level first — since that's where most bugs are detected anyway — and to start testing *as soon as possible,* even before most of the actual working code is written. This approach is referred to as *top-down testing,* a natural extension of top-down design and top-down coding. The dummy programs are referred to as program *stubs.* We built and tested `find` that way, a piece at a time, and it paid off. Despite a number of stupid mistakes (some of which we will admit), the program was written and debugged in short order.

Since a match can occur anywhere on a line, it seems easiest to factor the matching into two pieces. `match` looks for a match anywhere on a line, by repeatedly calling `amatch` to look for a match that begins at position i — an *anchored* match. This separates checking for a match from deciding what match to try next.

```
{ match -- find match anywhere on line }
function match (var lin, pat : string) : boolean;
var
    i, pos : integer;
#include "amatch.p"
begin
    pos := 0;
    i := 1;
    while (lin[i] <> ENDSTR) and (pos = 0) do begin
        pos := amatch(lin, i, pat, 1);
        i := i + 1
    end;
    match := (pos > 0)
end;
```

`amatch` will return some indication of where the matched string is, or zero if there was no match. Although later programs will eventually need to know what part of the text matched the pattern, all `find` cares about is whether or not there was a match. We do pass the position in `pat` to `amatch` because it will be used in later routines. This kind of fine-tuning is rarely done from the top down!

Leaving aside all metacharacters for the moment, `amatch` has to compare the pattern with the input, character by character, until it either finds a mismatch (in which case it returns zero), or until it gets to the end of the pattern successfully (in which case it can return the next position of the input, which is guaranteed not to be zero). Then the most basic version of `amatch` might be

```
{ amatch -- with no metacharacters }
function amatch (var lin : string; i : integer;
        var pat : string; j : integer) : integer;
begin
    while (pat[j] <> ENDSTR) and (i > 0) do
        if (lin[i] <> pat[j]) then
            i := 0  { no match }
        else begin
            i := i + 1;
            j := j + 1
        end;
    amatch := i
end;
```

Here the pattern characters are stored in successive elements of `pat`.

The metacharacters ?, % and $ add only minor complications. Character classes, however, bring up a question of representation. Clearly we don't want to have to interpret shorthand like [a-z] for every character position within every line of input. It looks as if text patterns are sufficiently complicated to warrant encoding. That way, we can go over the pattern once, carefully check it for illegal specifications, expand shorthand, and rewrite it in a more convenient form. We anticipate looking through rather large files with find, so we would like to detect a match or mismatch reasonably quickly. Encoding the pattern is a specific example of a general principle — the more time you're willing to spend preprocessing your data, the faster you can use it later.

Each text pattern type will be represented in `pat` by a special code. Literal characters are represented by two entries — the indicator LITCHAR in position j and the character itself in position j+1. The metacharacters %, $ and ? are represented by the single entries BOL, EOL and ANY respectively. Character classes are represented as either CCL (for [...]) or NCCL (for [^ ...]), followed by a count of the number of characters in the class and the characters themselves, after any shorthand has been expanded. We will ignore closures for a while yet, until the easier part is under control. Thus the pattern

```
%[^x]?[0-9]x$
```

is encoded in `pat` as

```
BOL
NCCL 1 'x'
ANY
CCL 10 '0' '1' '2' '3' '4' '5' '6' '7' '8' '9'
LITCHAR 'x'
EOL
```

(The first 1 and the 10 are numbers in the encoding, not characters.) Conversion of an input pattern to this encoded form is done by getpat and its subordinates, to which we shall return.

Given this much complexity in the representation of a pattern, it's also worthwhile to put the testing and matching of single characters into a separate routine, to keep amatch down to manageable size. omatch will test whether a single input character matches the current pattern position, and advance the input position by the right amount if it does. amatch can then concentrate on walking through the pattern in proper synchronization with the text to be matched. Now we can write another version of amatch:

```
{ amatch -- with some metacharacters }
function amatch (var lin : string; i : integer;
        var pat : string; j : integer) : integer;
#include "omatch.p"
begin
    while (pat[j] <> ENDSTR) and (i > 0) do
        if (omatch(lin, i, pat, j)) then
            j := j + patsize(pat, j)
        else
            i := 0; { no match possible }
    amatch := i
end;
```

omatch handles everything but closures. patsize returns the length of an entry in pat, so that it can be skipped over. We will get back to both of these routines once we deal with closures.

Closures cause all of the difficulty. In the text changing program near the end of this chapter and in the editor of Chapter 6, we are going to write code that replaces the matched text by something else. For that purpose, the most useful behavior is to match the longest possible pattern if there is a choice, so encountering a * should cause a loop on the pattern to be replicated, eating up as many occurrences as possible, until the match fails. Scanning then resumes from the point of failure by trying to match the rest of the pattern against the rest of the input line.

But what if the rest of the pattern fails? It does *not* necessarily mean that there is no match. The pattern b*b, for instance, does match the line bb, but only if the b* part is confined to the first b (or to the null string before the first b). What this means is, every time a match fails, we have to go back to the previous closure, shorten it by one and try matching the rest of the pattern once more. Only when the pattern fails with the closure matching a null string can we give up.

And we're *still* not done, for there may be more than one closure in a pattern. (Remember, we said go back to the *previous* closure.) So to handle patterns correctly, we must backtrack systematically through *all possible* closure matches, until we either find a match or fail utterly.

A powerful method for reducing apparent complexity is recursion. In a recursive procedure, the method of solution is defined in terms of itself: each part of the routine handles only a piece of the strategy, then calls other parts (or itself) to handle the rest. The trick is to reduce each hard case to one that is handled simply elsewhere.

Closure matching is a natural for recursion: after a closure is matched, the entire matching procedure is called to check the rest of the input against the rest of the pattern. The advantage of recursion is that the compiler generates code to handle many of the bookkeeping details that complicate a non-recursive program. For example, we could sketch amatch like this:

```
for each pattern element
    if it's a closure indicator
        n := as many omatches as possible
        for i := n downto 0
            if amatch(rest of input, rest of pattern) succeeds
                return with success
        return with failure
    else if omatch fails on non-closure
        return with failure
return with success if we get here
```

There are some details to be filled in, of course, and some complications because Pascal doesn't have a return statement to permit an early exit from a function. Most of the complication in the real amatch comes from circumventing that omission.

```
{ amatch -- look for match of pat[j]... at lin[offset]... }
function amatch (var lin : string; offset : integer;
        var pat : string; j : integer) : integer;
var
    i, k : integer;
    done : boolean;
#include "omatch.p"
#include "patsize.p"
begin
    done := false;
    while (not done) and (pat[j] <> ENDSTR) do
        if (pat[j] = CLOSURE) then begin
            j := j + patsize(pat, j);   { step over CLOSURE }
            i := offset;
            { match as many as possible }
            while (not done) and (lin[i] <> ENDSTR) do
                if (not omatch(lin, i, pat, j)) then
                    done := true;
            { i points to input character that made us fail }
            { match rest of pattern against rest of input }
            { shrink closure by 1 after each failure }
            done := false;
            while (not done) and (i >= offset) do begin
                k := amatch(lin, i, pat, j+patsize(pat,j));
                if (k > 0) then { matched rest of pattern }
                    done := true
                else
                    i := i - 1
            end;
            offset := k;   { if k = 0 failure else success }
            done := true
        end
        else if (not omatch(lin, offset, pat, j)) then begin
            offset := 0;          { non-closure }
            done := true
        end
        else    { omatch succeeded on this pattern element }
            j := j + patsize(pat, j);
    amatch := offset
end;
```

For a closure, the pattern to be repeated is assumed to *follow* the closure
entry in pat, so that when pat is scanned the closure indicator will be encountered before the pattern itself; we will have to arrange this order when we build
the pattern array. The pattern is matched as many times as possible, then
amatch is called recursively to try to match the rest of the pattern. The recursion occurs in the line

```
    k := amatch(lin, i, pat, j+patsize(pat,j));
```

The recursion stack will get only as deep as the number of closures.

If a pattern entry fails, and if the last closure match can still be made shorter, amatch shortens it by one match and retries from there. Otherwise, it goes back to the previous closure (by returning from one level of recursion) and tries to shorten that one. Only when it exhausts all alternatives does it report failure. And of course if it fails before the first closure, there are no alternatives.

Recursion represents no saving of time or storage. Somewhere in the computer must be maintained a list of all the places a recursive routine is called, so the program can eventually find its way back. But the storage for that list is shared among different uses. More important, it is managed automatically; many of the burdens of storage management and control flow are placed on the compiler, not on the programmer. And since bookkeeping details are hidden, the program will be much easier to understand. Learning to think recursively takes some effort, but it is repaid with smaller and simpler programs.

Not every problem benefits from a recursive approach, and sometimes you cannot use recursion. But if you find yourself administering a last-in first-out list in any form, however, then your problem *is* intrinsically recursive. Even if recursion is not possible, you will find it valuable to do the original design as a recursive program, then unfold the recursion, simulating the last-in first-out storage with your own linked lists or indexed data structures. The resulting program should be cleaner and easier to understand than if you start from scratch.

The accompanying routines patsize and omatch can now be spelled out:

```
{ patsize -- returns size of pattern entry at pat[n] }
function patsize (var pat : string; n : integer) : integer;
begin
    if (not (pat[n] in
       [LITCHAR, BOL, EOL, ANY, CCL, NCCL, CLOSURE])) then
         error('in patsize: can''t happen')
    else
       case pat[n] of
          LITCHAR:
             patsize := 2;
          BOL, EOL, ANY:
             patsize := 1;
          CCL, NCCL:
             patsize := pat[n+1] + 2;
          CLOSURE:
             patsize := CLOSIZE
       end
end;
```

```
{ omatch -- match one pattern element at pat[j] }
function omatch (var lin : string; var i : integer;
        var pat : string; j : integer) : boolean;
var
    advance : -1..1;
#include "locate.p"
begin
    advance := -1;
    if (lin[i] = ENDSTR) then
        omatch := false
    else if (not (pat[j] in
      [LITCHAR, BOL, EOL, ANY, CCL, NCCL, CLOSURE])) then
        error('in omatch: can''t happen')
    else
        case pat[j] of
            LITCHAR:
                if (lin[i] = pat[j+1]) then
                    advance := 1;
            BOL:
                if (i = 1) then
                    advance := 0;
            ANY:
                if (lin[i] <> NEWLINE) then
                    advance := 1;
            EOL:
                if (lin[i] = NEWLINE) then
                    advance := 0;
            CCL:
                if (locate(lin[i], pat, j+1)) then
                    advance := 1;
            NCCL:
                if (lin[i] <> NEWLINE)
                    and (not locate(lin[i], pat, j+1)) then
                    advance := 1
        end;
    if (advance >= 0) then begin
        i := i + advance;
        omatch := true
    end
    else
        omatch := false
end;
```

advance is the amount to advance the input position if omatch finds a match.
This is zero for patterns that match null strings and one otherwise.
    locate looks for a character in a character class:

```
{ locate -- look for c in character class at pat[offset] }
function locate (c : character; var pat : string;
        offset : integer) : boolean;
var
    i : integer;
begin
    { size of class is at pat[offset], characters follow }
    locate := false;
    i := offset + pat[offset];   { last position }
    while (i > offset) do
        if (c = pat[i]) then begin
            locate := true;
            i := offset { force loop termination }
        end
        else
            i := i - 1
end;
```

The "can't happen" messages in patsize and omatch are interesting. Since the program builds its own patterns, we know precisely what sorts of entries can be encountered, and so there is no need to verify that the pattern entry is one of the labels in the case.

Or is there?

pat is a hodgepodge. The pat array contains a variety of objects in close proximity:

BOL, EOL, ANY, CLOSURE	identifying code
LITCHAR	identifying code, character to match
CCL, NCCL	identifying code, size of class, list of characters in class

Keeping all of this straight during some complicated processing is not trivial. We can expect problems, therefore, and should prepare for them. There are many common coding and design errors that will botch what gets put into pat. If we blindly assume that all is well, patsize and omatch will treat garbage as a valid pattern and act on it. (A careful implementation of Pascal will catch an invalid case for you, but not all implementations are that careful.) Garbage is bad enough, but garbage that is expected to contain a count to tell you how long it is can be much worse. So we test explicitly for all the possible conditions and print "can't happen" when the impossible occurs.

The first time we ran this code, it said "can't happen." We got that message embarrassingly often in the process of adding the rest of the code and shaking it down. This experience speaks for itself: if you're going to walk a high-wire, use a net. You might meditate upon how much harder it would have been to debug a program that just silently went crazy whenever it was run.

Even after the initial development period, various pieces of find were modified, sometimes quite dramatically. Whenever a change was made with more enthusiasm than caution, "can't happen" brought us back on the track again. We finally decided to leave the messages in for all time instead of pretending to be perfect. Removing the error messages "now that the program is working" is like wearing a parachute on the ground, but taking it off once you're in the air.

As an aside, notice that the standard case statement provides no way to handle a "default" or "none of the above" condition, so we were forced to add a separate range test before the case. A chain of else if's would serve as well in this situation, because it eliminates the duplicate test. We could equally well write patsize as

```
{ patsize -- returns size of pattern entry at pat[n] }
function patsize (var pat : string; n : integer) : integer;
begin
    if (pat[n] = LITCHAR) then
        patsize := 2
    else if (pat[n] in [BOL, EOL, ANY]) then
        patsize := 1
    else if (pat[n] = CCL) or (pat[n] = NCCL) then
        patsize := pat[n+1] + 2
    else if (pat[n] = CLOSURE) then
        patsize := CLOSIZE
    else
        error('in patsize: can''t happen')
end;
```

Similar comments apply to omatch.

Exercise 5-6. Estimate or measure how much execution time is added by leaving the debugging tests in patsize and omatch. What fraction of the total time spent by the program does this constitute? How is it affected by how often different patterns occur in everyday use? How many extra storage locations are added by the extra code? What fraction of the total size of the program is it? □

Exercise 5-7. How would you test match and its sub-modules? List, in order of increasing difficulty, ten text patterns you should try. Try them. (Hint: What kinds of patterns do you have to write to visit *every* part of the code?) □

5.3 Building Patterns

Now that we have most of a working pattern finder, let's concentrate on reading and encoding the pattern. Although find is always concerned with a pattern that begins at position one and terminates with an ENDSTR, we would still prefer a more general pattern builder — one which terminates on an arbitrary delimiter and which tells us where to continue scanning if we want. (We prefer it partly on general principles and partly because we know where we are going in this chapter and the next.) So getpat is a trivial routine that interfaces between find and makepat, which does the real work.

```
{ getpat -- convert argument into pattern }
function getpat (var arg, pat : string) : boolean;
#include "makepat.p"
begin
    getpat := (makepat(arg, 1, ENDSTR, pat) > 0)
end;
```

As we were writing makepat, it became clear that we could modify it to make find easier to use. If a % is not at the beginning of a pattern, it loses its special meaning, as does a $ not at the end, or a * at the very beginning. In many cases this eliminates the need to escape these characters when we are looking for literal occurrences of them. (It also eliminates the need for an error message, which is nice.) A * that does not occur at the beginning of the line is checked to make sure it never calls for repetition of anything that can match a null string, since the rest of the program is not prepared to handle that situation. In this case, however, the * is not taken literally; instead the pattern is abandoned and a diagnostic is printed. This seems to be the safer course in practice.

We emphasize that these "features" are *ad hoc* decisions made as we implemented the pattern builder. A number of curious situations turned out to be unspecified, as is often the case, and had to be resolved during coding. We chose to complete the specification in what appeared to be the most convenient way for the user.

There is no question, however, that too much of this sort of thing is bad. Our goal is always to write to clear, unambiguous functional specifications that are easy to remember, as opposed to writing routines any old way and trying to live with them. Too many exceptions, too much *ad hoc*-ery, can lead to programs that are hard to get right and hard to use. It is necessary to strike a careful balance.

Here is makepat, which converts the pattern argument into its encoded form in the array pat. makepat does the easy cases itself, and leaves the complicated ones to sub-procedures.

```
{ makepat -- make pattern from arg[i], terminate at delim }
function makepat (var arg : string; start : integer;
        delim : character; var pat : string) : integer;
var
    i, j, lastj, lj : integer;
    done, junk : boolean;
#include "getccl.p"
#include "stclose.p"
begin
    j := 1; { pat index }
    i := start; { arg index }
    lastj := 1;
    done := false;
    while (not done) and (arg[i] <> delim)
      and (arg[i] <> ENDSTR) do begin
        lj := j;
        if (arg[i] = ANY) then
            junk := addstr(ANY, pat, j, MAXPAT)
        else if (arg[i] = BOL) and (i = start) then
            junk := addstr(BOL, pat, j, MAXPAT)
        else if (arg[i] = EOL) and (arg[i+1] = delim) then
            junk := addstr(EOL, pat, j, MAXPAT)
        else if (arg[i] = CCL) then
            done := (getccl(arg, i, pat, j) = false)
        else if (arg[i] = CLOSURE) and (i > start) then begin
            lj := lastj;
            if (pat[lj] in [BOL, EOL, CLOSURE]) then
                done := true    { force loop termination }
            else
                stclose(pat, j, lastj)
        end
        else begin
            junk := addstr(LITCHAR, pat, j, MAXPAT);
            junk := addstr(esc(arg, i), pat, j, MAXPAT)
        end;
        lastj := lj;
        if (not done) then
            i := i + 1
    end;
    if (done) or (arg[i] <> delim) then  { finished early }
        makepat := 0
    else if (not addstr(ENDSTR, pat, j, MAXPAT)) then
        makepat := 0            { no room }
    else
        makepat := i            { all is well }
end;
```

All entries in the pat array are made via calls to addstr. This is the same routine used in translit to check for overwrites, store an entry, and update the store index. `esc` was also described with `translit`; it handles an escape character if one is present.

Rather than test each call to `addstr` to see if there was room for the new character, we ignore the status return (by assigning it to `junk`, as in Chapter 2), since `addstr` will never write beyond the specified limit. Normally, `makepat` returns the index of the closing delimiter. If there is room for the `ENDSTR` that terminates the pattern, all is well; if not, something went wrong and `makepat` returns zero, which is never a valid index.

Character classes are encoded by `getccl`. We have organized `getccl` so that it uses `dodash` (and all its sub-modules) to build character class entries as in `translit`. That way, we avoid writing a lot of new code, we have some assurance that the code is correct, and we *know* `find` and `translit` will apply the same rules for specifying character classes.

```
{ getccl -- expand char class at arg[i] into pat[j] }
function getccl (var arg : string; var i : integer;
         var pat : string; var j : integer) : boolean;
var
    jstart : integer;
    junk : boolean;
#include "dodash.p"
begin
    i := i + 1; { skip over '[' }
    if (arg[i] = NEGATE) then begin
        junk := addstr(NCCL, pat, j, MAXPAT);
        i := i + 1
    end
    else
        junk := addstr(CCL, pat, j, MAXPAT);
    jstart := j;
    junk := addstr(0, pat, j, MAXPAT);    { room for count }
    dodash(CCLEND, arg, i, pat, j, MAXPAT);
    pat[jstart] := j - jstart - 1;
    getccl := (arg[i] = CCLEND)
end;
```

CCLEND is, of course, a].

Since a closure entry must be rearranged so the CLOSURE flag appears before the object to be repeated, `makepat` uses a separate routine `stclose` to move things around in `pat`. When a * is encountered, we have to move the previous pattern over far enough that we can stick in a closure entry, to be seen *first* when `amatch` scans. `stclose` does this, being careful not to move anything off the end of `pat` inadvertently.

```
{ stclose -- insert closure entry at pat[j] }
procedure stclose (var pat : string; var j : integer;
       lastj : integer);
var
    jp, jt : integer;
    junk : boolean;
begin
    for jp := j-1 downto lastj do begin
        jt := jp + CLOSIZE;
        junk := addstr(pat[jp], pat, jt, MAXPAT)
    end;
    j := j + CLOSIZE;
    pat[lastj] := CLOSURE  { where original pattern began }
end;
```

CLOSIZE is 1, the size of a closure entry. The const declarations for find are grouped in a separate file:

```
{ findcons -- const declarations for find }
const
    MAXPAT = MAXSTR;
    CLOSIZE = 1;     { size of a closure entry }
    CLOSURE = STAR;
    BOL = PERCENT;
    EOL = DOLLAR;
    ANY = QUESTION;
    CCL = LBRACK;
    CCLEND = RBRACK;
    NEGATE = CARET;
    NCCL = EXCLAM;   { cannot be the same as NEGATE }
    LITCHAR = LETC; { ord('c') }
```

When we built find, the identifying codes stored in pat were the actual characters from the argument, wherever possible. (This may not have been entirely obvious because we used symbolic constants like EOL and CLOSURE instead of DOLLAR and STAR, in case you want to replace them with characters of your own choosing.) We always try to use printable internal codes, so we can insert debugging lines like

```
    putstr(pat, STDERR)
```

and get out something more or less readable. Thus we defined LITCHAR to be the letter c and CCL to be [. Counts come out funny, but most patterns tend to be readable.

We only mentioned three testing plateaus in the process of building find, but actually there were many more. As we designed the mechanism for handling each type of pattern, we stuck it in and tried it out with the existing skeleton. Since we are presenting you with a finished design, however, it would be artificial to go through the several false starts we discarded. When you build your own designs top-down, plan on more than three tests!

Getting closures right was the hardest part, for the logic involved in handling them constitutes about half the code. Most of the errors were made, as expected, in the `pat` array, trying to keep track of where things were during the recursive search for closures. Either an entry was built wrong or it was not read as it should have been in `amatch` and its subordinates. In either event the program responded by saying "can't happen" when we tried a new feature. That made it easy to locate and correct mistakes.

`find` is not a big program, only about 240 lines, excluding the contribution of `translit`, but it is big enough to warrant a diagram of the relationship among the procedures and functions, just as we did with `archive` in Chapter 3.

```
find
    getpat
        makepat
            getccl
                dodash
            stclose
    match
        amatch
            omatch
                locate
            patsize
```

This picture excludes primitives like `getline` and `putstr`, and of course `dodash` calls several routines developed for `translit` in Chapter 2.

Notice how both major branches progress from the abstract to the specific as we get further from the root of the tree. This is a natural result of the way we wrote `find`. We took an abstract problem, to find all the occurrences of a pattern in the input, and refined it into two steps:

> get the pattern
> match input lines against the pattern

Each of these was refined in turn (although we attacked the second one first), until all of the details were filled in at the lowest levels. At each stage, if the operation to be performed was simple enough, it was coded directly. If not, part of it was coded in terms of calls on lower routines, which were expanded later on.

Starting at the top and working towards the bottom by filling in details is often called "successive refinement." It is a valuable approach even for programs of modest size. At no point does the design bog down in details, for they are deferred to later stages of refinement. Testing can begin early, because the "unrefined" parts of the design can be replaced by temporary stubs that implement very limited functions. (We did that in `find`.) And revisions are easier because different aspects of the implementation tend to appear at separate levels. The hard thing is to recognize the appropriate level of abstraction at each stage and to avoid mixing in lower-level details.

PROGRAM
    find   find patterns in text
USAGE
    find pattern
FUNCTION
    find reads its input a line at a time and writes to its output those lines that match the specified text pattern. A text pattern is a concatenation of the following elements:

c	literal character c
?	any character except newline
%	beginning of line
$	end of line (null string before newline)
[...]	character class (any one of these characters)
[^ ...]	negated character class (all but these characters)
*	closure (zero or more occurrences of previous pattern)
@c	escaped character (e.g., @%, @[, @*)

Special meaning of characters in a text pattern is lost when escaped, inside [...] (except @]), or for:

%	not at beginning
$	not at end
*	at beginning

A character class consists of zero or more of the following elements, surrounded by [and]:

c	literal character c, including [
c1−c2	range of characters (digits, lower or upper case letters)
^	negated character class if at beginning
@c	escaped character (e.g., @^ @- @@ @])

Special meaning of characters in a character class is lost when escaped or for:

^	not at beginning
−	at beginning or end

An escape sequence consists of the character @ followed by a single character:

@n	newline
@t	tab
@c	c (including @@)

EXAMPLE
    To print lines ending in a Pascal keyword or identifier:
        find [a-zA-Z][a-zA-Z0-9]*$

Exercise 5-8. Add multiple file capabilities to find, so that

       find *pattern file1 file2* ...

will read the specified files in order or, if no file arguments are given, read the standard input. Print the file name before each matched line if there is more than one file argument. Would you ever want to turn this extra printout off? □

Exercise 5-9. Modify find so that

       find ^*pattern*

will print *all* those lines that do *not* match the pattern. To what routine should the test be added? How do you specify a pattern beginning with a literal ^? Modify find to permit searching for lines that contain all of a set of patterns, or any one of a set. □

Exercise 5-10. Add to find the metacharacter +, which stands for "one or more occurrences" of a pattern in the same way that * stands for zero or more. □

Exercise 5-11. Invent a syntax for specifying an arbitrary character-sized bit string in a pattern so as to be able to match non-graphic characters; modify find to scan for such patterns. (See the discussion of esc in Chapter 2.) Add a metacharacter to match non-printing characters. □

Exercise 5-12. An alternate design for find is to turn all metacharacters off by default, and require that each must be preceded by @ when its special meaning is desired. Implement this variation and experiment to see which is easier to explain and use. □

5.4 Some Measurements

We ran find with a number of patterns on an input of 784 lines and 17,713 characters (the source for find with all its supporting code). Here are some CPU times as measured on a DEC VAX 11/780.

pattern:	% (start of line)	1 character (not present)	3-letter word	?*x x not present
total time:	4.0 sec	5.7 sec.	6.2 sec.	131.5 sec.
getline	59.2%	38.8%	33.5%	1.9%
putstr	33.8	0.0	4.8	0.0
match	0.0	7.6	6.7	0.4
amatch	1.7	24.8	23.0	34.4
omatch	1.7	25.1	25.4	42.0
patsize	0.4	0.0	0.5	16.6

As is often the case, the CPU time for simple patterns is dominated by I/O processing. (Our getline calls getcf to construct the line, thus incurring all possible overhead on every input character.) In the same manner, putstr calls putcf. The pattern ?*x, where x is a character not present in the input, is a bad case, since find must backtrack through each character position on each line before deciding that the character doesn't occur. Of course a pattern like ?*?*x would be even worse.

To decide whether find is efficient enough, you have to weight its performance on different patterns by the frequency with which they occur and by the size of the inputs being searched. If the workload consists entirely of nasty patterns and large texts, then clearly find needs a better algorithm. As written, find cannot be readily improved because it would require a complete backtrack through all matches to guarantee finding the leftmost longest. It is possible, however, to recognize any regular expression with no backtracking whatsoever. The most efficient methods convert the regular expression into a "machine" that looks for all possible matches in parallel as it reads the input, and signals whenever one is found. The construction of such a machine is of course a more time-consuming encoding than the one we used, and can take a lot more space, but it has a correspondingly greater payoff in running time: once the machine is built, the running time is independent of the complexity of the pattern. For more details, see Chapter 3 of Aho and Ullman's *Principles of Compiler Design*, referenced at the end of this chapter.

Fortunately the combination of difficult pattern and large input seems to be infrequent in practice. Much more common is a search for a particular word, for which `find` is acceptably efficient.

5.5 Changing Text

Now that we know how to identify patterns in text, let's consider a useful tool for making selective changes. Change usually implies one of three different operations. When we discard what we found, we call it a *deletion;* when we put something new in its place, we call it a *replacement;* and when we leave what we found intact and stick something before or after, we call it an *insertion*. Many "update" utilities make quite a thing out of preserving these distinctions, but the differences are often irrelevant.

There is a simple notation that lets us express all these operations plus a few additional interesting alternatives. The program `change` lets us say

    change *from to*

to look for all occurrences of text patterns that match *from* and replace each with the substitution string *to*. The substitution string can be just a string of replacement characters:

    change mispell misspell

Or it can be null, to effect a deletion:

    change "very, "
    change " *$"

Or it can include the special "ditto" character & to put back the matched stuff and thus do an insertion:

    change active in&

The last example changes all instances of `active` to `inactive`.

The ditto character can appear at either end:

    change able &-bodied

in the middle:

    change a+b (&)

or more than once:

    change very "&, &"

It can also be used literally with the help of an escape:

    change and @&

For change, it is important to know not only what line matches a pattern but also what *substring* of the line caused the match to succeed. The task is to make the specified changes in that substring, then look for additional matches on the remainder of the line. Our matching process finds the leftmost longest match; once that match is located, we can resume scanning the input at the first character after the matched substring and so pick up all disjoint instances of a given pattern in a text file. We never rescan replacement text; this avoids any possibility of looping.

Very little code need be added to what was written for find in order to implement change. From the start we were careful to specify exactly how text patterns match pattern strings, so the size of the match string is well defined; and we wrote amatch so that it returns the index of the first character past the end of the match. Here is the top level.

```
{ change -- change "from" into "to" on each line }
procedure change;
#include "findcons.p"
    DITTO = -1;
var
    lin, pat, sub, arg : string;
#include "getpat.p"
#include "getsub.p"
#include "subline.p"
begin
    if (not getarg(1, arg, MAXSTR)) then
        error('usage: change from [to]');
    if (not getpat(arg, pat)) then
        error('change: illegal "from" pattern');
    if (not getarg(2, arg, MAXSTR)) then
        arg[1] := ENDSTR;
    if (not getsub(arg, sub)) then
        error('change: illegal "to" string');
    while (getline(lin, STDIN, MAXSTR)) do
        subline(lin, pat, sub)
end;
```

Arguments are analyzed and converted into the appropriate forms by getpat, which we wrote for find, and getsub, to which we will return shortly. The actual substitution and printing is done by subline:

```
{ subline -- substitute sub for pat in lin and print }
procedure subline (var lin, pat, sub : string);
var
    i, lastm, m : integer;
    junk : boolean;
#include "amatch.p"
#include "putsub.p"
begin
    lastm := 0;
    i := 1;
    while (lin[i] <> ENDSTR) do begin
        m := amatch(lin, i, pat, 1);
        if (m > 0) and (lastm <> m) then begin
            { replace matched text }
            putsub(lin, i, m, sub);
            lastm := m
        end;
        if (m = 0) or (m = i) then begin
            { no match or null match }
            putc(lin[i]);
            i := i + 1
        end
        else    { skip matched text }
            i := m
    end
end;
```

amatch is attempted for every starting position on each line. If there is a
match (m>0) and if it is not the same match as the last time (lastm<>m),
putsub outputs the expanded substitution string, and the entire matched string
is skipped over. If there is no match (m=0) or if the match was to a null string
(m=i), one character is copied to the output and skipped over on input.

The main problem is what to do with null string matches, because unless one
is careful, there can be unexpected null strings. We have arranged change so
there are never two adjacent null strings. This ensures that the pattern a*
matches the line xy at three points — before x, between x and y, and after y.
We are also careful that a* matches xay at exactly three places as well; this is
proper behavior even though it may not be immediately obvious.

getsub, like getpat, divides the work of building the substitution string
into two pieces, one specific and one more general.

```
{ getsub -- get substitution string into sub }
function getsub (var arg, sub : string) : boolean;
#include "makesub.p"
begin
    getsub := (makesub(arg, 1, ENDSTR, sub) > 0)
end;
```

makesub copies the substitution pattern into sub until it finds an

occurrence of the delimiter, in this case an ENDSTR. Any instances of the ditto
character & are replaced by a special code DITTO, which must be distinct from
all representable characters, just like ENDFILE and ENDSTR.

```
{ makesub -- make substitution string from arg in sub }
function makesub (var arg : string; from : integer;
        delim : character; var sub : string) : integer;
var
    i, j : integer;
    junk : boolean;
begin
    j := 1;
    i := from;
    while (arg[i] <> delim) and (arg[i] <> ENDSTR) do begin
        if (arg[i] = ord('&')) then
            junk := addstr(DITTO, sub, j, MAXPAT)
        else
            junk := addstr(esc(arg, i), sub, j, MAXPAT);
        i := i + 1
    end;
    if (arg[i] <> delim) then    { missing delimiter }
        makesub := 0
    else if (not addstr(ENDSTR, sub, j, MAXPAT)) then
        makesub := 0
    else
        makesub := i
end;
```

All that remains is putsub, which is straightforward:

```
{ putsub -- output substitution text }
procedure putsub (var lin : string; s1, s2 : integer;
        var sub : string);
var
    i, j : integer;
    junk : boolean;
begin
    i := 1;
    while (sub[i] <> ENDSTR) do begin
        if (sub[i] = DITTO) then
            for j := s1 to s2-1 do
                putc(lin[j])
        else
            putc(sub[i]);
        i := i + 1
    end
end;
```

PROGRAM
    change   change patterns in text
USAGE
    change pattern [newstuff]
FUNCTION
    change copies its input to its output except that each non-overlapping string that matches pattern is replaced by the string newstuff. A non-existent newstuff implies deletion of the matched string. The patterns accepted by change are the same as those used by find.

    The replacement string newstuff consists of zero or more of the following elements:
        c   literal character
        &   ditto, i.e., whatever was matched
        @*c*   escaped character *c* (e.g., @&)

EXAMPLE
    To parenthesize all sums and differences of identifiers:
        change "[a-zA-Z][a-zA-Z0-9]*[ ]*[+-][ ]*[a-zA-Z][a-zA-Z0-9]*" (&)

Exercise 5-13. What does

    change active in&

do to inactive, attractive, and radioactive? What procedures would you establish for verifying that "small" changes to a document actually have the desired effect? □

Exercise 5-14. What happens if you try to change something into a newline? What happens if you try to remove the newline at the end of a line? □

Exercise 5-15. Is there anything you can do with translit that you can't do with change? □

Exercise 5-16. Extend change to perform multiple changes; for example,

    change a b c d

changes all a's to b's, then changes all c's to d's on the resulting line. Is this equivalent to

    change a b ¦ change c d

for all possible patterns and substitution strings? □

Exercise 5-17. Consider a file in which each line consists of two fields separated by a tab. Write a pipeline to produce a new file with the fields interchanged on each line, i.e.,

    1234 5678

becomes

    5678 1234

(Hint: Try duplicating the contents of each line, with a separator between the two instances.) □

    Often useful is the ability to *tag* parts of a text pattern so that the pieces of a matched string can be put back selectively or rearranged. Suppose we invent two metacharacters { and } in a text pattern to "remember" the substring matched by that part of the pattern. For example in the pattern

```
%{???}{?*}
```

the first pair of braces will remember the three characters at the beginning of the line, whatever they are; the second braces remember the rest of the line. Now we need a notation to recall the saved substrings. Suppose that @*n* refers to the string remembered by the *n*th pair of braces, where *n* is a single digit. Then we can move a three-character sequence number from the beginning of a line to the end like this:

```
change %{???}{?*} @2@1
```

As a harder-to-read example,

```
change {[^@t]*}@t{?*} @2@t@1
```

reverses two tab-separated fields, as you did by brute force in the previous exercise.

Exercise 5-18. Rewrite the pattern-finding code as cleanly as possible to remember tagged patterns, then alter `change` to insert them on demand in the substitution string. Does your code handle nested braces? You might consider using @(and @) in place of { and }, particularly if your machine has a restricted character set. Why is this a better convention than making ordinary parentheses into metacharacters? □

Exercise 5-19. Given pattern tagging, how would you specify that only the leftmost integer in a line of integers is to be changed to zero? Only the rightmost? The second one from the left? □

Exercise 5-20. Add an option -n to `find`, to print the line number and a space before each line that matches. This is useful for subsequently identifying the matched lines. What is the effect of

```
find -n % | sort -r -n | change "%[0-9]* "
```

(Recall that `sort -r -n` calls for a *reverse* sort with a *numeric* field at the start of a line.) How hard would it be to write a special program to do this particular job for all file sizes? Would it be worth it? □

Exercise 5-21. A problem suggested by D. E. Knuth is to find the largest set of eight-letter words that have the same *middle* four letters. Assuming you have a machine-readable dictionary (with one word per line), how would you solve this problem with `find, change, sort` and `unique`? Do you need anything else? □

Bibliographic Notes

For a comprehensive discussion of how to recognize the broader class of text patterns called regular expressions, see Chapter 3 of A. V. Aho and J. D. Ullman, *Principles of Compiler Design* (Addison-Wesley, 1977). This also describes a program called LEX for mechanically generating lexical analyzers specified by regular expressions. You might also read J. F. Gimpel's "A theory of discrete patterns and their implementation in Snobol4," *CACM*, February,

1973).   Snobol is of course a widely used pattern-matching language.

An excellent treatise on recursion, when to use it, and how to avoid it, is D. W. Barron's *Recursive Techniques in Programming* (American-Elsevier, 1968).

find is modeled after the Unix utility grep (globally look for regular expressions and print) by K. L. Thompson.

Now that we have some pattern matching and changing code handy, we are ready to tackle the more general problem of text editing — creating and modifying textual information like programs, data, documents, what have you. All interactive computing systems (and some batch systems) have some form of editing facility, but it is often rudimentary. The ability to do context searches with regular expressions, make global changes, or do arbitrary file I/O is often left out of even "advanced" editors. Those that include these features often have a command syntax so cumbersome that it is largely unused.

The editor we present here is modeled after the latest in a long family of conversational text editors that have achieved wide acceptance. Concern for human engineering dominates the design — edit tries to be concise, regular and powerful. Because edit is primarily intended for interactive use, it is streamlined and terse, but easy to use. This is especially important for a text editor: for most users it is the primary interface to the system. (On our Unix system, the editor accounts for fifteen percent of all commands executed, more than three times the nearest competitor.) edit is *not* confined to conversational editing, however. It can be driven from prepared scripts and from other programs. It is frequently used to select results from programs or to prepare input to still other programs. It is a tool.

Error recovery is a second major influence on the design of the editor. Like the archive program of Chapter 3, edit maintains precious files, so it must be cautious. Not only that, but when it is used interactively it cannot just throw up its hands and quit when a user enters an erroneous command. It must recover gracefully, for otherwise some trifling mistake could cause the loss of valuable information.

Third, since the editor is inherently a big program, its code must be well organized, or it will get utterly out of hand (and thus probably fail to achieve the goals of good human engineering and reliability). Accordingly we will design the editor top-down, and push to the lowest possible level any information about how files are handled or how text is represented. As much as possible, details of implementation will be hidden from routines that don't need to know about them, so they can be changed or improved without upsetting the

169

bulk of the program.

The editor we present here is not a "screen editor" — it takes no advantage of the ability of many terminals to add, delete and change characters and lines on a screen with a cursor. Such editors are often convenient, but they are typically bigger, slower and harder to make portable than ones that make no assumptions about terminals. They also make more demands on the underlying operating system than we are prepared to deal with here. The bibliographic notes suggest further reading on the topic of screen editors.

6.1 What the User Sees

Although it is generally wise to start small and evolve, an editor, like a programming language, is so heavily used that it should be really good, so that you don't spend all your time fighting its deficiencies. Accordingly, `edit` provides a relatively rich set of facilities, much more than the bare minimum.

This section contains a synopsis of `edit`, enough to give you a feeling for what design decisions were made and why, and for what commands are available. We will expand upon individual commands as we come to them during implementation.

To get started, you type

```
edit
```

or

```
edit file
```

In the latter case, if *file* already exists, it's assumed you want to access its contents, so they are copied into an internal buffer, whose implementation is left unspecified for now. In any case, text is modified in the buffer and perhaps eventually written back to some external file. Files are never modified except by explicit command. This proves to be a safer procedure than working on a file in place, for if you botch an edit you can always read in a fresh copy and start anew.

`edit` is basically "line oriented," in that most editing commands operate on groups of one or more lines in the buffer. This is a natural organization, since text intrinsically comes in lines. Other units might be selected — characters, words, sentences, or arbitrary strings — but lines seem to be most suitable for a wide variety of applications. It is certainly possible to access parts of lines as well; we'll get to that in a moment.

We should emphasize that the editor imposes no structure on lines. It doesn't know that columns 7 and 72 are especially significant in a Fortran program, for instance, nor does it know about any other special format. In our experience, editors that presume to know a lot about what you're doing are more hindrance than help.

As we said, `edit` tries to be concise and regular. Each editing command consists of a single letter, which may be optionally preceded by one or two "line numbers," which specify the inclusive range of lines in the buffer over which the command is to act. Thus for the *print* command p,

      1p

calls for the printing of the first line, and

      1,3p

prints lines 1, 2, and 3. Only one command per line is permitted, since this reduces the possibility that erroneous input will cause serious damage.

    The *delete* command d is analogous to p; it deletes the lines in the specified range:

      1,3d

deletes the first three lines from the buffer. It is always an error to refer to a line that doesn't exist; edit complains when you do.

    Line numbers are *relative* to the beginning of the buffer. After the first three lines have been deleted, the first remaining line (the old line 4) becomes the new line 1, and all other lines are renumbered correspondingly. This behavior may be unfamiliar if you're used to an editor where "line numbers" have a physical existence as part of text lines themselves. Our line numbers are not part of the file, and indeed have no physical representation anywhere; they are just the relative positions of the lines in the buffer. As you will see shortly, this organization gives invaluable flexibility in specifying and rearranging lines.

    Although it is possible to edit entirely in terms of line numbers, be they relative or absolute, it's often an unwieldy nuisance, so edit lets you specify the lines in which you're interested in several other ways. For instance, the editor always keeps track of the *current line,* typically the most recent line affected by the previous command. The current line is specified by the character . (period or "dot"), which you can use anywhere you would have used an integer line number. The *last line* in the buffer is also known; it is called $. So

      .,$p

would print the current line and any subsequent lines through to the end of the buffer;

      1,$p

prints everything; and

      1,$d

deletes everything.

    Dot is altered by many commands. In particular, it is set to the last line printed after a p command and to the next undeleted line after d, except that it never moves past $. Thus a single

```
d
```

deletes the current line, and leaves dot pointing to the next line, while

```
.,$d
p
```

deletes all lines from here to the end, and prints the new last line.

The purpose of . and $ is to reduce the need for specific line numbers. This is further helped by the ability to do line number arithmetic. To print the last few lines of the buffer (perhaps to see how far you got in a previous editing session), say

```
$-10,$p
```

Or you can say

```
.-5,.+5p
```

to print a group of lines around where you're working.

Even when augmented by ., $ and arithmetic, line number editing is still clumsy. When you're editing, you want to be able to say, "Find me an occurrence of this string," so you can work on it without first having to know precisely where it occurs. In edit you can do a *context search* to find a line, simply by writing a pattern between slashes.

```
/abc/
```

means: Starting with the next line after the current line, scan forward until you find a line which matches the pattern abc. The pattern is of course anything of the sort that we described in Chapter 5; we will use the same pattern matching code to ensure this. The search wraps around from line $ to line 1 if necessary. Thus

```
/abc/,$p
```

would locate the next line (after the current line) that matches abc, and print from there to the end of the buffer. If a context search proceeds forward around the ring back to the current line without finding a match, an error is signaled.

Similarly, you can scan backwards by writing a pattern between backslashes. \def\ means: Starting with the line right before the current line, scan backward until you find a line which matches the specified pattern (def). Again, the search wraps around from line 1 to line $, and if no line satisfies the search, an error is signaled. Editing a Pascal program, for instance, you might say

```
\%begin\,/%end/p
```

to print the code part of the routine in which the current line is imbedded.

A line number standing by itself (i.e., followed only by a newline) is taken as a request to print that line, so

```
$
```

prints the last line, and the common case of "Find me the next line with an abc" is

```
/abc/
```

It finds the line, prints it, and sets dot to that line so you can begin to work there. As a special case, a newline all by itself is a request to print the next line, to make it easy to step through the buffer a line at a time.

It is hard to overstate the importance of context searching. Most of the time you use context searches to get to the next place where you want to do some editing. Even when you know the source line numbers, it's often better to scan. If you've used an identifier two different ways, for instance, you might overlook an instance or two while correcting the listing. A context search, however, will lead you in turn to every place in the source where the offending identifier is referred to.

Placing line numbers before the command instead of after it may seem unnatural at first, but one adapts rapidly. This choice lets individual commands use different syntaxes for optional information after the command letter without destroying the regularity with which a range of lines is specified.

The most important of the commands which take further information is the *substitute* command s, used for changing characters within a line.

```
s/bgein/begin/
```

changes the *first* occurrence of bgein to begin on the current line. If there should be more than one on that line (which is unlikely in this case), you can say

```
s/bgein/begin/g
```

to do it *globally* (i.e., everywhere) on the line. Of course the left side of an s command can be any legal pattern, since the same pattern-matching code is used for context searches and substitutions. The right hand side can include the ditto character & as shorthand for whatever was matched by the left hand side, as in the change program of Chapter 5.

An s command, with or without g, can be followed by a p to print the last affected line, to verify that the desired substitution was made. Printing is not automatic for any of the commands, so edit is only as chatty as you want to make it. (You can also follow a delete command by a p; the first undeleted line is printed.) An s command can be preceded by one or two line numbers, to indicate that the substitution is to be done on a range of lines:

```
.+1s/bgein/begin/
```

fixes the mistake on the next line, and

```
1,$s/bgein/begin/g
```

does it everywhere on all lines. (This is handy for consistent misspellers.) Dot is left pointing to the last line which was changed.

s is probably the most useful command in the editor, since it permits you to specify changes in a line or lines succinctly. It is frequently used to add text to the end of a line

```
s/$/ new end/
```

or the beginning

```
s/%/new beginning /
```

or the middle

```
s/and/& furthermore/p
```

The character that delimits the pieces of a substitute command need not be a slash; any character will do, so

```
s:/::g
```

deletes all slashes in a line. Of course you could achieve the same effect by "escaping" the slash, as in

```
s/@///g
```

but this can be confusing.

The last pattern used in a context search or substitute is remembered, and can be specified by a null pattern like // or \\. If you say /begin/ to find a begin keyword, and it's not the one you want, you can say // to get to the next one, or \\ to go back to the previous one. The remembered pattern eliminates a lot of tedious and error-prone re-typing. A typical use of remembered patterns while substituting is

```
/bgein/s//begin/p
//s//begin/p
//s//begin/p
...
```

to walk (slowly) through a document, picking up the misspellings one by one. You know you have them all when a search fails. You can change them all at once with

```
1,$s/bgein/begin/gp
```

but this prints only the last one for verification.

We return now to operations that affect whole lines of text. Most important is the *append* command a, to add new lines of text to the buffer. It is the basic mechanism for adding text to a file, or for making a file to begin with. This entire book and all the programs that go with it were at one time or another appended to the buffer of a text editor very similar to the one we are presenting here.

Since it is used so much, the append mechanism tries to be as unobtrusive as possible. Once it encounters the command a, the editor enters a special *append mode* where everything following is tucked away in the appropriate part of the buffer. Escapes and all other characters lose their special meaning, until a line is encountered that contains *only* a period. This signal, which is easy to type, and unlikely to appear in ordinary text, marks the end of append mode and is not itself copied into the buffer. Subsequent lines are interpreted as commands once again.

So to add text to the buffer, you specify where you want to put it and do an append. To tack stuff on to the end, for instance,

```
$a
```
anything you want to type
except a line containing only a .
as in the following line:

```
.
```

This adds three lines to the buffer, then resumes looking for commands. It was not necessary to escape the period at the end of the second line, since that character is magic only when it stands alone at the beginning of a line. To add something at the beginning of the buffer, you can use the line number zero, as in 0a. If no line number is specified, the text is appended after the current line (dot).

The *insert* command i is identical to a, except that it inserts lines before the line named, instead of after it. The *change* command c replaces one or more lines with a fresh group of zero or more lines:

```
line1, line2  c
```
stuff

```
.
```

replaces *line1* through *line2* with whatever lines follow the c. If no line numbers are given, dot is used by both i and c.

Clearly if you have a and d, you don't need either c or i. The extra flexibility appears to be worthwhile, however, and the amount of additional code turns out to be insignificant.

Dot is left at the last line of text appended, changed or inserted, so you can correct errors as you go, as in this sequence. (The annotations in italics are to clarify what is going on.)

```
a                                      append some text
      if (i < 3) then bgein           oops!
.                                      stop appending
s/bge/beg/                             fix it
a                                      resume appending right after corrected line
... more text ...
botched line                           oops again
.                                      stop appending
c                                      just replace it entirely
... corrected stuff ...               and continue typing
```

The behavior of dot and the default line numbers may seem like a minor concern, but in fact proper choices are crucial for smooth editing. The example above works naturally, without any explicit line numbers, because dot and the default line numbers are "right" each time. We have tried to take similar care with other commands.

The *move* command m lets you move a block of one or more lines to any place in the buffer, and thus provides for "cut and paste" editing. The command

> *line1, line2* m *line3*

moves *line1* through *line2* inclusive to after *line3*. Thus

> `. , . + 1m$`

moves the current line and the one following to the end of the buffer, and

> `$m0`

moves the last line to the beginning ("after line zero"). If no *line1* or *line2* is present, line dot is moved. Dot is left pointing to the last line moved.

You can add the contents of any file to the buffer with the *read* command r:

> `r file`

reads `file`, places its contents right after line dot, and sets dot to the last line read in. Lines already in the buffer are not altered. If a line number is specified with the r command, the text is read in after that line.

Any part of the buffer can be written onto any file with the *write* command w;

> `\procedure\,/%end/w test`

writes the current procedure on `test`, assuming that a line that begins with end marks the end. If no lines are given, a w command writes out the entire contents of the buffer, and if you omit the file name (a bare w command), it writes on the file name used in the original `edit` *file* command. w does not change dot, nor does it alter the buffer.

The *edit* command

```
e file
```

reinitializes the editor buffer just as if you had quit and typed

```
edit file
```

Finally, the *quit* command q lets you leave the editor gracefully. The file you were working on is *not* saved automatically — if you want it saved, you have to issue an appropriate w command before the q.

Any editor command except a, c, i and q can be preceded by a *global prefix*:

```
g/pattern/command
```

specifies that *command* is to be performed for each line in the buffer that contains an instance of *pattern*. g, like w, has a default range of all lines, but a smaller range can be given. A common use of the global prefix is to print all lines containing an interesting pattern:

```
g/interesting/p
```

(which is what the program find does), or to delete all lines with an undesirable pattern:

```
g/undesirable/d
```

For example,

```
g/% *$/d
```

deletes empty lines and lines that contain *only* blanks. You could use

```
g/bgein/s//begin/gp
```

to find all bgein's, fix them, and print *each* corrected line as a check. Since the command that follows a global prefix can have a range of lines, we can even print all lines near ones that contain an interesting pattern:

```
g/interesting/.-1,.+1p
```

The g prefix is definitely an advanced feature, not the concern of a first-time user, but it's worth learning.

There is also a x command which is identical to g except that it operates only on those lines that *do not* contain the pattern (x is for "exclude"):

```
x/% *$/p
```

prints *only* non-blank lines.

That pretty much covers the commands, but before we get into the code, here are a few more notes on line numbers, since much of editing is concerned with specifying the lines you want to do things to.

A semicolon may be used to separate line numbers just as a comma does, but it has the additional effect of setting dot to the latest line number before evaluating the next argument.

```
/abc/;.+1p
```

scans forward to the next line containing abc, then prints that line and the one following it (.+1).

A line number expression may be arbitrarily complex, so long as its value lies between 0 and $, inclusive. And there can be any number of expressions, so long as the last one or two are legal for the particular command. Thus

```
\function\;\\
```

finds the second previous function declaration, and

```
/begin/;//;//;//p
```

prints from the third succeeding line containing begin to the fourth, inclusive.

You can do a lot of editing without global prefixes, semicolons and multiple context searches, and indeed there is seldom call for anything as elaborate as the last example. But as you gain familiarity with the editor, more and more of these things become natural. And when you write scripts to perform complex editing sequences on a series of files, these facilities are invaluable.

Here is the manual page for edit so you can see where we are going.

PROGRAM
    edit   edit text files
USAGE
    edit [file]
FUNCTION
    edit is an interactive text editor that reads command lines from its input and writes display information, upon command, to its output. It works by reading text files on command into an internal "buffer" (which may be quite large), displaying and modifying the buffer contents by other commands, then writing all or part of the buffer to text files, also on command. The buffer is organized as a sequence of lines, numbered from 1; lines are implicitly renumbered as text is added or deleted.

    Context searches and substitutions are specified by writing text patterns, following the same rules for building patterns as used by find. Substitutions specify replacement text following the same rules as used by the program change.

    Line numbers are formed from the following components:

n	a decimal number
.	the current line ("dot")
$	the last line
/pattern/	a forward context search
\pattern\	a backward context search

Components may be combined with + or −, as in, for example,

.+1	sum of . and 1	
$-5	five lines before $	*(continued on next page)*

Line numbers are separated by commas or semicolons; a semicolon sets the current line to the most recent line number before proceeding.

Commands may be preceded by an arbitrary number of line numbers (except for e, f and q, which require that none be present). The last one or two are used as needed. If two line numbers are needed and only one is specified, it is used for both. If no line numbers are specified, a default rule is applied:

(.)	use the current line
(. + 1)	use the next line
(. , .)	use the current line for both line numbers
(1 , $)	use all lines

In alphabetical order, the commands and their default line numbers are:

(.)	a	append text after line (text follows)
(. , .)	c	change text (text follows)
(. , .)	dp	delete text
	e *file*	edit *file* after discarding all previous text, remember file name
	f *file*	print file name, remember file name
(.)	i	insert text before line (text follows)
(. , .)	m *line3* p	move text to after *line3*
(. , .)	p	print text
	q	quit
(.)	r *file*	read *file*, appending after line
(. , .)	s/*pat*/*new*/gp	substitute *new* for occurrence of *pat*
		(g implies for each occurrence across line)
(1 , $)	w *file*	write *file* (leaves current state unaltered)
(.)	=p	print line number
(. + 1)	*newline*	print one line

The trailing p, which is optional, causes the last affected line to be printed. Dot is set to the last affected line, except for f, w, and =, for which it is unchanged.

Text entered with a, c and i is terminated with a line containing just a '.'.

The global prefixes cause repeated execution of a command, once for each line that matches (g) or does not match (x) a specified text pattern:

(1 , $)	g/*pattern*/*command*
(1 , $)	x/*pattern*/*command*

command can be anything but a, c, i or q, and may be preceded by line numbers as usual. Dot is set to the matched line before *command* is done.

If the command line argument file is present, then the editor behaves as if its input began with the command e file. The first filename used is remembered, so that a subsequent e, f, r, or w command can be written with no filename to refer to the remembered filename. A filename given with e or f replaces any remembered filename.

EXAMPLE

Don't be silly.

Exercise 6-1. Compare the external characteristics of edit with the editing facilities available on your system. □

6.2 Line Numbers

A warning: edit is a big program; at 950 lines (excluding contributions from translit, find and change), it is fifty percent bigger than anything else in this book. Although we have done our best to write it well and to present it well, it will take study to assimilate fully. Bear with us as you read and be willing to take a couple of passes over difficult parts.

Input to the editor is a series of command lines, each of which looks like

   line1, line2 command stuff

where *line1*, *line2* and *stuff* are all typically optional. Thus the main loop of the editor is

```
while (getline(lin, STDIN, MAXSTR))
    get list of line numbers from lin
    if (status is OK)
        do command
```

We observed earlier that edit is among those programs that *must* be absolutely reliable and robust. It can't just exit, even when the most ghastly errors happen, because giving up might cost the user whatever work has been accomplished so far. An editor that dies without a struggle will not be used much.

Nearly all parts of edit pass back status, sometimes as both the value of the function and in the argument status. We introduce the enumerated type stcode, with three status values: OK if all is well, ERR if not, and ENDDATA if any sub-module has consumed the last of the input.

```
type
    stcode = (ENDDATA, ERR, OK);      { status returns }
```

"Doing the command" is a multi-way decision with one entry for each command. Most commands validate line numbers, set up defaults if appropriate, then act, usually by calling further procedures and functions. Underpinning all of this are routines that maintain the text in the buffer.

Let us begin with the code for obtaining line numbers for a command. This is an isolated piece that we can understand and get working before doing much else. That way, when the time comes to start checking editing functions, we can use it to poke around in the lines of text at will.

The input line is held in the array lin, with lin[i] the next character to be examined. The top level for handling line numbers is getlist, which gets whatever line numbers there are on the input line, updates i so it points one position beyond the last number, and returns status (OK or ERR) both as the value of the function and in status.

getlist reads a whole list of line numbers by repeatedly calling on getone, and remembers the last two in line1 and line2. It ensures that if no lines were specified, line1 and line2 are both set to curln, the current line (dot). If one line is given, line1 and line2 are both set to it. getlist also records in nlines the number of line numbers actually entered (zero, one, or two) and updates curln whenever a semicolon is encountered.

There are too many control variables to pass around on each call (although that is often the preferred way of making data known to sub-modules), so we will pass things by block structure inheritance. As we mentioned before, it is also possible to use a record, i.e., an aggregate of related variables, perhaps of different types, which can be referenced by one name, but this doesn't really solve the problems either. All the declarations for global variables are held in a file which is included in the main procedure. The following variables are used for line number control:

```
line1 : integer;     { first line number }
line2 : integer;     { second line number }
nlines : integer;    { # of line numbers specified }
curln : integer;     { current line -- value of dot }
lastln : integer;    { last line -- value of $ }
```

Here is getlist, which obtains the line numbers that precede a command:

```
{ getlist -- get list of line nums at lin[i], increment i }
function getlist (var lin : string; var i : integer;
    var status : stcode) : stcode;
var
    num : integer;
    done : boolean;
begin
    line2 := 0;
    nlines := 0;
    done := (getone(lin, i, num, status) <> OK);
    while (not done) do begin
        line1 := line2;
        line2 := num;
        nlines := nlines + 1;
        if (lin[i] = SEMICOL) then
            curln := num;
        if (lin[i] = COMMA) or (lin[i] = SEMICOL) then begin
            i := i + 1;
            done := (getone(lin, i, num, status) <> OK)
        end
        else
            done := true
    end;
    nlines := min(nlines, 2);
    if (nlines = 0) then
        line2 := curln;
    if (nlines <= 1) then
        line1 := line2;
    if (status <> ERR) then
        status := OK;
    getlist := status
end;
```

All the arithmetic and general validity checking for line numbers occurs in getone, which returns a value of type stcode, i.e., OK for a valid number, ERR for error conditions, and eventually ENDDATA when it sees something that is not a line number. Note that getlist, like many other functions in the editor, also returns values of type stcode.

Why do we divide up the code this way? For much the same reason we separated out the functions of match in Chapter 5 — each level is preoccupied with a rather different aspect of control; mixing different aspects in one module only serves to confuse. Here, getlist has quite enough to do keeping track of how many line numbers have been seen and whether a semicolon has been encountered. Reading the code at this level, we couldn't care less how an individual line number is obtained, so we defer that to getone.

And it is clear that obtaining a line number is not all that easy either, for getone in turn passes on some of the work to a subordinate getnum, which collects a single number in a line number expression. First, here is getone.

```
    { getone -- get one line number expression }
    function getone (var lin : string; var i, num : integer;
            var status : stcode) : stcode;
    var
        istart, mul, pnum : integer;
    begin
        istart := i;
        num := 0;
        if (getnum(lin, i, num, status) = OK) then   { 1st term }
            repeat  { + or - terms }
                skipbl(lin, i);
                if (lin[i] <> PLUS) and (lin[i] <> MINUS) then
                    status := ENDDATA
                else begin
                    if (lin[i] = PLUS) then
                        mul := +1
                    else
                        mul := -1;
                    i := i + 1;
                    if (getnum(lin, i, pnum, status) = OK) then
                        num := num + mul * pnum;
                    if (status = ENDDATA) then
                        status := ERR
                end
            until (status <> OK);
        if (num < 0) or (num > lastln) then
            status := ERR;
        if (status <> ERR) then begin
            if (i <= istart) then
                status := ENDDATA
            else
                status := OK
        end;
        getone := status
    end;
```

skipbl merely skips blanks and tabs; it is used in getone to permit spaces

between terms of a line number expression. We could have used it in ctoi
(Chapter 2) and getword (Chapter 3), for it performs a common operation. It
will be used regularly from now on.

```
{ skipbl -- skip blanks and tabs at s[i]... }
procedure skipbl (var s : string; var i : integer);
begin
    while (s[i] = BLANK) or (s[i] = TAB) do
        i := i + 1
end;
```

getnum evaluates one number in a line number expression, where a number
is either an integer, . (dot), $, or a context search.

```
{ getnum -- get single line number component }
function getnum (var lin : string;  var i, num : integer;
        var status : stcode) : stcode;
begin
    status := OK;
    skipbl(lin, i);
    if (isdigit(lin[i])) then begin
        num := ctoi(lin, i);
        i := i - 1  { move back; to be advanced at end }
    end
    else if (lin[i] = CURLINE) then
        num := curln
    else if (lin[i] = LASTLINE) then
        num := lastln
    else if (lin[i] = SCAN) or (lin[i] = BACKSCAN) then begin
        if (optpat(lin, i) = ERR) then  { build pattern }
            status := ERR
        else
            status := patscan(lin[i], num)
    end
    else
        status := ENDDATA;
    if (status = OK) then
        i := i + 1; { next character to be examined }
    getnum := status
end;
```

optpat builds a scan pattern; if the pattern in lin is empty, the previous
pattern will be used. patscan performs the actual context search.

```
{ optpat -- get optional pattern from lin[i], increment i }
function optpat (var lin : string; var i : integer) : stcode;
#include "makepat.p"
begin
    if (lin[i] = ENDSTR) then
        i := 0
    else if (lin[i+1] = ENDSTR) then
        i := 0
    else if (lin[i+1] = lin[i]) then  { repeated delimiter }
        i := i + 1  { leave existing pattern alone }
    else
        i := makepat(lin, i+1, lin[i], pat);
    if (pat[1] = ENDSTR) then
        i := 0;
    if (i = 0) then begin
        pat[1] := ENDSTR;
        optpat := ERR
    end
    else
        optpat := OK
end;
```

The chain of else if's ensures that the tests are performed in exactly the
right order. (We don't want to look at lin[i+1] if lin[i] is ENDSTR.) A
chain of tests is appropriate when the tests are expressions, not constants, and
the order of evaluation must be controlled.

makepat and its supporting routines were defined in Chapter 5. At that
time we wrote makepat to use an arbitrary delimiter to stop the scan. optpat
is the first place that uses the facility; here the delimiter is the character at
lin[i], which is either \ or / for context searches.

patscan starts at .+1 or .-1, depending on direction, and scans around
the buffer until it either finds a match or gets back to curln. Searching begins
one line away from the current line because presumably we just did something
to the current line and we'd like to get on with the next one. Testing for a pattern match is done by match and its subordinates, also from Chapter 5.

```
{ patscan -- find next occurrence of pattern after line n }
function patscan (way : character; var n : integer) : stcode;
var
    done : boolean;
    line : string;
begin
    n := curln;
    patscan := ERR;
    done := false;
    repeat
        if (way = SCAN) then
            n := nextln(n)
        else
            n := prevln(n);
        gettxt(n, line);
        if (match(line, pat)) then begin
            patscan := OK;
            done := true
        end
    until (n = curln) or (done)
end;
```

optpat and patscan must know about the pattern array pat, which is
another global variable:

```
        pat : string;          { pattern }
```

In addition, patscan must be able to obtain actual lines of text for match. It
does so by invoking gettxt, which returns the line in its second argument.
gettxt is part of the interface to the buffer management. Since patscan
needs only the text, gettxt need only be mentioned here; we will discuss
implementation later.

prevln and nextln are functions for walking around the buffer, one line
at a time. It turns out to be convenient to have in the buffer at all times a
"line zero" that contains nothing (so no pattern will match it). Line zero can
serve as a legal line number for commands like a, m and r, which must be able
to put things before the first line. Line zero is an instance of a useful technique
— simplifying a program by adding a dummy element to a data structure, to
make the boundary conditions easier to work with.

```
        { nextln -- get line after n }
        function nextln (n : integer) : integer;
        begin
            if (n >= lastln) then
                nextln := 0
            else
                nextln := n + 1
        end;
```

```
{ prevln -- get line before n }
function prevln (n : integer) : integer;
begin
    if (n <= 0) then
        prevln := lastln
    else
        prevln := n - 1
end;
```

To summarize the line number code, here is the tree of calls for the major procedures and functions so far.

```
edit
    getlist
        getone
            getnum
                optpat
                    makepat
                patscan
                    gettxt, match, nextln, prevln
```

Once again the progression is from the general (getlist) to the specific (optpat, patscan) in several stages. Each level of the hierarchy handles a progressively smaller part of the whole problem, eliminating the need to know many details at any level.

makepat and match in turn call upon additional routines that we wrote in Chapters 2 and 5. Of course this saves us a fair amount of coding, but much more important is consistency. translit, find, change and edit all use the same rules and conventions for patterns; there is no need to learn and remember separate rules for each. This reduces the burden on users and encourages those who know one program to try the others.

6.3 Control Program

Let's go back to the top now, and specify command handling in detail. Basically, the editor is a loop, reading command lines, decoding them and carrying them out. We want to ensure that as much as possible each command line is completely sensible before carrying out any irreversible action, for otherwise a small slip could destroy a whole file. This means that, like expand in Chapter 2, the control structure of edit will mostly reflect error checking.

edit will accept only one command per line, although that command may optionally be preceded by a global prefix. We will fill in the details of global processing later, after learning more about what can be done with the basic commands. For now, we can write the main processing loop of edit as

```
while (getline(lin, STDIN, MAXSTR))
    i := 1
    cursave := curln
    if (getlist(lin, i, status) = OK)
        if (ckglob(lin, i, status) = OK)
            status := doglob(lin, i, cursave, status)
        else if (status <> ERR)
            status = docmd(lin, i, false, status)
        { else error, do nothing }
    if (status = ERR)
        message('?')
        curln := min(cursave, lastln)
    else if (status = ENDDATA)
        break out of loop
    { else OK, loop }
```

ckglob looks for g/.../ or x/.../; if either is found, ckglob marks the lines for processing by doglob, which does the desired command on each marked line. We will get back to these later; for now we can assume a dummy ckglob that returns ENDDATA (no global command seen). If no global prefix is found, and if there was no error, docmd executes the command for the range of lines found by getlist. The false argument to docmd says that it is not being called from within a global prefix.

The main routine must restore curln on an error (unless it goes past lastln), since it is changed with each semicolon found by getlist and may be altered by commands done by doglob and docmd.

The editor's response to all errors is a terse ?. This brevity is acceptable only because the error is almost always obvious, usually a slip in typing or a search that failed. In such cases an error message impedes getting on with the job. edit is structured so that wordier error messages could readily be inserted, however; one of the exercises is concerned with filling in the details.

Most of the code in docmd is in a long if ... else if ... else if to identify which command is to be performed; each case is followed by a few lines to perform the task, most often by procedure call.

The entry for *print* (p), for example, is

```
if (lin[i] = PCMD) then begin
    if (lin[i+1] = NEWLINE) then
        if (default(curln, curln, status) = OK) then
            status := doprint(line1, line2)
end
```

This checks for a valid command format, verifies that the line numbers are reasonable, then performs the appropriate routine. Most of the tests in this procedure use two or more if's of the form

```
if (...) then
   if (...) then
      ...
```

We emphasize that a sequence of tests must be performed *in the given order*. Pascal, like many languages, does not guarantee any particular order for evaluation of logical expressions (or any other expressions, for that matter), nor does it guarantee that evaluation of a logical expression will terminate as soon as the truth value is known. We cannot use

```
if (lin[i] = PCMD)          { wrong! }
   and (lin[i+1] = NEWLINE)
   and (default(curln, curln, status) = OK) then ...
```

because we do not want a call to `default` to set `status` to `OK` after we have established that `lin[i+1]` is not a `NEWLINE`. We are also careful to surround each `if...then if` sequence with `begin-end` so the next `else` is associated with the proper `if`.

The `p` command expects two line numbers. If only one is given, it is used for both line numbers (i.e., print only one line). If none are given, the current line is used for both line numbers. Our notation for this is `(.,.)p`, the parentheses indicating that line numbers are optional, and the two dots showing the default values. `default` sets defaulted line numbers to the specified values.

```
{ default -- set defaulted line numbers }
function default (def1, def2 : integer;
        var status : stcode) : stcode;
begin
   if (nlines = 0) then begin
       line1 := def1;
       line2 := def2
   end;
   if (line1 > line2) or (line1 <= 0) then
       status := ERR
   else
       status := OK;
   default := status
end;
```

In no case is it permissible to print line zero or wrap around the end of the buffer, so `default` flags this as an error. (`getlist` has already ensured that `line2` is not beyond `lastln`.)

The actual printing is straightforward:

```
{ doprint -- print lines n1 through n2 }
function doprint (n1, n2 : integer) : stcode;
var
    i : integer;
    line : string;
begin
    if (n1 <= 0) then
        doprint := ERR
    else begin
        for i := n1 to n2 do begin
            gettxt(i, line);
            putstr(line, STDOUT)
        end;
        curln := n2;
        doprint := OK
    end
end;
```

doprint is called from several places in docmd, so it is necessary to check for line zero here as well as in default. We use the same mechanism as in patscan to locate actual text, by calling on gettxt to get the line we want to print.

Note that there is no printing of gratuitous noise like "end of file" when line $ is printed. Indeed edit is quiet in most ways. Just because a program is used interactively, it does not mean that you should be forced to listen to it babble. One trouble with chatty programs is that you can't turn them off when you want to use them with other programs. Thus printing should occur only when you specify it, so that commands can work silently. But it is called for often enough to warrant some extra notation and shorthand. s, m and d commands can be followed by a p, to print the (last) line affected. And a command line containing only line numbers (no command) causes the last line specified to be printed. Most commonly, this will be a single line, as in 1 or $ or /abc/-2, but it also could be many:

        /abc/;//;//;//

will print only the fourth occurrence of abc, not the third through the fourth as when the trailing p is present. And finally, a completely empty command line (newline only) is taken as .+1p, so you can walk through the buffer by typing newlines.

docmd is the first routine in this book which is longer than one page (when we show it all). Although it is foolish to set arbitrary limits, it does seem wise to keep individual routines shorter than a page, for the shorter a program is, the easier it is to grasp. (And once a page boundary is crossed, it's hard to keep track of indentation.) The median size of our routines is 15 lines; the mean is 19 lines. Even our bigger-than-a-page procedures are designed to be easy to understand — each is just a chain of else if's that chooses among a large set

of alternatives; each alternative is readily comprehended. docmd is shown in its
entirety later in this chapter; for now, the part that controls printing is

```
{ docmd -- handle all commands except globals }
function docmd (var lin : string; var i : integer;
        glob : boolean; var status : stcode) : stcode;
var
    fil, sub : string;
    line3 : integer;
    gflag, pflag : boolean;
begin
    pflag := false; { may be set by d, m, s }
    status := ERR;
    if (lin[i] = PCMD) then begin
        if (lin[i+1] = NEWLINE) then
          if (default(curln, curln, status) = OK) then
            status := doprint(line1, line2)
    end
    else if (lin[i] = NEWLINE) then begin
        if (nlines = 0) then
            line2 := nextln(curln);
        status := doprint(line2, line2)
    end
    else if (lin[i] = QCMD) then begin
        if (lin[i+1]=NEWLINE) and (nlines=0) and (not glob) then
            status := ENDDATA
    end
    else if (lin[i] = ACMD) then begin
        ...
    { and so on for other commands ... }
        ...
    { else status is ERR }

    if (status = OK) and (pflag) then
        status := doprint(curln, curln);
    docmd := status
  end;
```

This also shows the code for the *quit* command q, which is called for by a
command line containing only q. It causes the editor to exit, just as if it had
encountered an ENDFILE while reading commands. Nothing is printed, for the
same reasons that most commands are silent.

Furthermore, nothing is written onto any file after a q command. You
might ask whether it would be better to write out the editing buffer automatically, or at least to ask the user for confirmation before exiting. The latter
guards against embarrassing mistakes, but it should only ask for confirmation if
the buffer has been modified since the last write and there should be some way
to suppress the query when the editor is used noninteractively. This is more
mechanism than we want to describe initially, however, so we will leave it as an

exercise.

It is hard to decide how much to protect users from their own behavior, but in our experience, it is generally wisest to keep out of people's way: assume they know what they are doing and let them do it with as few prohibitions and warnings as you can manage. You will hear from them quickly enough when you do something wrong.

6.4 Buffer Representations

In this section we will deal with how the buffer of lines being edited is actually represented. We begin by discussing the command *append*, which adds text to the buffer. The lines to be appended are placed in the buffer right after the line specified, or right after the current line if no line number is provided. Our shorthand for this rule is (.)a. It should be clear why we want to be particular about what is acceptable as a command. If you forget to enter append mode before typing text, you don't want arbitrary letters in a word to cause changes in the text. Instead a ? will bring you up short after just one line of nonsense.

The code in docmd that calls append is

```
else if (lin[i] = ACMD) then begin
    if (lin[i+1] = NEWLINE) then
        status := append(line2, glob)
end
```

and append itself is

```
{ append -- append lines after "line" }
function append (line : integer; glob : boolean) : stcode;
var
      inline : string;
      stat : stcode;
      done : boolean;
begin
      if (glob) then
            stat := ERR
      else begin
            curln := line;
            stat := OK;
            done := false;
            while (not done) and (stat = OK) do
                  if (not getline(inline, STDIN, MAXSTR)) then
                        stat := ENDDATA
                  else if (inline[1] = PERIOD)
                     and (inline[2] = NEWLINE) then
                        done := true
                  else if (puttxt(inline) = ERR) then
                        stat := ERR
      end;
      append := stat
end;
```

Appending text under control of a global prefix is more code than we want to handle right now; if necessary, you can achieve the same effect with an r command. This version of append outlaws global appends, but the possibility of special treatment for them later is left open.

The work of inserting each new line and updating curln to point at it is done by the routine puttxt. To see how it works, we must learn a little more about how the buffer is organized.

We want to be able to rearrange lines freely, and to scan in either direction efficiently. Several organizations are possible. For instance, we could use a two-way linked list of text lines where each line entry contains pointers to the previous line and to the next line. (With links in both directions operations like scanning backwards do not pay a time penalty.) That way, we could rewrite pointer information to move lines around as needed. Appending and deleting entire sections would also be easy. But finding the nth line requires a scan down a list.

Alternatively, we could keep a single array of positions of text lines, and rearrange the position values as lines are deleted or moved, as we did for sort in Chapter 4. Since appending, deleting and reading all change the number of lines, bookkeeping is needed to keep the active positions in a compact set. But finding any given line is fast.

As it turns out, the position-array organization is substantially easier to work with than the linked list (we tried that once before and it was a mess), and for most operations is just as efficient. Therefore that is what we will use.

Where should the lines be stored? The easiest thing is to hold everything in memory, but that can put a severe limit on the size of file we can deal with. We could compromise and put the text out on some working file, keeping the positions in memory along with enough information to locate each text line in the file. That limits the total number of lines we can handle, but allows for many more characters of text. Or we could keep the position vector on a file, and access only what we need through a fixed size "window."

However we choose to do it, the important thing is to isolate the implementation as much as possible from the rest of the program. That way we can optimize a given implementation, even change the entire strategy, just by altering a handful of low-level buffer management routines.

In this particular case, we can implement *any* of the possibilities mentioned above by writing seven functions:

- `setbuf` initializes the buffer to contain only a valid line zero, and creates a scratch file if necessary.
- `clrbuf` discards the scratch file, if one is used.
- `puttxt(lin)` copies the text in `lin` into the buffer immediately after the current line and sets `curln` to the last line added.
- `gettxt(n,s)` copies the contents of line n into the string s.
- `blkmove(n1,n2,n3)` rearranges lines by moving the block of lines n1 through n2 to after line n3. n3 must not be between n1 and n2.
- `putmark(n,m)` places the mark m on line n for global prefix processing.
- `getmark(n)` returns the mark on line n.

It is not necessary to know (and there is no way of knowing) whether the text resides in memory, or the positions do, or anything. So long as one line of text is available, we can do everything we have to in the way of editing. That means that the buffer in memory can contain all the data, or it can be a fixed size window on a much larger world. Once we have a working editor it's easy to change buffer management, because the interface to the buffer manager is well specified and the code for it is isolated.

We should stress that we didn't start with these routines right at the beginning. Instead we "discovered" them as we wrote the editor from top to bottom. (And to be honest, we discovered different versions as we re-thought the program from time to time — the first draft is rarely the best.) By seeing at each stage what operations we wanted to perform on the text, we were able to abstract this handful of basic functions. It also helped that we wanted to put off deciding the actual implementation as long as possible — that goal steered us away from a number of more restrictive designs. Given this set of basic operations, and measurements showing where the editor spends its time, we can improve `edit`'s efficiency as it becomes necessary, without touching the bulk of the code.

But the first order of business is to get a working editor, so we pick the easiest form of buffer management to implement, keeping everything in memory in

an array of strings buf. Since we also have to look ahead to marks, we will use
a record to hold both the text and the mark.

```
type
    buftype =    { in-memory edit buffer entry }
        record
            txt : string;    { text of line }
            mark : boolean   { mark for line }
        end;

var
    buf : array [0..MAXLINES] of buftype;
```

Thus the text for a particular line is accessed as buf[i].txt and the mark as
buf[i].mark. Each text line occupies an array position in buf; no attempt is
made to use space efficiently. Marks are stored as booleans; we will return to
this later.

We can now write in-memory versions of the buffer management routines.
clrbuf is easiest, when there is no scratch file.

```
{ clrbuf (in memory) -- initialize for new file }
procedure clrbuf;
begin
    { nothing to do }
end;
```

gettxt isn't much harder:

```
{ gettxt (in memory) -- get text from line n into s }
procedure gettxt (n : integer; var s : string);
begin
    scopy(buf[n].txt, 1, s, 1)
end;
```

blkmove moves lines around; it does most of its work with the help of a
subordinate, reverse, which reverses part of an array. Three well-chosen
reversals cause the desired group of lines to move. We have illustrated one case
here; you should verify the other yourself.

n1 ... n2	x y z n3	*original positions*
n2 ... n1	x y z n3	*first reversal*
n2 ... n1	n3 z y x	*second reversal*
x y z n3	n1 ... n2	*third reversal*

```
{ blkmove -- move block of lines n1..n2 to after n3 }
procedure blkmove (n1, n2, n3 : integer);
begin
    if (n3 < n1-1) then begin
        reverse(n3+1, n1-1);
        reverse(n1, n2);
        reverse(n3+1, n2)
    end
    else if (n3 > n2) then begin
        reverse(n1, n2);
        reverse(n2+1, n3);
        reverse(n1, n3)
    end
end;

{ reverse -- reverse buf[n1]...buf[n2] }
procedure reverse (n1, n2 : integer);
var
    temp : buftype;
begin
    while (n1 < n2) do begin
        temp := buf[n1];
        buf[n1] := buf[n2];
        buf[n2] := temp;
        n1 := n1 + 1;
        n2 := n2 - 1
    end
end;
```

setbuf sets up the buffer initially, by creating line zero. Line zero regularizes the code — appending after line zero is not a special case, for instance. As currently written, the program never looks at the contents of line zero, but we have chosen to make it a null string nonetheless. This was originally put in as insurance, then left in to appease a gnawing sense of insecurity, just in case someday a programmer modifying edit inadvertently does look at it. Programmers have the right to be ignorant of many details of your code and still make reasonable changes.

```
{ setbuf (in memory) -- initialize line storage buffer }
procedure setbuf;
var
    null : string;   { value is '' }
begin
    null[1] := ENDSTR;
    scopy(null, 1, buf[0].txt, 1);
    curln := 0;
    lastln := 0
end;
```

puttxt adds the new line at the end (if it fits), then calls blkmove to move it into place. puttxt also updates curln and lastln appropriately.

```
{ puttxt (in memory) -- put text from lin after curln }
function puttxt (var lin : string) : stcode;
begin
    puttxt := ERR;
    if (lastln < MAXLINES) then begin
        lastln := lastln + 1;
        scopy(lin, 1, buf[lastln].txt, 1);
        putmark(lastln, false);
        blkmove(lastln, lastln, curln);
        curln := curln + 1;
        puttxt := OK
    end
end;
```

putmark will appear shortly, when we discuss global prefixes.

We can now show some more of the procedure hierarchy, to help you keep track of who calls whom.

```
edit
    setbuf
    getlist
    docmd
        append
            getline
            puttxt
                blkmove, putmark
        default
        doprint
            gettxt
    clrbuf
```

Most of the growth will be in docmd as we add more cases.

Exercise 6-2. Change the quit command so it will prompt for reassurance if the buffer has been changed since the last write. How do you turn prompting off? □

Exercise 6-3. What happens to the current line when you append nothing, that is, when you write the command sequence

```
a
.
```

Is this reasonable? □

Exercise 6-4. Is there any circumstance under which a context search could match line zero? □

6.5 More Commands: Delete, Insert, Change, Print line number, Move

Another important capability besides appending is making unwanted text go away. This is done with the *delete* command (. , .)d. In docmd we add:

```
else if (lin[i] = DCMD) then begin
    if (ckp(lin, i+1, pflag, status) = OK) then
        if (default(curln, curln, status) = OK) then
        if (lndelete(line1, line2, status) = OK) then
        if (nextln(curln) <> 0) then
            curln := nextln(curln)
end
```

The *delete* command removes the line or lines specified and leaves curln pointing at the next line after the stuff removed, unless that would be off the end of the buffer, in which case curln is set to lastln. The optional p, to print this line as a check, is checked and recorded in pflag by ckp:

```
{ ckp -- check for "p" after command }
function ckp (var lin : string; i : integer;
        var pflag : boolean; var status : stcode) : stcode;
begin
    skipbl(lin, i);
    if (lin[i] = PCMD) then begin
        i := i + 1;
        pflag := true
    end
    else
        pflag := false;
    if (lin[i] = NEWLINE) then
        status := OK
    else
        status := ERR;
    ckp := status
end;
```

The actual work is done in the function lndelete, which leaves curln pointing to the line just *before* the lines removed, and resets lastln to the new last line. (We use lndelete to avoid a name conflict with the delete procedure of archive.)

```
{ lndelete -- delete lines n1 through n2 }
function lndelete (n1, n2 : integer; var status : stcode)
      : stcode;
begin
    if (n1 <= 0) then
        status := ERR
    else begin
        blkmove(n1, n2, lastln);
        lastln := lastln - (n2 - n1 + 1);
        curln := prevln(n1);
        status := OK
    end;
    lndelete := status
end;
```

Note that lines are "deleted" by moving them to the end of the buffer, then abandoning them by decreasing lastln. This implies that we are not going to attempt to reclaim text storage while a given file is being edited, no matter what set of primitives we use.

Three other commands are easily implemented using existing routines. *Insert* or (.)i injects text immediately *before* the specified line number.

```
else if (lin[i] = ICMD) then begin
    if (lin[i+1] = NEWLINE) then begin
        if (line2 = 0) then
            status := append(0, glob)
        else
            status := append(prevln(line2), glob)
    end
```

Change or (. , .)c deletes the lines in the specified range, then injects text in their place.

```
else if (lin[i] = CCMD) then begin
    if (lin[i+1] = NEWLINE) then
        if (default(curln, curln, status) = OK) then
            if (lndelete(line1, line2, status) = OK) then
                status := append(prevln(line1), glob)
    end
```

And (.)= is used to print the value of a line number expression (or of the current line number), so you can see where some line is. It is often used as $=
to tell how many lines are in the buffer.

```
      else if (lin[i] = EQCMD) then begin
          if (ckp(lin, i+1, pflag, status) = OK) then begin
              putdec(line2, 1);
              putc(NEWLINE)
          end
      end
end
```

The *move* command m rearranges lines of text:

　　(. , .)m *line3*

causes the specified line or lines to be taken from wherever they currently reside
and placed immediately after *line3*. Since getone is used to obtain *line3*, any
valid expression can be used, such as

```
/const/m\function\p
```

which moves the next line containing const to immediately after the closest
previous line containing function. curln is left pointing at the last line
moved, which would contain const in this case. The optional trailing p prints
this line. The code in docmd is

```
      else if (lin[i] = MCMD) then begin
          i := i + 1;
          if (getone(lin, i, line3, status) = ENDDATA) then
              status := ERR;
          if (status = OK) then
            if (ckp(lin, i, pflag, status) = OK) then
            if (default(curln, curln, status) = OK) then
              status := move(line3)
      end
```

and the work is done in move:

```
      { move -- move line1 through line2 after line3 }
      function move (line3 : integer) : stcode;
      begin
          if (line1<=0) or ((line3>=line1) and (line3<line2)) then
              move := ERR
          else begin
              blkmove(line1, line2, line3);
              if (line3 > line1) then
                  curln := line3
              else
                  curln := line3 + (line2 - line1 + 1);
              move := OK
          end
      end;
```

Exercise 6-5. How would you test that part of the editor built so far? Pay particular
attention to behavior at the "boundaries," such as 0i, m0, m.-1, m., and 1,$d. □

Exercise 6-6. Implement a *copy* command k

> (. , .)k *line3* p

which makes a copy of a block of lines after *line3*, instead of moving them. (The mnemonic k for "copy" is strained but we're running out of letters, and it seems worthwhile to retain the single-letter convention for command names.) □

6.6 The Substitute Command

So far we have dealt with entire lines of text. But we have the change pro-gram of Chapter 5 to draw upon, so we can easily add a *substitute* command s that selectively replaces text matched by a text pattern.

The format of a *substitute* command is

> (. , .)s/*pattern*/*new*/g

where the delimiter / can actually be any character other than newline. The g suffix is used when you want to alter *all* matching substrings, as in change; if the g is absent only the leftmost match is altered.

The code in docmd that checks for *substitute* is

```
        else if (lin[i] = SCMD) then begin
            i := i + 1;
            if (optpat(lin, i) = OK) then
                if (getrhs(lin, i, sub, gflag) = OK) then
                if (ckp(lin, i+1, pflag, status) = OK) then
                if (default(curln, curln, status) = OK) then
                    status := subst(sub, gflag, glob)
        end
```

It uses optpat, as does getnum, to encode the pattern, then calls on getrhs ("get right hand side") to encode the replacement string and look for a g. getrhs in turn relies on makesub, which we wrote for change, to do most of the work. Both makepat and makesub were written so the delimiter can be any character. This permits substitute commands to be delimited by any con-venient character, not necessarily the slashes we have used in most of our exam-ples. (This is handy when you want to substitute instances of / and don't feel like escaping it every time.) ckp again checks for the optional trailing p that prints the resulting line, and default sets the default line numbers if neces-sary.

```
{ getrhs -- get right hand side of "s" command }
function getrhs (var lin : string; var i : integer;
        var sub : string; var gflag : boolean) : stcode;
begin
    getrhs := OK;
    if (lin[i] = ENDSTR) then
        getrhs := ERR
    else if (lin[i+1] = ENDSTR) then
        getrhs := ERR
    else begin
        i := makesub(lin, i+1, lin[i], sub);
        if (i = 0) then
            getrhs := ERR
        else if (lin[i+1] = ord('g')) then begin
            i := i + 1;
            gflag := true
        end
        else
            gflag := false
    end
end;
```

All that remains is the code for subst, which is modeled after subline, from change in Chapter 5.

```
{ subst -- substitute "sub" for occurrences of pattern }
function subst (var sub : string; gflag, glob : boolean) : stcode;
var
    new, old : string;
    j, k, lastm, line, m : integer;
    stat : stcode;
    done, subbed, junk : boolean;
begin
    if (glob) then
        stat := OK
    else
        stat := ERR;
    done := (line1 <= 0);
    line := line1;
    while (not done) and (line <= line2) do begin
        j := 1;
        subbed := false;
        gettxt(line, old);
        lastm := 0;
        k := 1;
        while (old[k] <> ENDSTR) do begin
            if (gflag) or (not subbed) then
                m := amatch(old, k, pat, 1)
            else
                m := 0;
            if (m > 0) and (lastm <> m) then begin
                { replace matched text }
                subbed := true;
                catsub(old, k, m, sub, new, j, MAXSTR);
                lastm := m
            end;
            if (m = 0) or (m = k) then begin
                { no match or null match }
                junk := addstr(old[k], new, j, MAXSTR);
                k := k + 1
            end
            else    { skip matched text }
                k := m
        end;
        if (subbed) then begin
            if (not addstr(ENDSTR, new, j, MAXSTR)) then begin
                stat := ERR;
                done := true
            end
            else begin
                stat := lndelete(line, line, status);
                stat := puttxt(new);
                line2 := line2+curln-line;
                line := curln;
```

```
                    if (stat = ERR) then
                        done := true
                    else
                        stat := OK
                end
            end;
            line := line + 1
        end;
        subst := stat
    end;
```

It is considered an error for a substitute command to make no substitutions at all, since that often indicates that you didn't type the right pattern, or that you applied it to the wrong line. But under the control of a g or x prefix, subst can be called many times and a failure in one of them does not mean that the whole thing has failed. The first test in subst checks for the global prefix.

   catsub is much the same as putsub in Chapter 5.

```
{ catsub -- add replacement text to end of new }
procedure catsub (var lin : string; s1, s2 : integer;
        var sub : string; var new : string;
        var k : integer; maxnew : integer);
var
    i, j : integer;
    junk : boolean;
begin
    i := 1;
    while (sub[i] <> ENDSTR) do begin
        if (sub[i] = DITTO) then
            for j := s1 to s2-1 do
                junk := addstr(lin[j], new, k, maxnew)
        else
            junk := addstr(sub[i], new, k, maxnew);
        i := i + 1
    end
end;
```

Exercise 6-7. How would you get a line containing only a dot into the buffer? □

Exercise 6-8. What is the meaning of each occurrence of // in

   /abc/;//;//s///

What does the command do? □

Exercise 6-9. What happens when you delete all the characters on a line, as in

   s/?*//

What if you then delete the newline, as in

   s/@n//

What happens if you delete the newline at the end of a non-empty line? What happens if you substitute additional newlines into existence? Express desirable behavior in one or two concise rules, then implement it. □

Exercise 6-10. Modify the s command so users can specify which substitutions are wanted; for example, "s3/x/y/" could mean "change the third x into y," and "s1-5/x/y/" would change the first 5 instances. How ornate should such a feature be? □

Exercise 6-11. Implement the *transliterate* command (. , .)t, which maps one character set into another, as in the translit program of Chapter 2. That is

        1,$t/a-z/A-Z/

would convert lower case letters to upper case on all lines. Why would you want this facility in addition to translit? Why would you want translit in addition to this facility? □

Exercise 6-12. How would you implement an *undo* command u, which would undo the effect of the last substitute command (that is, replace the new line by the old one)? Can you extend it to other commands? □

6.7 Input/Output

We could quit right about now and have a pretty comprehensive text editor. By adding a little more code, we could have a program we could invoke as

        edit *file*

which reads *file* into its internal buffer for processing and, just before exiting, writes it back.

Instead, we are going to add a few more commands that will let us read and write files explicitly, so we can selectively merge and split files or make multiple copies without going outside the editor. These extra commands greatly increase the ease with which you can do "cut and paste" editing.

The *edit* command e *file* clears the internal buffer and copies *file* into it. There is also a *read* command (.)r *file*, which appends the contents of *file* right after the specified line, as if they had been typed after an a command, without altering text already in the buffer. Files are created or rewritten with the *write* command (1 , $)w *file*, which copies the specified range of lines onto *file*, replacing its previous contents. The default for this command is to write the entire buffer if there are no line numbers, or to write one line if there is only one line number. Dot is set to the last line read on e and r commands. The w command does not change dot or the buffer contents, so you can write intermediate versions of the file without interfering with editing.

A filename is remembered from the argument in edit *file*, or from the first r or w command that specifies one, or from the most recent e command. An I/O command with no *file* uses the remembered name, so an unadorned e, r or w command refers to the file you began with. The *filename* command f prints the remembered name for inspection, or sets it if a name is given, as in the command f *file*. We introduce another global variable called savefile to hold the remembered file name.

```
savefile : string;  { remembered file name }
```

The code in docmd for filename processing is

```
else if (lin[i] = ECMD) then begin
    if (nlines = 0) then
      if (getfn(lin, i, fil) = OK) then begin
        scopy(fil, 1, savefile, 1);
        clrbuf;
        setbuf;
        status := doread(0, fil)
      end
end
else if (lin[i] = FCMD) then begin
    if (nlines = 0) then
      if (getfn(lin, i, fil) = OK) then begin
        scopy(fil, 1, savefile, 1);
        putstr(savefile, STDOUT);
        putc(NEWLINE);
        status := OK
      end
end
else if (lin[i] = RCMD) then begin
    if (getfn(lin, i, fil) = OK) then
        status := doread(line2, fil)
end
else if (lin[i] = WCMD) then begin
    if (getfn(lin, i, fil) = OK) then
      if (default(1, lastln, status) = OK) then
        status := dowrite(line1, line2, fil)
end;
```

The (1,$) line number rule for the w command is enforced by default, described earlier.

Filenames are obtained and checked by getfn, which insists on at least one space and a filename, or nothing at all.

```
    { getfn -- get file name from lin[i]... }
    function getfn (var lin : string; var i : integer;
            var fil : string) : stcode;
    var
        k : integer;
        stat : stcode;
    #include "getword.p"
    begin
        stat := ERR;
        if (lin[i+1] = BLANK) then begin
            k := getword(lin, i+2, fil);       { get new filename }
            if (k > 0) then
                if (lin[k] = NEWLINE) then
                    stat := OK
        end
        else if (lin[i+1] = NEWLINE)
          and (savefile[1] <> ENDSTR) then begin
            scopy(savefile, 1, fil, 1);
            stat := OK
        end;
        if (stat = OK) and (savefile[1] = ENDSTR) then
            scopy(fil, 1, savefile, 1); { save if no old one }
        getfn := stat
    end;
```

doread and dowrite both print the number of lines transmitted, as a check and to signal completion of the operation. This design is inconsistent with our earlier lecture about programs that talk too much, but it has been our experience that users prefer some feedback for operations like r and w which involve a significant change in the status of either local or external file copy. The line count provides a rough confirmation that you transmitted what you really wanted to. It also tells you when the command is done. A design principle like "avoid excessive chatter" is a guideline to be applied intelligently, not an absolute rule to be followed blindly. (It's a straightforward but useful exercise to add an option to turn the count off when it isn't wanted.)

```
{ doread -- read "fil" after line n }
function doread (n : integer; var fil : string) : stcode;
var
    count : integer;
    t : boolean;
    stat : stcode;
    fd : filedesc;
    inline : string;
begin
    fd := open(fil, IOREAD);
    if (fd = IOERROR) then
        stat := ERR
    else begin
        curln := n;
        stat := OK;
        count := 0;
        repeat
            t := getline(inline, fd, MAXSTR);
            if (t) then begin
                stat := puttxt(inline);
                if (stat <> ERR) then
                    count := count + 1
            end
        until (stat <> OK) or (t = false);
        close(fd);
        putdec(count, 1);
        putc(NEWLINE)
    end;
    doread := stat
end;
```

```
{ dowrite -- write lines n1..n2 into file }
function dowrite (n1, n2 : integer; var fil : string) : stcode;
var
    i : integer;
    fd : filedesc;
    line : string;
begin
    fd := create(fil, IOWRITE);
    if (fd = IOERROR) then
        dowrite := ERR
    else begin
        for i := n1 to n2 do begin
            gettxt(i, line);
            putstr(line, fd)
        end;
        close(fd);
        putdec(n2-n1+1, 1);
        putc(NEWLINE);
        dowrite := OK
    end
end;
```

Exercise 6-13. Modify the r and w commands so they produce no confirming line count. Experiment with both versions. Which do you prefer? Add an option to control it. Modify the w command so that it can optionally *append* the information to the file instead of overwriting. □

6.8 Global Commands

We have now specified everything in the editor except the details of the global prefix g, which has the format

     (1 , $) g/*pattern*/*command*

Default line numbers are the same as for the w command: if none are given the entire buffer is examined. For every line that matches *pattern* the *command* will be obeyed. But sometimes it is more convenient to specify a pattern that matches those lines we want to leave alone, so we define the complement of g to be **x**:

     (1 , $) x/*pattern*/*command*

does *command* on every line that *does not* contain *pattern*. (The mnemonic significance of **x** is "exclude." The code is written entirely in terms of symbolic constants, however, only one of which needs to be changed to alter our selection if you prefer something else.)

command can be any edit command except q, and a, c or i, whose operation in global commands we have left as an exercise. Furthermore, it may be preceded by line numbers with context searches and so on. For example,

```
g/%{/p
```

prints lines that begin with a {, such as the comment lines that introduce our procedures and functions, and

```
g/%{/ .,/%begin/-1p
```

prints from the comment line to just before the `begin` that terminates the declaration part.

Since we allow d, m and r after a global prefix, executing a command can cause all sorts of rearrangements of the lines in the buffer, so we must be precise in defining the order in which lines are examined and acted upon. We must also take care that the editor does not get into infinite loops, yet still does more or less what we want and expect.

The scheme we settled on may not be perfect, but it is simple and it works. First we go through the entire range marking lines that match (g) or do not match (x) the `pattern`. We also erase any leftover marks on all other lines. All this is done in `ckglob`, which picks off the global prefix if it exists.

```
{ ckglob -- if global prefix, mark lines to be affected }
function ckglob (var lin : string; var i : integer;
        var status : stcode) : stcode;
var
    n : integer;
    gflag : boolean;
    temp : string;
begin
    if (lin[i] <> GCMD) and (lin[i] <> XCMD) then
        status := ENDDATA
    else begin
        gflag := (lin[i] = GCMD);
        i := i + 1;
        if (optpat(lin, i) = ERR) then
            status := ERR
        else if (default(1,lastln,status) <> ERR) then begin
            i := i + 1; { mark affected lines }
            for n := line1 to line2 do begin
                gettxt(n, temp);
                putmark(n, (match(temp, pat) = gflag))
            end;
            for n := 1 to line1-1 do      { erase other marks }
                putmark(n, false);
            for n := line2+1 to lastln do
                putmark(n, false);
            status := OK
        end
    end;
    ckglob := status
end;
```

getmark and putmark are trivial:

```
{ getmark -- get mark from nth line }
function getmark (n : integer) : boolean;
begin
    getmark := buf[n].mark
end;

{ putmark -- put mark m on nth line }
procedure putmark(n : integer; m : boolean);
begin
    buf[n].mark := m
end;
```

The rest of the work is done in doglob, which is called (from the main routine) if ckglob finds a valid global prefix. doglob begins examining lines for marks, starting at line1. If one is found doglob erases it, sets curln, and obeys the command by calling docmd. Otherwise, it proceeds around the buffer, keeping careful count of how many lines have been examined since the

last success. When it makes a complete pass without seeing a mark
(count>lastln) it is done.

```
{ doglob -- do command at lin[i] on all marked lines }
function doglob (var lin : string; var i, cursave : integer;
        var status : stcode) : stcode;
var
    count, istart, n : integer;
begin
    status := OK;
    count := 0;
    n := line1;
    istart := i;
    repeat
        if (getmark(n)) then begin
            putmark(n, false);
            curln := n;
            cursave := curln;
            i := istart;
            if (getlist(lin, i, status) = OK) then
              if (docmd(lin, i, true, status) = OK) then
                count := 0
        end
        else begin
            n := nextln(n);
            count := count + 1
        end
    until (count > lastln) or (status <> OK);
    doglob := status
end;
```

For each marked line, dot is set to that line, then the command is executed with
docmd. (The true argument indicates that the command is being done under
control of a global prefix. Only a, c, i, s and q worry about this.) The command itself can modify dot, access multiple lines, and so forth. For example,

```
g/procedure/.,/%end$/p
```

prints all procedures (assuming religious formatting) — each time a line containing procedure is found, all lines from there to an unindented end are
printed.

As a more difficult example,

```
g/%/m0
```

marks *every* line, then goes back and moves each line to the beginning of the
buffer. The effect is to reverse the order of the lines. Another example, based
on the same operation, is this one which we use from time to time:

```
g/thing/m0
0;\\=
```

which moves all lines with `thing` on them to the beginning, then finds the last one. The net result is to count the `thing`'s, at the expense of scrambling the buffer. You can also count `thing`'s with

```
x/thing/d
$=
```

if you don't mind deleting lines from the buffer.

Exercise 6-14. One operation that does not work properly is this attempt to separate even and odd numbered lines in the buffer:

```
g/%/.+1m$
```

What does it actually do? How would you change `move` so this works properly (and no other useful operation gets messed up)? □

Exercise 6-15. Prove that `doglob` cannot loop forever. □

Exercise 6-16. How would you improve the efficiency of `g` processing? (Consider `g/%/d`.) Is it worth it? □

6.9 The Main Routine

We are now in a position to present the main routine for `edit`. Before we do, however, here is the entire code for `docmd`, so you can see it all at once and refresh your memory. As we said, though it is long, it is only a multi-way branch that selects one of many alternatives.

```
{ docmd -- handle all commands except globals }
function docmd (var lin : string; var i : integer;
        glob : boolean; var status : stcode) : stcode;
var
    fil, sub : string;
    line3 : integer;
    gflag, pflag : boolean;
begin
    pflag := false; { may be set by d, m, s }
    status := ERR;
    if (lin[i] = PCMD) then begin
        if (lin[i+1] = NEWLINE) then
            if (default(curln, curln, status) = OK) then
                status := doprint(line1, line2)
    end
    else if (lin[i] = NEWLINE) then begin
        if (nlines = 0) then
            line2 := nextln(curln);
        status := doprint(line2, line2)
    end
    else if (lin[i] = QCMD) then begin
        if (lin[i+1]=NEWLINE) and (nlines=0) and (not glob) then
            status := ENDDATA
    end
    else if (lin[i] = ACMD) then begin
        if (lin[i+1] = NEWLINE) then
            status := append(line2, glob)
    end
    else if (lin[i] = CCMD) then begin
        if (lin[i+1] = NEWLINE) then
            if (default(curln, curln, status) = OK) then
            if (lndelete(line1, line2, status) = OK) then
                status := append(prevln(line1), glob)
    end
    else if (lin[i] = DCMD) then begin
        if (ckp(lin, i+1, pflag, status) = OK) then
            if (default(curln, curln, status) = OK) then
            if (lndelete(line1, line2, status) = OK) then
            if (nextln(curln) <> 0) then
                curln := nextln(curln)
    end
    else if (lin[i] = ICMD) then begin
        if (lin[i+1] = NEWLINE) then begin
            if (line2 = 0) then
                status := append(0, glob)
            else
                status := append(prevln(line2), glob)
        end
    end
```

```
    else if (lin[i] = EQCMD) then begin
        if (ckp(lin, i+1, pflag, status) = OK) then begin
            putdec(line2, 1);
            putc(NEWLINE)
        end
end
else if (lin[i] = MCMD) then begin
    i := i + 1;
    if (getone(lin, i, line3, status) = ENDDATA) then
        status := ERR;
    if (status = OK) then
      if (ckp(lin, i, pflag, status) = OK) then
      if (default(curln, curln, status) = OK) then
        status := move(line3)
end
else if (lin[i] = SCMD) then begin
    i := i + 1;
    if (optpat(lin, i) = OK) then
      if (getrhs(lin, i, sub, gflag) = OK) then
      if (ckp(lin, i+1, pflag, status) = OK) then
      if (default(curln, curln, status) = OK) then
        status := subst(sub, gflag, glob)
end
else if (lin[i] = ECMD) then begin
    if (nlines = 0) then
      if (getfn(lin, i, fil) = OK) then begin
        scopy(fil, 1, savefile, 1);
        clrbuf;
        setbuf;
        status := doread(0, fil)
    end
end
else if (lin[i] = FCMD) then begin
    if (nlines = 0) then
      if (getfn(lin, i, fil) = OK) then begin
        scopy(fil, 1, savefile, 1);
        putstr(savefile, STDOUT);
        putc(NEWLINE);
        status := OK
    end
end
else if (lin[i] = RCMD) then begin
    if (getfn(lin, i, fil) = OK) then
        status := doread(line2, fil)
end
else if (lin[i] = WCMD) then begin
    if (getfn(lin, i, fil) = OK) then
      if (default(1, lastln, status) = OK) then
        status := dowrite(line1, line2, fil)
end;
```

```
    { else status is ERR }

    if (status = OK) and (pflag) then
        status := doprint(curln, curln);
    docmd := status
  end;
```

This is the main routine for edit, with its complete declarations. This code also handles the optional file name in edit *file*.

```
    { edit -- main routine for text editor }
    procedure edit;
    #include "editcons.p"
    #include "edittype.p"
    #include "editvar.p"
        cursave, i : integer;
        status : stcode;
        more : boolean;
    #include "editproc.p"
    begin
        setbuf;
        pat[1] := ENDSTR;
        savefile[1] := ENDSTR;
        if (getarg(1, savefile, MAXSTR)) then
            if (doread(0, savefile) = ERR) then
                message('?');
        more := getline(lin, STDIN, MAXSTR);
        while (more) do begin
            i := 1;
            cursave := curln;
            if (getlist(lin, i, status) = OK) then begin
                if (ckglob(lin, i, status) = OK) then
                    status := doglob(lin, i, cursave, status)
                else if (status <> ERR) then
                    status := docmd(lin, i, false, status)
                { else ERR, do nothing }
            end;
            if (status = ERR) then begin
                message('?');
                curln := min(cursave, lastln)
            end
            else if (status = ENDDATA) then
                more := false;
            { else OK }
            if (more) then
                more := getline(lin, STDIN, MAXSTR)
        end;
        clrbuf
    end;
```

To refresh your memory, here are the variables from editvar:

```
{ editvar -- variables for edit }
var
     buf : array [0..MAXLINES] of buftype;

     line1 : integer;      { first line number }
     line2 : integer;      { second line number }
     nlines : integer;     { # of line numbers specified }
     curln : integer;      { current line -- value of dot }
     lastln : integer;     { last line -- value of $ }

     pat : string;         { pattern }
     lin : string;         { input line }
     savefile : string;    { remembered file name }
```

The constants for edit are in editcons and the procedure inclusions in editproc:

```
{ editproc -- procedures for edit }
#include "edprim.p" { editor buffer primitives }
#include "amatch.p"
#include "match.p"
#include "skipbl.p"
#include "optpat.p"
#include "nextln.p"
#include "prevln.p"
#include "patscan.p"
#include "getnum.p"
#include "getone.p"
#include "getlist.p"
#include "append.p"
#include "lndelete.p"
#include "doprint.p"
#include "doread.p"
#include "dowrite.p"
#include "move.p"
#include "makesub.p"
#include "getrhs.p"
#include "catsub.p"
#include "subst.p"
#include "ckp.p"
#include "default.p"
#include "getfn.p"
#include "docmd.p"
#include "ckglob.p"
#include "doglob.p"
```

```
{ editcons -- const declarations for edit }
const
    MAXLINES = 100; { set small for testing }
    MAXPAT = MAXSTR;
    CLOSIZE = 1;      { size of a closure entry }
    DITTO = -1;
    CLOSURE = STAR;
    BOL = PERCENT;
    EOL = DOLLAR;
    ANY = QUESTION;
    CCL = LBRACK;
    CCLEND = RBRACK;
    NEGATE = CARET;
    NCCL = EXCLAM;
    LITCHAR = LETC;
    CURLINE = PERIOD;
    LASTLINE = DOLLAR;
    SCAN = SLASH;
    BACKSCAN = BACKSLASH;

    ACMD = LETA;      { = ord('a') }
    CCMD = LETC;
    DCMD = LETD;
    ECMD = LETE;
    EQCMD = EQUALS;
    FCMD = LETF;
    GCMD = LETG;
    ICMD = LETI;
    MCMD = LETM;
    PCMD = LETP;
    QCMD = LETQ;
    RCMD = LETR;
    SCMD = LETS;
    WCMD = LETW;
    XCMD = LETX;

{ edittype -- types for in-memory version of edit }
type
    stcode = (ENDDATA, ERR, OK);     { status returns }
    buftype =    { in-memory edit buffer entry }
        record
            txt : string;    { text of line }
            mark : boolean   { mark for line }
        end;
```

Finally, here is an outline of the procedure hierarchy for edit. As before, a number of low level service routines have been omitted to keep it down to manageable size.

```
edit
    setbuf
    doread
    getlist
        getone
            getnum
                optpat
                    makepat
                patscan
                    gettxt, match
    ckglob
        optpat, match, gettxt, getmark, putmark, default
    doglob
        getlist, docmd, getmark, putmark
    docmd
        append
            puttxt
                blkmove
        default
        lndelete
            blkmove
        ckp
        getone
        move
            blkmove
        optpat
        getrhs
            makesub
        subst
            gettxt, amatch, lndelete, puttxt, catsub
        getfn
        doread
            puttxt
        dowrite, doprint
            gettxt
    clrbuf
```

docmd knows about a large number of routines, but this is not as bad as it seems, for on any call to docmd we need only concern ourselves with one case. In that light, the hierarchy for edit is straightforward.

Exercise 6-17. Add a *next* command (., .)n*k* that will print the next *k* lines starting at line2. The default value of *k* is slightly less than one screenful. A negative *k* should print the *k* previous lines. What should happen if there are less than *k* lines in the specified direction? □

Exercise 6-18. Do you think it would be better if edit told you more about what it is doing? If so, modify append to print a prompting * before reading each line, and force a print after every command. Try both versions for a while and see which you prefer. You might consider an *options* command o, that lets you run the editor in verbose mode (ov) with prompts or in silent mode (os). In which state should the editor start? □

Exercise 6-19. Add a command to turn off the significance of metacharacters like ?, [ ], and so on. If the metacharacters are turned off, it should be possible to restore the special meaning temporarily by preceding the character with an escape character. Should metacharacters be on or off by default? □

Exercise 6-20. Implement a *list* command l, which is identical to the *print* command p, except that it prints some visible representation of otherwise invisible characters like backspaces, tabs, blanks at the ends of lines, and non-graphics. □

Exercise 6-21. Some people object (with justification) to a bald ? as the sole diagnostic. Implement a ? command that concisely describes the most recent error. □

Exercise 6-22. How would you specify a global append so that you only have to enter the text to be appended (or changed or inserted) once? How would you implement it? How would you allow an arbitrary number of commands to be controlled by a global prefix? How would you implement nested global prefixes? Would recursion simplify the job? □

Exercise 6-23. If your system requires or strongly encourages line numbers semi-permanently attached to lines, or if you prefer them on esthetic grounds, modify the editor to handle them. The "absolute" line numbers need to be usable with any command, generated somehow by a, c, and i, treated appropriately by s and m, and dealt with by r and w. Should relative line numbers remain? □

6.10 Scratch Files

Now that we have a working editor, we can concentrate on making it better. Our first concern is the buffer storage, which is intentionally rudimentary in the current version. We can gain considerable capacity by keeping only position information in memory and maintaining the bulkier text on a *scratch file*.

The main change is to separate the text of the lines from the position information, because not all the text will be in memory at once. Most of it is off on a scratch file, stored in a manner we haven't yet described. What we must do is organize the in-memory information so that (with the help of another primitive) we can treat the scratch file as an unlimited extension of memory, albeit with a longer access time.

Consider a substitute command. The text of the line must be accessed, which means it must be found on the scratch file, unless we're lucky and it's already in memory. The current version of the line must be deleted from the scratch file, which can be done by simply forgetting about it — the text remains on the scratch file, but nothing points to it. Then the replacement line is added, which is most easily by adding it to the end of the scratch file. Clearly to make all of this work we still require position information such as we had with the in-memory version so we can deduce what line follows what; we need to know where the current version of a line is on the scratch file so it can be read; we have to be able to move to that point on the scratch file to access it; and we have to be able to move to the end to write out a new version.

The organization this time is a bit different.

```
{ edittype -- types for scratch-file version of edit }
type
    stcode = (ENDDATA, ERR, OK);
    buftype =
        record
            txt : integer;  { text of line }
            mark : boolean  { mark for line }
        end;

var
    buf : array [0..MAXLINES] of buftype;
    scrout : filedesc;  { scratch input fd }
    scrin : filedesc;   { scratch output fd }
    recin : integer;    { next record to read from scrin }
    recout : integer;   { next record to write on scrout }
    edittemp : string;  { temp file name 'edtemp' }
```

This time the buftype record contains a record number where the corresponding text can be found on the scratch file. scrin and scrout are file descriptors for reading and writing the scratch file, and recin and recout are the numbers of the next input and output records on the file.

Rather than restrict ourselves to some specific storage medium such as tape or disk for the scratch file, we introduce an additional primitive called seek to provide a standard interface.

>   seek(*pos*, *filedesc*)

positions the specified file for a subsequent read or write beginning at the file position *pos*. *filedesc* is a file descriptor returned by open or create. In our implementation, we keep track of the record simply by counting how much has been read or written.

We found it easiest to express *pos* in terms of records (that is, lines of text), but in a different environment, you might use the number of characters as the positioning information. Since seek depends very strongly on peculiarities of individual systems, we will not present a version here; it must be considered a primitive.

In any case, seek does whatever is necessary to find its way back to a line of text written earlier or forward to one further down the file. The program can thus view a file as a randomly addressable array of lines, leaving it up to primitives to worry about making it work. This is as it should be.

puttxt is much as before:

```
{ puttxt (scratch file) -- put text from lin after curln }
function puttxt (var lin : string) : stcode;
begin
    puttxt := ERR;
    if (lastln < MAXLINES) then begin
        lastln := lastln + 1;
        putstr(lin, scrout);
        putmark(lastln, false);
        buf[lastln].txt := recout;
        recout := recout + 1;
        blkmove(lastln, lastln, curln);
        curln := curln + 1;
        puttxt := OK
    end
end;
```

All new text is added at the end of the file, at record number `recout`; `scrout` is the file descriptor for writing the scratch file, returned by `create`.

`gettxt` again fetches a line of text; in our implementation, it must `seek` to the proper place on the scratch file, then read the line into `txt`.

```
{ gettxt (scratch file) -- get text from line n into s }
procedure gettxt (n : integer; var s : string);
var
    junk : boolean;
begin
    if (n = 0) then
        s[1] := ENDSTR
    else begin
        seek(buf[n].txt, scrin);
        recin := recin + 1;
        junk := getline(s, scrin, MAXSTR)
    end
end;
```

Our scratch file scheme works with just one line of text in memory at any one time, although this is not very efficient, and we could do much better by keeping more lines around. One of the exercises is concerned with making better use of memory.

Now that we know the steady state workings of the scratch file routines, we can set up the initialization and termination routines. It is usually best to proceed this way, saving initialization and termination to the last, for it is only then that you have a proper appreciation for what has to be done.

```
{ setbuf (scratch file) -- create scratch file, set up line 0 }
procedure setbuf;
begin
    { setstring(edittemp, 'edtemp'); }
        edittemp[1] := ord('e');
        edittemp[2] := ord('d');
        edittemp[3] := ord('t');
        edittemp[4] := ord('e');
        edittemp[5] := ord('m');
        edittemp[6] := ord('p');
        edittemp[7] := ENDSTR;
    scrout := mustcreate(edittemp, IOWRITE);
    scrin := mustopen(edittemp, IOREAD);
    recout := 1;
    recin := 1;
    curln := 0;
    lastln := 0
end;

{ clrbuf (scratch file) -- dispose of scratch file }
procedure clrbuf;
begin
    close(scrin);
    close(scrout);
    remove(edittemp)
end;
```

The other buffer routines — `blkmove`, `reverse`, `getmark` and `putmark` — are unchanged.

Exercise 6-24. Replace the existing buffer control primitives with the scratch file set (plus `seek`). Measure the mean line length of a sample of your files (what tools would you use to do this?) and use this data to estimate the relative capacities of the two versions of the editor. □

Exercise 6-25. Run various editions of the editor against a standard script of commands and compare response times. Use this information to determine how elaborate your buffer mechanism should be. □

Exercise 6-26. On most systems, `edit` can be made faster by trying to anticipate the lines that will be used in the immediate future and reading several lines at one time. Modify `gettxt` or a subordinate to read a group of lines when `gettxt` is called, unless the line is already present in memory. The challenge is to organize things so that for common editing operations the line *is* already present with high probability. What are the common operations that are worth improving? How much code has to be changed? How much will this speed up various operations? □

Exercise 6-27. No attempt is made to reclaim space used by deleted lines on the scratch file. What problems can this cause? How would you implement a *garbage collection* scheme, modifying `lndelete` as little as possible? (`lndelete` is the only routine where space is thrown away; it is called for by the c, d and s commands.) Is it better to recycle collected garbage as soon as possible, or only when necessary, or never? What measurements would you make to justify your prejudice? □

Exercise 6-28. Magnetic tape has the property that you can never read information past the latest stuff written (i.e., you dare not rewrite patches in the middle). Does our scratch file maintenance scheme work properly with magnetic tape? Why would you want to be able to use tape with the text editor? What are its drawbacks? □

Exercise 6-29. How would you implement an editor that keeps *all* information on a scratch file, including line pointers? Can you still use magnetic tape? Is garbage collection worthwhile? □

Exercise 6-30. If your system provides a `run` primitive that lets you execute a command from within a running program, implement an "escape" command @ that lets you type an operating system command from within the editor. For instance,

        @edit *file*

would invoke a fresh instance of `edit` on *file*; when that instance is finished, execution resumes in the current editor. What modifications are necessary in `setbuf` and `clrbuf` if nested editors are to work correctly? □

One aspect of system environment we have not mentioned is handling signals from the outside world, primarily *interrupts*. In an editor it is desirable that the user be able to stop the current command, for example to terminate a long print command, without losing any information. In general, interrupts arrive at unpredictable and probably inconvenient times, so the editor must be prepared to maintain its integrity as it deals with them. For a print command, this is not much of a problem, but you can imagine the difficulties when an interrupt occurs in the middle of a move command done under a global prefix. The problem is to stop the current action as soon as possible, yet remain sane enough that subsequent editing proceeds properly.

Exercise 6-31. If your system provides a primitive for catching interrupts, modify `edit` so it handles them properly, without losing information or buffer consistency. What can you do if there is no way to intercept an interrupt? What happens if a user hangs up the phone? □

Once a file gets too big, it may be too much trouble to provide some of the nice features of `edit`, like global commands and reverse searching with \\. But it is still vital to be able to perform most editing tasks on big files. One possibility is to cannibalize `edit` to make a "stream editor." A stream editor digests a set of commands, then copies its standard input to its standard output, applying all the commands to each input line in turn. The set of editing transformations is necessarily limited. For example, any command that implies backwards or repeated scanning of the file would be disallowed; this includes \\, some aspects of the global prefix, the move command, and minus signs in line number arithmetic (no /begin/-1).

The command

> *line1* , *line2 command*

would be taken to mean, "Attempt this command on the first line that matches the first line number, and on all subsequent lines until you find one that matches the second; then begin watching for a match of the first line number again." A single line number would imply doing the command on each line that matched the pattern; a missing line number would perform the command on every line. Multiple commands should be allowed after any selection pattern.

If you have a stream editor, find and change are special cases, respectively

        sedit */pattern/*p

and

        sedit */pattern/*s*//replacement/*gp

Should find and change be retained as separate programs nonetheless?

Exercise 6-32. Design and implement a stream editor based on the suggestions above. □

6.11 Summary

It is hard to get a proper perspective on the design or code of anything as large as a text editor, particularly without some experience using it.

One useful approach is to make a list of common editing tasks, then compare how they are expressed in several editors. Here is one example of a task which we do regularly, yet which is far beyond the capabilities of many editors. The text and programs for this book are stored in more than four hundred files in the file system on our computer. From time to time, we need to go through the entire book making some change wherever it occurs in this set of files. Doing each file by hand would be intolerably slow and error-prone, so instead we can use edit, like this.

First we make a *script* — the set of commands that we want to do on each file. (And of course we make it with edit!) One of our scripts, for instance, converted the word EOF to ENDFILE globally, so we could avoid a potential conflict with the name of the standard procedure eof. The script was

        f
        g/EOF/s//ENDFILE/gp
        w

The f command echoes the name of the file we're editing, in case something goes wrong; the s command with global prefix makes the change and prints all affected lines; and the w command writes the new version back on the file it came from.

Then we run a program listcat ("list catalog") to prepare a list of all our files, one file name per line:

```
listcat >filelist
```

places the file list in a file called `filelist`. (Recall that we discussed the `>` operation in Chapter 3.)

Next we edit `filelist`. All of the files in our book contain the letters book as part of their name, so we first delete all file names that are not part of the book with an x command:

```
x/book/d
```

Then we convert each file name to an e command by putting "e " before it:

```
1,$s/%/e /
```

This leaves each line in the buffer in the form

    e *filename*

Then we read in a copy of the script after each file name:

```
g/?/.r script
```

At this point each of the original book filenames has been converted into a group of editing commands consisting of e *filename* followed by whatever the script specifies.

We write the whole thing into a file called `command`:

```
w command
q
```

Now the single command

```
edit <command
```

invokes the editor with its input coming from the set of editor commands in the file `command`. Thus `edit` does the script, whatever it is, on each of the files in turn.

In practice, this goes faster than we can describe it. And of course, if you stop to think about it, you will realize that the editing operations to make the command file can be placed in another file, perhaps `commandmaker`, and this process run whenever a new file of commands is needed. It is a good test of an editing system to see whether it can accomplish the same function with as little fuss.

Bibliographic Notes

The earliest traceable version of the editor presented here is TECO, written for the first PDP-1 timesharing system at MIT. It was subsequently implemented on the SDS-940 as the "quick editor" QED by L. P. Deutsch and B. W. Lampson; see "An online editor," *CACM*, December, 1967. K. L. Thompson adapted QED for CTSS on the IBM 7090 at MIT, and later D. M.

Ritchie wrote a version for the GE-635 (now Honeywell 6070) at Bell Labs.

The latest version is ed, a simplified form of QED for the Unix operating system, written by Ritchie and Thompson. Our editor closely resembles ed, at least in outward appearance.

C. W. Fraser, "A Compact, Portable, CRT-based Text Editor," *Software Practice and Experience*, February, 1979, describes the construction of a screen editor that uses edit for the editing functions, with a moderate amount of extra code to handle the terminal. Fraser's paper "A generalized text editor" (*CACM*, March, 1980) describes some interesting non-text applications of an editor very much like edit. The proceedings of the SIGPLAN Conference on Text Manipulation, Portland (June, 1981), contains several papers describing innovative text editors; it is a good place to start further reading.

CHAPTER 7: **FORMATTING**

Our next task is to write a text formatter — a program for neatly formatting a document on a suitable printer. Naturally the precise meanings of "neatly," "formatting," and "suitable" will vary according to your aspirations and your budget. Our formatter provides a bare minimum of formatting controls, those which we have observed people actually use when preparing documents. It produces output for devices like terminals and line printers, with automatic right margin justification, pagination (skipping over the fold in the paper), page numbering and titling, centering, underlining, indenting, and multiple line spacing.

A formatter is an important tool for anyone who writes (including programmers describing their programs), because, once correct, material is never retyped. This has some obvious cost benefits, and helps ensure that the number of errors decreases with time. Machine formatting eases the typing job, since margin alignment, centering, underlining and similar tedious operations are handled by the computer, not by the typist. It also permits drastic format changes in a document without altering any text. But perhaps most important, it seems to encourage writers to improve their product, since the overhead of making an improvement is small and there is an esthetic satisfaction in having a clean copy.

Freedom from errors may sometimes be the primary concern. For instance, this book was produced on a phototypesetter driven by a (very) sophisticated big brother of the formatter we are going to write now. The programs are stored in the same file system as the text is. When a chapter is printed, programs are included at the point where they are referred to (by a mechanism much like the `include` processor of Chapter 3), sometimes using a stream editor like the one described in Chapter 6 to select a subset of the lines. In this way, the tested programs are combined with the text, untouched by human hands. We are fairly confident that what is printed is what was actually tested.

The `format` program described in this chapter is quite conventional. It accepts text to be formatted, interspersed with formatting commands telling `format` what the output is to look like. A command consists of a period, a two-letter name, and perhaps some optional information. Each command must

227

appear at the beginning of a line, with nothing on the line but the command and its arguments. For instance,

```
.ce
```

centers the next line of output, and

```
.sp 3
```

generates three spaces (blank lines).

Most of the time, however, the `format` user should have to know little about commands and arguments — most formatting happens automatically. This is merely good human engineering. Ideally a document containing *no* commands should be printed sensibly. Default parameter settings and formatting actions are intended to be reasonable and free of surprises. For instance, words fill up output lines as much as possible, regardless of the length of input lines. Blank lines cause fresh paragraphs. Input is correctly spaced across page boundaries, with top and bottom margins.

At the same time the design has to be sufficiently flexible that it can be augmented with more advanced features for sophisticated use. Knowledgeable users should of course be able to change parameter settings as desired. Ultimately it should be possible for users to define new formatting operations in terms of those already provided. We will explore these possibilities in the exercises at the end of the chapter.

7.1 Commands

As we said, all commands consist of a period at the beginning of a line, which is an unlikely occurrence in ordinary text, and have two-letter names. It has been our experience that users prefer concise commands in most languages, so this seems a reasonable compromise between brevity and mnemonic value. In any case, the code is written so that some other choice could be made with minimal changes.

By default `format` *fills* output lines, by packing as many input words as possible onto an output line before printing it. The lines are also *justified* (right margins made even) by inserting extra blanks into the filled line before output. People normally want filled text, which is why we choose it as the default behavior. It can be turned off, however, by the *no-fill* command

```
.nf
```

and thereafter lines will be copied from input to output without any rearrangement. Filling can be turned back on with the *fill* command

```
.fi
```

When an `.nf` is encountered, there may be a partial line collected but not yet output. The `.nf` will force this line out before anything else happens. The action of forcing out a partially collected line is called a *break*. The break concept pervades `format`; many commands implicitly cause a break. To force a break explicitly, for example to separate two paragraphs, use

```
.br
```

Of course you may want to add an extra blank line between paragraphs. The *space* command

```
.sp
```

causes a break, then produces a blank line. To get *n* blank lines, use

```
.sp n
```

(A blank is always required between a command and its argument.) If the bottom of a page is reached before all of the blank lines have been printed, the excess ones are thrown away, so that all pages will normally start at the same first line.

By default output will be single spaced, but the line spacing can be changed at any time:

```
.ls n
```

sets line spacing to *n*. (*n*=2 is double spacing.) The `.ls` command does not cause a break.

The *begin page* command `.bp` causes a skip to the top of a new page and also causes a break. If you use

```
.bp n
```

the next output page will be numbered *n*. A `.bp` that happens to occur at the bottom of a page has no effect except perhaps to set the page number; no blank page is generated. The current page length can be changed (without a break) with

```
.pl n
```

To center the next line of output,

```
.ce
line to be centered
```

The `.ce` command causes a break. You can center *n* lines with

```
.ce n
```

and, if you don't like to count lines (or can't count correctly), say

```
.ce 1000
lots of lines
to be centered
    ...
.ce 0
```

The lines between the `.ce` commands will be centered. No filling is done on centered lines.

Underlining is much the same as centering:

```
.ul n
```

causes the text on the next *n* lines to be underlined upon output. But `.ul` does *not* cause a break, so words in filled text may be underlined by

```
words and words and
.ul
lots more
words.
```

to get

```
words and words and lots more words.
```

Centering and underlining may be intermixed in any order:

```
.ce
.ul
This is a Title
```

gives a centered and underlined title.

The *indent* command controls the left margin:

```
.in n
```

causes all subsequent output lines to be indented *n* positions. (Normally they are indented by 0.) The command

```
.rm n
```

sets the *right margin* to *n*. The line length of filled lines is the difference between right margin and indent values. `.in` and `.rm` do not cause a break.

The traditional paragraph indent is produced with *temporary indent* command:

```
.ti n
```

breaks and sets the indent to position *n* for one output line only.

To put running header and footer titles on every page, use `.he` and `.fo`:

```
.he this becomes the top of page (header) title
.fo this becomes the bottom of page (footer) title
```

The title begins with the first non-blank after the command, but a leading single or double quote will be discarded if present, so you can produce titles that begin with blanks. If a title contains the character #, it will be replaced by the current page number each time the title is actually printed. `.he` and `.fo` do not cause a break.

Since absolute numbers are often awkward, format allows *relative* values as command arguments. All commands that allow a numeric argument *n* also allow $+n$ or $-n$ instead, to signify a *change* in the current value. For instance,

```
.rm -10
.in +10
```

shrinks the right margin by 10 from its current value, and moves the indent 10 places further to the right. Thus

```
.rm 10
```

and

```
.rm +10
```

are quite different.

    Relative values are particularly useful with `.ti`, to temporarily indent relative to the current indent:

```
.in +5
.ti +5
```

produces a left margin indented by 5, with the first line indented by a further 5. And

```
.in +5
.ti -5
```

produces a "hanging indent," as in a numbered paragraph:

```
(1)   There   is   no warranty of merchantability nor
      any warranty  of  fitness  for  a  particular
      purpose   nor   any  other  warranty,  either
      express or implied, as to the accuracy of the
      enclosed materials or as to their suitability
      for any particular purpose.
```

    A line that begins with blanks is a special case. If there is no text at all, the line causes a break and produces a number of blank lines equal to the current line spacing. If a line begins with n blanks followed by text, it causes a break and a temporary indent of $+n$. These special actions help ensure that a document that contains no formatting commands will still be reasonably formatted.

    To summarize, then, here is the manual page for `format`. This is a reasonable set of capabilities, but others will undoubtedly have occurred to you. We will suggest further possibilities as we go along.

PROGRAM
    `format`   produce formatted output
USAGE
    `format`
FUNCTION
    `format` reads its input a line at a time and writes a neatly formatted version of the input text to the output, with page headers and footers and with output lines filled to a uniform right margin. Input text lines may have interspersed among them command lines that alter this default mode of formatting. A command line consists of a leading period, followed by a two letter code, possibly with optional arguments following the first sequence of blanks and tabs.

    Certain commands cause a "break" in the processing of input text lines, i.e., any partially filled line is output and a new line is begun. In the following command summary, the letter n stands for an optional numeric argument. If a numeric argument is preceded by a + or -, the current value is *changed* by this amount; otherwise the argument represents the new value. If no argument is given, the default value is used.

command	break?	default	function
`.bp` n	yes	$n=+1$	begin page numbered n
`.br`		yes	cause break
`.ce` n	yes	$n=1$	center next n lines
`.fi`	yes		start filling
`.fo` *str*	no	empty	footer title
`.he` *str*	no	empty	header title
`.in` n	no	$n=0$	indent n spaces
`.ls` n	no	$n=1$	line spacing is n
`.nf`	yes		stop filling
`.pl` n	no	$n=66$	set page length to n
`.rm` n	no	$n=60$	set right margin to n
`.sp` n	yes	$n=1$	space down n lines or to bottom of page
`.ti` n	yes	$n=0$	temporary indent of n
`.ul` n	no	$n=1$	underline words from next n lines

    A blank input line causes a break and is passed to the output unchanged. Similarly, an input line that begins with blanks causes a break and is written to the output with the leading blanks preserved. Thus a document formatted in the conventional manner by hand will retain its original paragraph breaks and indentation.

Exercise 7-1. Discuss criteria for which commands should cause a break and which should not. An alternative design is to have two characters that introduce commands, instead of one, so that, for instance, `.sp` causes a break as before, while `,sp` does not. Discuss this design. □

Exercise 7-2. Write a pipeline to count the words but not the `format` commands in a document. □

7.2 Construction

    The text formatter is another good candidate, like the editor and file archiver, for incremental construction — making the minimum amount that will do something useful, and then, with this part operational, fleshing out the skeleton a piece at a time. This divides a big job into smaller, more manageable pieces. Testing the first part is easier because it is smaller. If the design is good, later pieces should not interact much with what has gone before, so for the most part they may be tested independently. There is also a morale boost in having *something* working early.

On bigger projects, friendly users can try out a partial program with limited functions. Their reactions provide vital feedback to evaluate what already exists and what is yet to come. Often you will learn that what the user wants is less ornate than either of you thought at first, so some of the hard work can be postponed indefinitely. Or you may learn that what the user wants is quite different than you thought. It is foolish to build the whole thing in a closet before revealing any part of it. (Innocent users are also marvelous at stumbling into bugs, because they exercise programs in ways you never thought of.)

The text formatter is a case in point. Once a certain minimum capability has been built, additions can be made without affecting previous code very much (assuming sensible design in the first place). We will sketch out how the construction might proceed, now that we know what facilities are to be provided.

There are several choices for program organization, of which two seem promising. One is to handle the input one word at a time, and assemble lines out of words for line-oriented tasks like no-fill and centering. Or we could input a line at a time and break the line into words when filled text is being processed. Given the number of formatting operations that are based on lines — no-fill mode, centering, underlining, and commands themselves — the line-at-a-time structure seems to be easier. It's a good mental exercise to work out details of the word-at-a-time design, however. You will find that neither organization is ideal — each has its awkward parts.

7.3 Command Decoding

The main routine reads input a line at a time and separates it into text and formatting commands. This much we can write before anything else.

```
begin
    initfmt;
    while (getline(inbuf, STDIN, MAXSTR)) do
        if (inbuf[1] = CMD) then
            command(inbuf)
        else
            text(inbuf)
end;
```

CMD is the character period (.), unless you prefer something else. initfmt sets all parameters to their default initial values; we will show it later when we have discussed what the parameters are.

We begin with command, the routine that decides what kind of command has appeared, since most of the command interpreting code can be written before anything else is done. Temporarily text can be a stub which does nothing more than copy text lines from inbuf to the standard output with putstr.

```
{ command -- perform formatting command }
procedure command (var buf : string);
var
    cmd : cmdtype;
    argtype, spval, val : integer;
begin
    cmd := getcmd(buf);
    if (cmd <> UNKNOWN) then
        val := getval(buf, argtype);
    case cmd of
    FI: begin
        break;
        fill := true
        end;
    NF: begin
        break;
        fill := false
        end;
    BR:
        break;
    LS:
        setparam(lsval, val, argtype, 1, 1, HUGE);
    CE: begin
        break;
        setparam(ceval, val, argtype, 1, 0, HUGE)
        end;
    UL:
        setparam(ulval, val, argtype, 1, 0, HUGE);
    HE:
        gettl(buf, header);
    FO:
        gettl(buf, footer);
    BP: begin
        page;
        setparam(curpage,val,argtype,curpage+1,-HUGE,HUGE);
        newpage := curpage
        end;
    SP: begin
        setparam(spval, val, argtype, 1, 0, HUGE);
        space(spval)
        end;
    IND:
        setparam(inval, val, argtype, 0, 0, rmval-1);
    RM:
        setparam(rmval, val, argtype, PAGEWIDTH,
            inval+tival+1, HUGE);
    TI: begin
        break;
        setparam(tival, val, argtype, 0, -HUGE, rmval)
```

```
           end;
    PL: begin
           setparam(plval, val, argtype, PAGELEN,
             m1val+m2val+m3val+m4val+1, HUGE);
           bottom := plval - m3val - m4val
           end;
    UNKNOWN:
           { ignore }
       end
  end;
```

The structure of command is a multi-way branch on the command type; we will explain details as we come to them. Most commands just set the new value of a parameter, perhaps after causing a break. If one is needed, **break** is called to flush out partially filled lines. For the moment we can write a dummy version which returns without doing anything; since we are currently dealing only with unfilled text, there will never be any partially filled lines anyway.

The type cmdtype is an enumeration of the possible commands:

```
type
      cmdtype = (BP, BR, CE, FI, FO, HE, IND, LS, NF, PL,
                 RM, SP, TI, UL, UNKNOWN);
```

We use IND instead of IN to avoid a possible collision with the keyword in.

The majority of the parameters are kept in global variables in the main routine, since they are needed throughout the program and there are far too many to pass around as arguments.

```
    fill : boolean;        { fill if true; init=true }
    lsval : integer;       { current line spacing; init=1 }
    spval : integer;       { # of lines to space }
    inval : integer;       { current indent; >= 0; init=0 }
    rmval : integer;       { right margin; init=PAGEWIDTH=60 }
    tival : integer;       { current temporary indent; init=0 }
    ceval : integer;       { # of lines to center; init=0 }
    ulval : integer;       { # of lines to underline; init=0 }
```

command calls getcmd to decode the command name and getval to evaluate any arguments to the command.

```
{ getcmd -- decode command type }
function getcmd (var buf : string) : cmdtype;
var
    cmd : packed array [1..2] of char;
begin
    cmd[1] := chr(buf[2]);
    cmd[2] := chr(buf[3]);
    if (cmd = 'fi') then
        getcmd := FI
    else if (cmd = 'nf') then
        getcmd := NF
    else if (cmd = 'br') then
        getcmd := BR
    else if (cmd = 'ls') then
        getcmd := LS
    else if (cmd = 'bp') then
        getcmd := BP
    else if (cmd = 'sp') then
        getcmd := SP
    else if (cmd = 'in') then
        getcmd := IND
    else if (cmd = 'rm') then
        getcmd := RM
    else if (cmd = 'ti') then
        getcmd := TI
    else if (cmd = 'ce') then
        getcmd := CE
    else if (cmd = 'ul') then
        getcmd := UL
    else if (cmd = 'he') then
        getcmd := HE
    else if (cmd = 'fo') then
        getcmd := FO
    else if (cmd = 'pl') then
        getcmd := PL
    else
        getcmd := UNKNOWN
end;
```

When there are relatively few commands, a direct search with a series of explicit tests is certainly easiest and entirely adequate. Ultimately it might prove desirable to replace the tests by a more general table lookup scheme, perhaps like the one described in Chapter 8.

Notice that getcmd does not check whether a command is exactly two letters long, only that the first two letters match a known command. This permits users to write .fill, .break, etc., if they prefer. The drawback is that any new commands introduced must differ in their first two letters from all others, which can lead to some strained mnemonics. You might therefore consider changing `getcmd` to check entire command names.

Since nearly all commands allow a numeric argument with an optional sign, it is best to write a separate routine to get the argument and the sign. `getval` skips over the command, records the presence or absence of a sign and digits in `argtype`, and converts a numeric argument to an integer with `ctoi`.

```
{ getval -- evaluate optional numeric argument }
function getval (var buf : string;
        var argtype : integer) : integer;
var
    i : integer;
begin
    i := 1; { skip over command name }
    while (not (buf[i] in [BLANK, TAB, NEWLINE])) do
        i := i + 1;
    skipbl(buf, i); { find argument }
    argtype := buf[i];
    if (argtype = PLUS) or (argtype = MINUS) then
        i := i + 1;
    getval := ctoi(buf, i)
end;
```

Even though at the moment all commands consist of a period and two letters, `getval` is written to skip an arbitrary command terminated by a blank, tab or newline. (Recall that `skipbl`, written in Chapter 6, skips blanks and tabs.) Similarly, a separate routine `getcmd` decodes the command type. These choices will make it easier to change the program if it becomes necessary later. Few programs remain static over their lifetime; it is wise to plan ahead so the inevitable changes are not traumatic.

Furthermore, `getval` is called for all commands, even those like `.he` and `.fo` which never have a numeric argument. It just isn't worth making a special case out of them: the formatter may do a microscopic amount of extra work in such cases, but the rest of the time it does less because the program is less complicated.

`setparam` is a general routine for updating a parameter, relatively or absolutely or to a default value. It also ensures that the resulting value lies within specified bounds. For instance, the line spacing is set with the code in `command` that reads

```
LS:
        setparam(lsval, val, argtype, 1, 1, HUGE);
```

This call to `setparam` will set `lsval` to `val` if there was no sign with the `.ls` command, as in `.ls 2`, or to `lsval±val` if there was, as in `.ls -1`, or to 1 if there was no argument at all. In any case the result is forced to lie between the last two arguments, 1 and `HUGE` (a large number).

```
{ setparam -- set parameter and check range }
procedure setparam (var param : integer;
            val, argtype, defval, minval, maxval : integer);
begin
    if (argtype = NEWLINE) then      { defaulted }
        param := defval
    else if (argtype = PLUS) then    { relative + }
        param := param + val
    else if (argtype = MINUS) then   { relative - }
        param := param - val
    else      { absolute }
        param := val;
    param := min(param, maxval);
    param := max(param, minval)
end;
```

We now have enough code to test command decoding, so we can use it and not worry about it while working on the rest of the program.

Exercise 7-3. format ignores unknown commands. It could just as well have treated them as normal text to be printed, or as errors to be reported. Discuss the merits of these alternatives. □

Exercise 7-4. Commands begin with a period in column 1, because that occurs infrequently in normal text. What are other plausible choices? How would you arrange to print a line that begins with a period? Suppose you want to mix commands and text on the same line. Is it a good idea? What is a syntax that is easy to type and edit? □

7.4 Page Layout

The next step is to subdivide text handling into reasonable increments. Regardless of whether it fills or not, centers or not, underlines or not, format has to get the right number of lines per page. So let us work on that, copying text lines from input to output, but with proper line spacing, titles and page numbers. This will almost dispose of no-fill mode. The code is similar to print in Chapter 3, so we can adapt some of the lessons we learned there. The main one is the importance of the boundaries — getting the right number of lines at the right places on each page, and preventing unwanted pages.

The parameters that describe the vertical dimensions of a page are: the page length plval; the top margins before and after the header line, m1val and m2val (m1val includes the header); the corresponding bottom margins m3val and m4val; and bottom, the last line upon which text may be placed. The following relationship holds:

```
bottom = plval - m3val - m4val
```

For 11 inch paper and standard six line per inch spacing, plval is 66. If each margin is two lines, there are 58 text lines per page and bottom is 62.

lineno is the next line to be printed on the output page; a value of zero indicates top of page, and a value greater than bottom indicates the end of a page. When lineno exceeds bottom, it is time to flush the current page. curpage is the number of the current page; newpage is the number that will go on the next page. All these values are kept in more global variables; we also include the running titles header and footer.

```
curpage : integer;    { current output page number; init=0 }
newpage : integer;    { next output page number; init=1 }
lineno : integer;     { next line to be printed; init=0 }
plval : integer;      { page length in lines; init=PAGELEN=66 }
m1val : integer;      { margin before and including header }
m2val : integer;      { margin after header }
m3val : integer;      { margin after last text line }
m4val : integer;      { bottom margin, including footer }
bottom : integer;     { last line on page, =plval-m3val-m4val }
header : string;      { top of page title; init=NEWLINE }
footer : string;      { bottom of page title; init=NEWLINE }
```

We no longer want to merely copy text lines to the standard output, so we make a small change in text, so it calls a new routine put instead of putstr:

```
{ text -- process text lines (interim version 1) }
procedure text (var inbuf : string);
begin
    put(inbuf)
end;
```

Except for header and footer titles, and blank lines produced by .sp and .bp commands, every line of text that goes out is controlled by put. put and its subordinates look after top and bottom margins, line spacing, setting the page number, and indenting, which we will get to shortly. The outline of put is

```
if (at top or past bottom of page)
    do top margins and top title
put out indent, if any
put out line
increment line number
if (past bottom)
    do bottom margins and bottom title
```

and the code becomes

```
{ put -- put out line with proper spacing and indenting }
procedure put (var buf : string);
var
    i : integer;
begin
    if (lineno <= 0) or (lineno > bottom) then
        puthead;
    for i := 1 to inval + tival do        { indenting }
        putc(BLANK);
    tival := 0;
    putstr(buf, STDOUT);
    skip(min(lsval-1, bottom-lineno));
    lineno := lineno + lsval;
    if (lineno > bottom) then
        putfoot
end;
```

skip(n) produces n empty lines (NEWLINE only) if n is positive, and does
nothing if n is less than one. We wrote it for print in Chapter 3. We have
also included the code for indenting in put; all it does is put out the right
number of leading blanks and reset any temporary indent, so ignore it for now.

put has to stay sane if handed bizarre parameters. In particular, the line
spacing lsval could conceivably be larger than the bottom margin values, so
after a line is produced, the skip that follows skips at most to bottom+1.
(put skips lsval-1 because the previous putstr has already produced one
line.) Since each page starts at the top, there will always be at least one output
line per page regardless of the line spacing, and we are guaranteed that format
will always make some progress through a document no matter how strange the
parameters.

puthead and putfoot print the top and bottom margins. puthead is
responsible for updating the current and new page numbers in curpage and
newpage.

```
{ puthead -- put out page header }
procedure puthead;
begin
    curpage := newpage;
    newpage := newpage + 1;
    if (m1val > 0) then begin
        skip(m1val-1);
        puttl(header, curpage)
    end;
    skip(m2val);
    lineno := m1val + m2val + 1
end;
```

```
{ putfoot -- put out page footer }
procedure putfoot;
begin
    skip(m3val);
    if (m4val > 0) then begin
        puttl(footer, curpage);
        skip(m4val-1)
    end
end;
```

The header title is the last line of the margin m1val and the footer title is the
first line of m4val, so either title, and in fact all pagination, can be turned off
by setting the appropriate margins to zero. This is a minor point, but it eliminates what would otherwise be a special case. Adding commands to make the
margin values accessible is an easy exercise.

puthead and putfoot call puttl to produce the top or bottom title as a
single line, inserting the page number with putdec if called for.

```
{ puttl -- put out title line with optional page number }
procedure puttl (var buf : string; pageno : integer);
var
    i : integer;
begin
    for i := 1 to length(buf) do
        if (buf[i] = PAGENUM) then
            putdec(pageno, 1)
        else
            putc(buf[i])
end;
```

PAGENUM is whatever character is to be replaced by the page number in titles;
we use a #, which has some mnemonic value.

Titles are originally extracted by gettl, called from command with

```
HE:
    gettl(buf, header);
FO:
    gettl(buf, footer);
```

and gettl itself is

```
{ gettl -- copy title from buf to ttl }
procedure gettl (var buf, ttl : string);
var
    i : integer;
begin
    i := 1; { skip command name }
    while (not (buf[i] in [BLANK, TAB, NEWLINE])) do
        i := i + 1;
    skipbl(buf, i); { find argument }
    if (buf[i] = SQUOTE) or (buf[i] = DQUOTE) then
        i := i + 1;       { strip leading quote }
    scopy(buf, i, ttl, 1)
end;
```

The title is assumed to begin with the first non-blank character, but a leading apostrophe or quote is stripped off, to permit a title to begin with blanks, for example, to right-justify it.

Notice that we wrote the calls to gettl as

```
gettl(buf, header);
gettl(buf, footer);
```

instead of passing the command type to gettl and letting it decide where to put the title. The latter way requires gettl to know more about variables, and increases the data connections in the program. Whenever possible, hide details from routines that don't need them.

space is called directly from command when a .sp is seen; if no argument is provided, a single blank line is produced. .sp 0 is perfectly legal; its only effect is to cause a break.

```
SP: begin
    setparam(spval, val, argtype, 1, 0, HUGE);
    space(spval)
    end;
```

A similar procedure, page, is called for a .bp command, to get to the top of the next page.

```
BP: begin
    page;
    setparam(curpage,val,argtype,curpage+1,-HUGE,HUGE);
    newpage := curpage
    end;
```

The code for .bp has to be exceedingly careful or some unpleasant behavior results. First, we must have .bp equivalent to .bp +1, since this is part of the specification. A .bp at the bottom of a page (even the last page) should have no effect except to cause the normal page number increment. You should also verify that beginning a document with any one of .bp, .bp 1, .bp +1, or plain text yields a first page numbered 1. Finally, the .bp command allows negative page numbers, not because we think that anyone will ever use them, but because they can do no conceivable harm. Arbitrary restrictions will some-day impede someone.

Once `put` works, `space` and `page` are written by analogy. `space(n)` does nothing if it occurs at the bottom of a page (`lineno>bottom`). Other-wise it skips n lines, or enough lines to get to the bottom of the page, whichever is smaller. If the bottom is reached, the bottom margins are produced.

```
{ space -- space n lines or to bottom of page }
procedure space (n : integer);
begin
    break;
    if (lineno <= bottom) then begin
        if (lineno <= 0) then
            puthead;
        skip(min(n, bottom+1-lineno));
        lineno := lineno + n;
        if (lineno > bottom) then
            putfoot
    end
end;
```

`page` also skips to the bottom, then sets the line number back to the top:

```
{ page -- get to top of new page }
procedure page;
begin
    break;
    if (lineno > 0) and (lineno <= bottom) then begin
        skip(bottom+1-lineno);
        putfoot
    end;
    lineno := 0
end;
```

It is quite important to distinguish between "bottom of the page" and "top of the next page"; they are not the same place. If a `.sp` occurs at the top of a page the spaces are produced, but any blank lines left over at the end of a page are discarded, since this is usually what is wanted. If spaces are actually needed at the top of a page they can be obtained by the sequence

```
.bp
.sp
```

`space`, `page` and `put` are all rather similar. It would be possible to modify `space` to call `put`. This would centralize the output, a desirable goal. The main problem is how to avoid getting `lsval` line spaces each time `put` is called from the proposed new `space`. We certainly don't want to change `lsval` in `space` before calling `put`, then restore it after — this is the worst kind of pathological data connection because it is the least obvious. We don't want to burden each call to put with a line-spacing argument, nor do we want leading blanks on each blank line produced by space when text is indented. In spite of the apparent repetition of code, it's preferable the way it is. Similarly, page and space are best kept separate.

We now have enough skeleton to test all the permutations of line spacing, blank lines, new pages, and so on. The .pl command is particularly useful for testing, since you can shorten the page down to the point where it's easy to count output lines by hand. The code in command for .pl is

```
PL: begin
        setparam(plval, val, argtype, PAGELEN,
            m1val+m2val+m3val+m4val+1, HUGE);
        bottom := plval - m3val - m4val
        end;
```

You might also find it convenient to modify skip temporarily to produce a visible character on each skipped line; this makes it easier to interpret output.

What are particularly nasty boundary conditions that might go wrong? There is at least one error — the last page of output is short, because there is no provision to print the extra lines needed to get to the bottom. To repair it we ask for a new page in the main routine, after the end of the input has occurred, in exactly the same way the .bp command does. Here is the revised version of format:

```
begin
    initfmt;
    while (getline(inbuf, STDIN, MAXSTR)) do
        if (inbuf[1] = CMD) then
            command(inbuf)
        else
            text(inbuf);
    page     { flush last output, if any }
end;
```

This works (i.e., does nothing) if we are already at the bottom of the last page, because no further spaces will be produced there. It also works for the less common case that we are at the top of a page; in particular, if there is no input, it produces no output.

We could have written special code to handle the end of the last page, but it is better to use existing mechanisms like this wherever possible. Doing so avoids having two slightly different ways of doing the same thing (one of which is going to be overlooked when the other is improved) and ensures that the standard mechanism is well thought out at an important boundary.

The basic structure of format is now pretty well established, so we can show the hierarchy as it currently stands:

```
format
    initfmt
    command
        getcmd, getval, break, setparam, gettl, space, page
    text
        put
            puthead, putfoot
                skip
                puttl
            skip
        space
            break, puthead, putfoot, skip
        page
            break, putfoot, skip
    page
```

`puthead` and `putfoot` call on the same routines; the hierarchy is shown once for both. Most new routines we are going to add will be called from `text`.

Exercise 7-5. Is it really necessary to have the two variables `curpage` and `newpage` to keep track of page numbers? Try to rewrite the code with only one. Make sure that `.bp` and `.bp +1` remain equivalent. □

7.5 Indenting

The next step is to implement settable left and right margins, which are required before we can do filled text properly. For each line of output, we need to know the indent `inval`, the right margin `rmval`, and the temporary indent `tival`. `tival` is the number of blanks to precede a line of output. The code in `command` that handles the `.in`, `.rm` and `.ti` commands is

```
IND:
    setparam(inval, val, argtype, 0, 0, rmval-1);
RM:
    setparam(rmval, val, argtype, PAGEWIDTH,
        inval+tival+1, HUGE);
TI: begin
    break;
    setparam(tival, val, argtype, 0, -HUGE, rmval)
    end;
```

Each line produced by `put` is preceded by `tival` blanks; after each line of output `tival` must be reset to zero so that only a single line is temporarily indented. This is done by the code in `put` that reads

```
for i := 1 to inval + tival do        { indenting }
    putc(BLANK);
tival := 0;
```

Leading blanks and empty lines are special cases detected in `text`, where we must add the test

```
if (inbuf[1] = BLANK) or (inbuf[1] = NEWLINE) then
    leadbl(inbuf);  { move left, set tival }
```

before the call to put. leadbl handles the leading blanks.

```
{ leadbl -- delete leading blanks, set tival }
procedure leadbl (var buf : string);
var
    i, j : integer;
begin
    break;
    i := 1;
    while (buf[i] = BLANK) do    { find 1st non-blank }
        i := i + 1;
    if (buf[i] <> NEWLINE) then
        tival := tival + i - 1;
    for j := i to length(buf)+1 do   { move line to left }
        buf[j-i+1] := buf[j]
end;
```

leadbl moves the entire line to the left so the first non-blank character is in
position 1. This ensures that leading blanks in no-fill mode don't get twice as
much indent as they should, once from the temporary indent and once from the
leading blanks themselves.

7.6 Filled Text

Now that unfilled text and margins work, we can do filled text; that is what
will be wanted most of the time. How does it work? Two routines, getword
and putword, work together as coroutines. getword breaks an input line into
words and passes them to putword. putword packs them and periodically
outputs a filled line. Thus text becomes

```
{ text -- process text lines (interim version 2) }
procedure text (var inbuf : string);
var
    wordbuf : string;
    i : integer;
begin
    if (inbuf[1] = BLANK) or (inbuf[1] = NEWLINE) then
        leadbl(inbuf);   { move left, set tival }
    if (inbuf[1] = NEWLINE) then     { all blank line }
        put(inbuf)
    else if (not fill) then      { unfilled text }
        put(inbuf)
    else begin   { filled text }
        i := 1;
        repeat
            i := getword(inbuf, i, wordbuf);
            if (i > 0) then
                putword(wordbuf)
        until (i = 0)
    end
end;
```

We wrote getword for the include program of Chapter 3. getword isolates words, that is, strings of non-blank characters. It is called with the index in inbuf where it is to start looking for a word; it returns with that index set just beyond the word it found, so it is ready for the next call. getword returns zero at the end of a line, and a positive index in the middle.

The other end of the chain is putword. If the new word does not fit on the current line, putword flushes the line with a call to break and resets for a fresh line. In any case the new word is tucked onto the end of the line. putword also adds a blank after the word, so the next word will be separated properly.

The call to page after ENDFILE in the main routine now serves a double function. Since it causes a break, it will force out any partially completed line collected by putword before skipping to the bottom of the last page. This is a benefit of using the high-level function page instead of coding an explicit "last page" routine.

```
{ putword -- put word in outbuf }
procedure putword (var wordbuf : string);
var
    last, llval, nextra, w : integer;
begin
    w := width(wordbuf);
    last := length(wordbuf) + outp + 1; { new end of outbuf }
    llval := rmval - tival - inval;
    if (outp > 0)
        and ((outw+w > llval) or (last >= MAXSTR)) then begin
            last := last - outp;      { remember end of wordbuf }
            break   { flush previous line }
        end;
    scopy(wordbuf, 1, outbuf, outp+1);
    outp := last;
    outbuf[outp] := BLANK;   { blank between words }
    outw := outw + w + 1;    { 1 for blank }
    outwds := outwds + 1
end;
```

The output line is collected in outbuf. outp is the last character position,
outw the width of the line, and outwds the word count.

```
outp : integer;      { last char pos in outbuf; init=0 }
outw : integer;      { width of text in outbuf; init=0 }
outwds : integer;    { number of words in outbuf; init=0 }
outbuf : string;     { lines to be filled collect here }
```

The width of the current line, outw, is not the same as outp, which points
to the last character on the line. Why? What happens if a line typed by some
innocent user contains a backspace, perhaps to underline a character by backspacing and underscoring? (We haven't built underlining yet, remember.)
Clearly the "width" of

xyz BACKSPACE BACKSPACE BACKSPACE ___

is 3 by any reasonable definition — it only occupies three columns of output —
but its "length" in actual storage space is 9 (characters). The two measures are
different.

   To handle this (and also looking ahead to underlining with .ul) we have
separated "width" from "number of characters" and isolated the width computation in a separate function.

```
{ width -- compute width of character string }
function width (var buf : string) : integer;
var
    i, w : integer;
begin
    w := 0;
    i := 1;
    while (buf[i] <> ENDSTR) do begin
        if (buf[i] = BACKSPACE) then
            w := w - 1
        else if (buf[i] <> NEWLINE) then
            w := w + 1;
        i := i + 1
    end;
    width := w
end;
```

width has two special characters to worry about: BACKSPACE has width -1 and NEWLINE has width zero. Everything else has width +1.

We are now in a position to specify break. Actually there isn't much to it — it outputs any text in outbuf with put, and resets the output pointer, width and word count to zero.

```
{ break -- end current filled line }
procedure break;
begin
    if (outp > 0) then begin
        outbuf[outp] := NEWLINE;
        outbuf[outp+1] := ENDSTR;
        put(outbuf)
    end;
    outp := 0;
    outw := 0;
    outwds := 0
end;
```

Exercise 7-6. What characters besides backspaces and newlines have zero width in your environment? Can you think of any characters whose width is not constant? □

Exercise 7-7. If your character set doesn't include a backspace, how would you provide it for format users nonetheless? □

7.7 Right Margin Justification

The only remaining loose end, so to speak, is justifying output lines, that is, squaring up the right margin. The best place is in putword, right before the call to break — at that point we have a full line, we know we're working on filled text, and we know how many words are in the line and what its width is. Thus we modify putword by calling a separate routine to spread out the line by adding extra spaces.

```
{ putword -- put word in outbuf; does margin justification }
procedure putword (var wordbuf : string);
var
    last, llval, nextra, w : integer;
begin
    w := width(wordbuf);
    last := length(wordbuf) + outp + 1; { new end of outbuf }
    llval := rmval - tival - inval;
    if (outp > 0)
       and ((outw+w > llval) or (last >= MAXSTR)) then begin
          last := last - outp;      { remember end of wordbuf }
          nextra := llval - outw + 1;
          if (nextra > 0) and (outwds > 1) then begin
              spread(outbuf, outp, nextra, outwds);
              outp := outp + nextra
          end;
          break   { flush previous line }
       end;
    scopy(wordbuf, 1, outbuf, outp+1);
    outp := last;
    outbuf[outp] := BLANK;  { blank between words }
    outw := outw + w + 1;   { 1 for blank }
    outwds := outwds + 1
end;
```

spread moves the words on the line to the right, starting with the rightmost.
Each time a word is moved, some of the extra blanks are parceled out, as uniformly as possible, until none are left. nextra is the number of extra blanks
needed to justify the line. Care is necessary in case nextra should be negative
because of a long input word, or in case there is only one word on the line.

As an esthetic matter, if the extra blanks do not distribute evenly, the
surplus ones are spread alternately from the right and from the left on successive
lines, to avoid "rivers" of white space down one margin or the other. dir
alternates between zero and one, selecting the side which gets the extra blanks.
Since dir has to retain its value from one call of spread to the next, it will
have to be another global variable:

```
dir : 0..1;      { direction for blank padding }
```

```
{ spread -- spread words to justify right margin }
procedure spread (var buf : string;
        outp, nextra, outwds : integer);
var
    i, j, nb, nholes : integer;
begin
    if (nextra > 0) and (outwds > 1) then begin
        dir := 1 - dir; { reverse previous direction }
        nholes := outwds - 1;
        i := outp - 1;
        j := min(MAXSTR-2, i+nextra); { room for NEWLINE }
        while (i < j) do begin       { and ENDSTR }
            buf[j] := buf[i];
            if (buf[i] = BLANK) then begin
                if (dir = 0) then
                    nb := (nextra-1) div nholes + 1
                else
                    nb := nextra div nholes;
                nextra := nextra - nb;
                nholes := nholes - 1;
                while (nb > 0) do begin
                    j := j - 1;
                    buf[j] := BLANK;
                    nb := nb - 1
                end
            end;
            i := i - 1;
            j := j - 1
        end
    end
end;
```

This code is tricky (which is not a compliment), but it performs an elaborate function and performs it correctly. The trickery lies in the computation of nb, which parcels out the extra blanks as uniformly as possible, while distributing the extras from one end or the other. There is no chance of division by zero even though nholes is continually decremented, because the code is executed only when nextra>0 and outwds>1, and the loop exits after nholes reaches 1.

By the way, we tested the condition

```
        if (nextra > 0) and (outwds > 1) then begin
```

in putword, then repeated the test in spread. Why not remove the redundant test from spread?

The reason is that this would require the calling program to know about the constraints on the arguments of the called program. This is another form of secret dependency or coupling. From the standpoint of maintenance it is a dangerous practice, because sooner or later someone modifying the caller will violate the constraints and perhaps introduce bugs. Thus we wrote `spread` to check its own arguments instead of relying on `putword`. Of course this sort of thing can be carried too far, but here the cost is insignificant, so it's well worth doing.

Exercise 7-8. Demonstrate that `spread` works properly, whether placing extra blanks on the right or on the left. Prove that it does something sane even at the extreme values of `outwds`, `nextra` and `outp`. How could you organize `format` differently so as to make `spread` easier? □

Exercise 7-9. Add the commands `.ju` (justify) and `.nj` (no justify) so justification can be turned on and off separately from filling. Should justification be permitted for unfilled lines? How would you add the ability to adjust lines to the right instead of the left? □

7.8 Centering and Underlining

Now that we have most of the formatter formatting, we can start to add bells and whistles.

Centering is a most useful addition, for it mechanizes a tedious and error-prone task that no human should ever have to do. Luckily it's dead easy. When a `.ce` command is seen, `command` computes the number of lines and places it in `ceval` with the code

```
CE: begin
      break;
      setparam(ceval, val, argtype, 1, 0, HUGE)
    end;
```

Each time a centered line is put out, `text` counts `ceval` down by one; when it reaches zero there is no more centering to be done. This code goes into `text`:

```
if (ceval > 0) then begin    { centering }
    center(inbuf);
    put(inbuf);
    ceval := ceval - 1
end
```

Finally, the line itself must be centered before it goes out. This is done by setting a temporary indent that moves the line to the right by the correct amount; when the line is output it will be positioned properly. We put this in a separate routine even though it is only a single line of code, because it seems to clutter up `text` less that way, but you can make a case for the other placement as well.

```
{ center -- center a line by setting tival }
procedure center (var buf : string);
begin
    tival := max((rmval+tival-width(buf)) div 2, 0)
end;
```

Underlining is also tedious to do manually; like centering, it's better mechanized. The sequence of events for underlining is essentially the same as for centering. `command` sets `ulval`:

```
UL:
      setparam(ulval, val, argtype, 1, 0, HUGE);
```

`text` decrements `ulval` for each underlined input line:

```
if (ulval > 0) then begin     { underlining }
    underln(inbuf, MAXSTR);
    ulval := ulval - 1
end;
```

A separate routine `underln` prepares the words to be underlined by converting each alphanumeric character into

UNDERLINE BACKSPACE *character*

On many video terminals, underlining a character erases it, so `format` prints the underline first. That way you get to see the character even if the underlining is erased.

```
{ underln -- underline a line }
procedure underln (var buf : string; size : integer);
var
    i, j : integer;
    tbuf : string;
begin
    j := 1; { expand into tbuf }
    i := 1;
    while (buf[i] <> NEWLINE) and (j < size-1) do begin
        if (isalphanum(buf[i])) then begin
            tbuf[j] := UNDERLINE;
            tbuf[j+1] := BACKSPACE;
            j := j + 2
        end;
        tbuf[j] := buf[i];
        j := j + 1;
        i := i + 1
    end;
    tbuf[j] := NEWLINE;
    tbuf[j+1] := ENDSTR;
    scopy(tbuf, 1, buf, 1)   { copy it back to buf }
end;
```

Backspaces and underlines are inserted as the line is copied into a temporary array, which is then copied back to the original place. You could also do it in place, but the code would be much less clear.

It is important to do all these functions in the proper order in `text`.

Underlining and checking for leading blanks must be done first, since all other cases force output. Centering must precede the test for a NEWLINE, so a centered blank line will decrement ceval. Putting the pieces together, we get the final version of text:

```
{ text -- process text lines (final version) }
procedure text (var inbuf : string);
var
     wordbuf : string;
     i : integer;
begin
     if (inbuf[1] = BLANK) or (inbuf[1] = NEWLINE) then
          leadbl(inbuf); { move left, set tival }
     if (ulval > 0) then begin   { underlining }
          underln(inbuf, MAXSTR);
          ulval := ulval - 1
     end;
     if (ceval > 0) then begin   { centering }
          center(inbuf);
          put(inbuf);
          ceval := ceval - 1
     end
     else if (inbuf[1] = NEWLINE) then   { all-blank line }
          put(inbuf)
     else if (not fill) then      { unfilled text }
          put(inbuf)
     else begin   { filled text }
          i := 1;
          repeat
               i := getword(inbuf, i, wordbuf);
               if (i > 0) then
                    putword(wordbuf)
          until (i = 0)
     end
end;
```

To be complete, here are format (complete) and initfmt.

```
{ format -- text formatter main program (final version) }
procedure format;
#include "fmtcons.p"
type
    cmdtype = (BP, BR, CE, FI, FO, HE, IND, LS, NF, PL,
                RM, SP, TI, UL, UNKNOWN);
var
    { page parameters }
    curpage : integer;   { current output page number; init=0 }
    newpage : integer;   { next output page number; init=1 }
    lineno : integer;    { next line to be printed; init=0 }
    plval : integer;     { page length in lines; init=PAGELEN=66 }
    m1val : integer;     { margin before and including header }
    m2val : integer;     { margin after header }
    m3val : integer;     { margin after last text line }
    m4val : integer;     { bottom margin, including footer }
    bottom : integer;    { last line on page, =plval-m3val-m4val }
    header : string;     { top of page title; init=NEWLINE }
    footer : string;     { bottom of page title; init=NEWLINE }

    { global parameters }
    fill : boolean;      { fill if true; init=true }
    lsval : integer;     { current line spacing; init=1 }
    spval : integer;     { # of lines to space }
    inval : integer;     { current indent; >= 0; init=0 }
    rmval : integer;     { right margin; init=PAGEWIDTH=60 }
    tival : integer;     { current temporary indent; init=0 }
    ceval : integer;     { # of lines to center; init=0 }
    ulval : integer;     { # of lines to underline; init=0 }

    { output area }
    outp : integer;      { last char pos in outbuf; init=0 }
    outw : integer;      { width of text in outbuf; init=0 }
    outwds : integer;    { number of words in outbuf; init=0 }
    outbuf : string;     { lines to be filled collect here }
    dir : 0..1;      { direction for blank padding }
    inbuf : string;      { input line }
#include "fmtproc.p"
begin
    initfmt;
    while (getline(inbuf, STDIN, MAXSTR)) do
        if (inbuf[1] = CMD) then
            command(inbuf)
        else
            text(inbuf);
    page      { flush last output, if any }
end;
```

```
{ initfmt -- set format parameters to default values }
procedure initfmt;
begin
    fill := true;
    dir := 0;
    inval := 0;
    rmval := PAGEWIDTH;
    tival := 0;
    lsval := 1;
    spval := 0;
    ceval := 0;
    ulval := 0;
    lineno := 0;
    curpage := 0;
    newpage := 1;
    plval := PAGELEN;
    m1val := 3; m2val := 2; m3val := 2; m4val := 3;
    bottom := plval - m3val - m4val;
    header[1] := NEWLINE;    { initial titles }
    header[2] := ENDSTR;
    footer[1] := NEWLINE;
    footer[2] := ENDSTR;
    outp := 0;
    outw := 0;
    outwds := 0
end;

{ fmtcons -- constants for format }
const
    CMD = PERIOD;
    PAGENUM = SHARP;
    PAGEWIDTH = 60;
    PAGELEN = 66;
    HUGE = 10000;
```

```
{ fmtproc -- procedures needed for format }
#include "skipbl.p"
#include "skip.p"
#include "getcmd.p"
#include "setparam.p"
#include "getval.p"
#include "gettl.p"
#include "puttl.p"
#include "puthead.p"
#include "putfoot.p"
#include "width.p"
#include "put.p"
#include "break.p"
#include "space.p"
#include "page.p"
#include "leadbl.p"
#include "spread.p"
#include "putword.p"
#include "getword.p"
#include "center.p"
#include "underln.p"
#include "initfmt.p"
#include "command.p"
#include "text.p"
```

The final calling tree of format reflects the additions we made.

```
format
    initfmt
    command
        getcmd
            getval
        setparam
        gettl
        space
        page
        break
            put
                puthead, putfoot
                    skip
                    puttl
                skip
    text
        leadbl
            break
        underln
        center
            width
        put
        getword
        putword
            width, spread, break
        space
            break, puthead, putfoot, skip
        page
            break, putfoot, skip
    page
```

Exercise 7-10. Investigate the behavior of format if a user underlines by backspacing and underscoring. What happens with backspacing across a blank in filled text? What about underlining a word containing backspaces? □

Exercise 7-11. Add a command to do continuous underlining: everything, spaces and all, is underlined until turned off. □

Exercise 7-12. Underlining a character at a time is the worst thing we can do to overstrike in Chapter 2. (It's also a test to destruction of some terminals.) Should we make underln more clever, or improve overstrike, or buy sturdier terminals? □

Exercise 7-13. Our underlining algorithm uses three characters in underln for every character to be underlined. Another way to do underlining is to surround each string to be underlined with magic "start underline" and "stop underline" characters of zero width. Discuss the merits and demerits of these organizations. □

Exercise 7-14. Add a command analogous to .ul to embolden output by overstriking it. Make sure it will embolden underlined material. □

7.9 Some Measurements

We ran `format` on some documents to measure where it spends its time. Here are some measurements for formatting Chapter 7, which consisted at that point of 3280 lines, or about 12,400 words, of which 878 lines were formatting commands; it produced 31 pages of single-spaced line-printer output.

As always, most of the CPU time (23.6 seconds) on the DEC VAX 11/780 where we did the timing was spent processing I/O requests: 35 percent in `getline` and functions below it (mostly in the latter), and 19.8 percent in `putstr` and its subordinates. These numbers so dominate the run time that until they are improved no other part of the program matters much. Let us assume, however, that they can be cut down to reasonable size by replacing `getline` and `putc` by more efficient routines. Then what parts of the program take the time?

The remaining significant routines are

`getword`	13.0%
`scopy`	5.5
`width`	4.2
`putword`	3.8
`spread`	3.5
`length`	2.9
`text`	2.1
`put`	1.1
`getcmd`	0.8
`getval`	0.8
`min`	0.8
`command`	0.6

After the I/O time has been removed, these routines account for most of the time taken by the formatter. (The numbers don't add up to quite 100 percent because of overhead in the measurement process.) The lesson is the same as before, but it is worth repeating. The best procedure for obtaining efficient code is to choose a good algorithm, write a program that implements it as cleanly as possible, then measure it. The measurements will lead you directly to the one or two routines that are worth making as efficient as possible — if they are clearly written and if they hide their information properly, they will be easy to change. Sacrificing readability for efficiency earlier than this, while the bulk of the code is being written, not only results in wasted effort but also leads to code that is hard to improve because it is hard to understand.

7.10 Extensions

As we said, this is not an elaborate formatter, and there are lots of things that could be added that would make it better without complicating it for unsophisticated users. Extensions to make more parameters settable by users are so straightforward that they don't even qualify as exercises. More involved, but valuable, are these functional enhancements.

Multiple Files

To follow good design principles format should read either from a list of files or, if none are specified, from its standard input, like the print program of Chapter 3. It should also be possible to include the contents of a file by a formatting command.

Exercise 7-15. Implement multiple files as arguments, and a file inclusion command. Since .in is already taken, you might use the name .so for "source"; the command

.so *filename*

will interpolate the contents of *filename* in the input at the point it is encountered. If you decided that the name would be better as .include, what changes would be needed in command and getcmd? Once .so is installed, you can use format for the same kind of formatting as was done by print in Chapter 3. Is it worthwhile to keep print around nonetheless? □

Exercise 7-16. Add optional arguments $+m$ and $-n$ to allow output to begin printing at page m and stop printing after page n. Thus

format +10 -20

prints pages 10 through 20 inclusive. Multiple uses of + and - should be legal. What is proper behavior if m or n is outside the range of pages in the document? □

Improved Running Titles

Our top and bottom running titles are sometimes awkward to use. Here is an alternative design: the syntax

.he */left/center/right/*

means the heading (top of page title) is to consist of the three parts separated by the (arbitrary) delimiter /. The *left* part is to be left-justified, the *right* part right-justified, and the *center* part centered. As before, any occurrence of the character # in the title is to be replaced by the current page number.

Exercise 7-17. Implement the extended .he and .fo commands. What right margin and indent values determine placement of the pieces? What should happen if the pieces overlap? How would you permit multi-line titles? Add the commands

.eh   .ef   .oh   .of

to allow different titles on even numbered and odd numbered pages. □

Escape Characters

It is sometimes necessary to force a character to be taken literally rather than as a command. One example is getting a literal period in the first column; another is creating a blank that cannot be padded.

Exercise 7-18. Add an escape character mechanism to format, so that the sequence @*c* will cause the character *c* to appear literally in the output. □

'Need' Command

Sometimes it is desirable to force output like a table or a program to appear all on one page; this was done for the programs in this book. Somehow a 'begin page' command must be simulated at the beginning of the table, but only if it would actually fall across a page boundary. One way is with a command

```
     .ne n
```

which says "I need n lines; if there aren't that many on this page, skip to a new page."

Exercise 7-19. Implement the `.ne` command. How would you use `.ne` commands for "widow" suppression? (A widow is an isolated line at the bottom or top of a page.) □

Exercise 7-20. Forcing people to count lines for a `.ne` command is obviously bad human engineering. Design and implement a mechanism to keep a group of lines together without requiring the user to count them. □

Extra Space after Sentence

Most people prefer an extra space after the period that terminates a sentence; it looks better.

Exercise 7-21. Implement this feature. Make sure it works when the period falls at the end of a line. What other characters and sequences terminate sentences? Is there a reasonable algorithm that doesn't put extra space after people's initials, abbreviations, and so on? □

Automatic Capitalization

Some computer centers have line printers with upper and lower case, but not upper and lower case terminals or keypunches. This need not discourage someone who wants neatly formatted output.

Exercise 7-22. Modify `format` so it detects plausible forms of end of sentence, like a period at the end of a line or followed by two or more spaces, and then capitalizes the next letter. You will also need "escape" characters that override the default action and force the next character to be explicitly lower or upper case. If you are clever about recognizing sentences, however, these will probably be little used. What is the width of these escape characters? □

7.11 Bigger Things

The suggestions in this closing section are major undertakings if done well, but they should suggest how the formatter may be increased in power. All of these facilities were available in some form in the formatter we used to prepare this book.

Hyphenation

`format` fills lines by packing as many words onto a line as will fit. Hyphenation increases this number on the average, and thus improves the appearance of the output. The problem is to design a reasonably accurate scheme for hyphenating English words by program.

First make up a list of suffixes that are potentially good hyphenation points, like *-tion*, *-ness*, and so on. (Remember that English hyphenates between syllables, so both suffix and prefix must contain a vowel.) Merely stripping these should provide a useful capability. Next, certain letter pairs ("digrams") should *never* be hyphenated — *qu* is the most obvious example — while others, like double letters, are often good bets. Build a 26×26 array (single bits are enough) whose entries show whether or not to hyphenate between particular pairs of letters. You might also experiment with prefix-stripping; our experience has been that this is less successful.

Experiment with these possibilities. Can you think of any other approaches? What programs would you write as tools to help you with this project? What tools have we already written for you in this book?

This book was hyphenated by a more complicated version of the suggested scheme. How many hyphenation gaffes can you find? (We did give our hyphenator a couple of hints.)

Macros

Although the next chapter will be devoted to macro processing, we should mention the possibility of adding macros, even in limited form, to the formatter. As the first step, you could allow a user to define shorthands for frequent sequences of commands. For example

```
.de pp
.sp
.ti +5
.en
```

would *define* a new command .pp (for "paragraph"). Thereafter, whenever the "command"

```
.pp
```

occurs, it is replaced by its defining text, everything between the .de and the .en. In this case, a space and a temporary indent result. And of course it should be possible to redefine any of the built-in names like .sp.

This much is easy. The next step is to allow macros to have arguments, so they can produce different results when called with different parameters. For example, you might define a title macro with

```
.de tl
.eh /#  SOFTWARE TOOLS IN PASCAL//CHAPTER $1/
.oh /CHAPTER $1//$2  #/
.en
```

The symbol $n means that when the macro is invoked, the *n*th argument is to replace the $n. Thus you might say

```
      .tl 7 FORMATTING
```
to create running titles like those in this chapter.

This syntax limits you to nine arguments, which is probably adequate. As a matter of good human engineering, missing arguments should be replaced by null strings; extra arguments should be ignored. We will return to this topic in Chapter 8.

Conditionals

A truly powerful formatter needs the ability to alter formatting actions depending on conditions that develop during a run. One possibility is a command like

```
      .if (condition) things
```

so you can dynamically test some condition, and take appropriate action if it is true. There is no limit to how extensive this can be made, but as a bare minimum, you will want to be able to test parameter values like output page number, line and page lengths, current position on the page, and whether or not you are in fill mode. You will also need arithmetic, variables to hold text and numbers, and string comparison operations. For example, both the section headings and the exercises in this book were numbered automatically by the formatter, using numeric variables and operations.

One of the best tests of whether you have enough tools in your formatter is whether you can construct with them a general footnote mechanism, where there can be multiple footnotes per page, and where footnotes are carried forward onto as many pages as are needed. Another test is whether you can do multi-column output. If you can do these cases well, you have enough power for most formatting situations.

These suggestions are intended to be vague, so that they will not bias you too strongly in any particular direction. As always, if you propose to build something, make sure it has some conceptual integrity — it should not be merely a collection of unrelated "features." And build it in increments, not all at once.

Bibliographic Notes

`format` is loosely based on J. Saltzer's Runoff program on CTSS. Runoff has gone through numerous versions; ours is most closely related to Roff, by M. D. McIlroy. There are many formatting programs available commercially, often as part of a "word processing system" that combines editing and formatting so that the display continuously shows the formatted appearance of the document. You might find it interesting to compare some of these offerings with `format` plus `edit`.

This book was typeset by a program called Troff, written for the Unix system by J. F. Ossanna. A typesetter has many more degrees of freedom than a line printer or terminal — multiple fonts, many sizes of type, and a much larger character set. A challenging problem is to design a language which permits access to these added facilities without unduly complicating things for naive users. We made extensive use of Troff's macro capabilities to conceal formatting details in macro commands which could be easily changed as necessary without touching the text itself.

Text formatting has become an active area of computer science research. Two particularly interesting examples are TEX, designed by D. E. Knuth, and described in *TEX and METAFONT,* Digital Press, 1979, and Scribe, by Brian K. Reid, described in "Scribe, a high-level approach to computer document formatting," ACM Symposium on Principles of Programming Languages, January, 1980. Scribe and TEX both have as a main design goal making it easy for users to separate the logical content of their documents from the formatting details.

Appendix H of the TEX manual cited above describe's TEX's hyphenation algorithm.

CHAPTER 8: **MACRO PROCESSING**

Macros are used to extend some underlying language — to perform a translation from one language to another. For example, many of our programs contain lines like

```
while (getc(c) <> ENDFILE) do
```

where `ENDFILE` is some unspecified constant value that indicates end of file. "Symbolic constants" like `ENDFILE` tell you what a number signifies in a way that the number itself could never do: if we had written some magic value like -1 you would not know what it meant without understanding the surrounding context. Besides, the value of `ENDFILE` may well differ from machine to machine, and it is much easier and safer to redefine the value of a constant in a single place than it is to go through an entire program finding all the -1's that really mean end of file.

In Pascal, the `const` declaration lets us define the value of `ENDFILE`, so long as it is a number (or a boolean or a quoted string). For most of the programs that we have written here, that is perfectly adequate. But there are other situations where this notion of a constant is too limited.

What we want is a program that lets us define symbolic constants like `ENDFILE` so that subsequent occurrences of the name are replaced by the defining string of characters, regardless of the contents of the definition or its context. Such a definition is called a *macro*, the replacement process is called *macro expansion*, and the program for doing it is called a *macro processor*. A macro processor copies its input to its output with the macro definitions deleted and the macro references expanded. This lets us use parameters even in places where a compiler would insist on numbers, and it permits more ambitious language extensions such as our `error` handler.

Our first step in this chapter is a program `define` for replacement of one string of text by another — the most elementary form of macro processing. This lets us say, for instance,

```
define(ENDFILE, -1)
```

and thereafter have all occurrences of `ENDFILE` replaced by -1. Although this is not much of a "language translation," it does make programs easier to read and change. This is about all the macro processing we would have needed for the programs in this book if `const` had not been available.

The second stage, a much bigger job, is to construct a processor that allows macros to have arguments, so we can say, for example,

```
define(putc(c), putcf(c, STDOUT))
```

to have all occurrences of `putc(x)` replaced by `putcf(x, STDOUT)` for whatever value the argument `x` might take.

The third stage is to add to the macro processor a handful of other built-in operations that materially assist in writing complicated macro operations. The most important of these are facilities for conditional testing and for evaluating arithmetic expressions. These give the macro processor the full capabilities of a programming language, at least in a formal sense.

The second and third stages are really luxuries: they are convenient to have, and it is instructive to see how to build them, but you can accomplish a great deal without them, as is evident from the utility of `const`.

We should also emphasize that this is not the only way to specify macros. Our notation is *functional*, i.e., it resembles the way function references are written in most programming languages, so macro calls mesh well with such languages. We could have borrowed syntax from Pascal:

```
define ENDFILE = -1
```

but that does not extend as well to multi-line definitions or to macros with arguments or to some of the other built-in operations we want to add. In Chapter 7 we suggested the form

```
define name
    body
endmarker
```

which is suitable for a language where input is handled a line at a time. Another possibility is a *template* macro processor, in which the macros correspond to operators (like the + and – in arithmetic expressions), and the arguments are the operands. Processors for template macros are sometimes easier to use, but are harder to write. The bibliographic notes at the end of the chapter suggest additional reading.

8.1 Simple Text Replacement

Let us begin with the easiest case. What we want is to copy input to output, except that when certain input strings appear they are to be replaced by previously defined replacement text. In a programming language like Pascal, the natural unit of replacement is the identifier, that is, a string of alphanumeric characters beginning with a letter and surrounded by non-alphanumerics. In the text

```
      while (getc(c) <> ENDFILE) do
```

ENDFILE is surrounded by non-alphanumerics and is thus a candidate for replacement. Of course so are while, getc, c, and do, but since they are presumably not defined to the macro processor, they should be copied unaltered.

The unit of replacement is called a *token*. In other situations, a token might be anything between "white space" (blanks, tabs, newlines) as it was in format, or anything between a pair of specified left and right markers. In any case, one part of the processor is a routine that reads input and divides it up into tokens according to some rule.

How are definitions provided? The syntax suggested above is convenient:

```
      define(name, replacement text)
```

defines *name* to be whatever text follows, up to a balancing right parenthesis; this allows the replacement text to be longer than one line. We will need modules to collect the name and replacement text, and to record new names and definitions as they are encountered.

Some of the implementation details are critical, because the order in which operations are done can make a big difference in the power and convenience of a macro processor. One significant decision is what should happen when one name is defined in terms of another one. For example, after the definitions

```
      define(x, 1)
      define(y, x)
```

does the input y produce x or 1? If the definitions are in reverse order,

```
      define(y, x)
      define(x, 1)
```

then what is y?

We don't want users of define to have to worry too much about the order in which their definitions appear. Accordingly, define is built so examples like this one will work in the more useful way — after a macro has been evaluated, its replacement text is *rescanned*. If it contains any further macros they in turn go through the same expansion process. (This introduces the chance of an infinite loop, of course, so we must be prepared for that eventuality.)

There are also several possibilities for *when* macro calls are evaluated. If we have already defined x with

```
      define(x, 1)
```

then when

```
      define(y, x)
```

is encountered, we can either replace x by 1 immediately, or we can ignore the fact that x is a macro and replace it later when y is invoked. In the example above these two methods produce the same result, but if x should subsequently be redefined, there would be a difference. Different choices here lead to somewhat different but equally useful processors. In our define processor, definitions are *not* scanned for macro calls while they are being copied into the table of definitions; the interpretation of macros is done as late as possible.

But first here is the outline of the no-argument macro processor.

```
while (gettok(token) <> ENDFILE)
    look up token
    if (token = 'define')
        install new token and value
    else if (token was found in table)
        switch input to definition of token
    else
        copy token to output
```

Since there are nested sources of input, in principle this is a recursive process. In define we will deal with recursion in a different way from the explicit recursion that we have used in other programs. We will get back to this shortly.

gettok is analogous to the getword routine we wrote in Chapter 3, but it must be made somewhat more complicated to handle non-alphabetic characters properly. For example, blanks are now significant and can't be ignored. The call

```
c := gettok(token, maxtok)
```

copies the next token from the standard input into token. A token is either a string of letters and digits, or a single non-alphanumeric character. The function value returned by gettok is the first character of the token; this determines whether or not the token is alphabetic.

```
    { gettok -- get token for define }
    function gettok (var token : string; toksize : integer)
            : character;
var
    i : integer;
    done : boolean;
begin
    i := 1;
    done := false;
    while (not done) and (i < toksize) do
        if (isalphanum(getpbc(token[i]))) then
            i := i + 1
        else
            done := true;
    if (i >= toksize) then
        error('define: token too long');
    if (i > 1) then begin    { some alpha was seen }
        putback(token[i]);
        i := i - 1
    end;
    { else single non-alphanumeric }
    token[i+1] := ENDSTR;
    gettok := token[1]
end;
```

Looking for tokens one character at a time, we don't know that we have seen the end of the token until we have gone one character too far. This is a classic example of an undesirable side effect, one that can tremendously complicate a program if we let it. Each time we need another character, we must check whether to read a new character or use the one we already have. Tangling this up with the logic of what to *do* with each character would make an unreadable mess.

Instead we hide the complication by introducing a pair of cooperating routines. getpbc delivers the next input character to be considered, both in its argument and as its function value. putback puts a character back on the input, so that the next call to getpbc will return it again. Now, every time gettok reads one character too many, it promptly pushes it back, so the rest of the code does not have to know about the problem.

One possibility is to make putback a primitive operation, so getpbc can be simply getc. We have separated them here to illustrate how the pushback can be done, since in general you will have to provide your own. putback puts the pushed-back characters into a buffer. getpbc reads from the buffer if there is anything there; it calls getc if the buffer is empty.

```
{ putback -- push character back onto input }
procedure putback (c : character);
begin
    if (bp >= BUFSIZE) then
        error('too many characters pushed back');
    bp := bp + 1;
    buf[bp] := c
end;


{ getpbc -- get a (possibly pushed back) character }
function getpbc (var c : character) : character;
begin
    if (bp > 0) then
        c := buf[bp]
    else begin
        bp := 1;
        buf[bp] := getc(c)
    end;
    if (c <> ENDFILE) then
        bp := bp - 1;
    getpbc := c
end;
```

bp is the index of the next character to be returned from buf; if bp is zero a fresh character is fetched by a call to getc. (bp must be initialized to zero.) The buffer and pointer used by getpbc and putback are global variables in define, and initialized by initdef.

```
buf : array [1..BUFSIZE] of character;  { for pushback }
bp : 0..BUFSIZE;    { next available character; init=0 }
```

As written, gettok never pushes back more than one character between calls to getpbc, so buf could have been an ordinary scalar variable instead of an array. But pushback is a useful mechanism, well worth generalizing. We can even write pbstr, which pushes back an entire string by repeated calls to putback.

```
{ pbstr -- push string back onto input }
procedure pbstr (var s : string);
var
    i : integer;
begin
    for i := length(s) downto 1 do
        putback(s[i])
end;
```

It is of course necessary to push a string back in reverse order.

Only getpbc and putback know about the data structure of buf and bp. pbstr could be faster if it also knew about them and could avoid the overhead of calling putback for each character, but as much as possible we try to minimize data connections between routines. This is one of the most effective ways we know of to write code that can be easily changed. Certainly if it later proves true that the overhead in `pbstr` is a bottleneck, then we can improve it. The important thing is to start with a good design. It is much easier to relax the standards for something written well than it is to tighten them for something done badly.

Since we can push back something different from what was read, it has probably occurred to you that `putback` provides an elegant way to implement the rescanning of macro replacement text. Suppose that after a defined name is found, we push its *replacement text* back onto the input. When that is read, if it in turn contains a defined name, the name will be looked up and translated just as if it had been in the input originally. This pushback is how we handle the recursion implicit in nested sources of input.

Now we can write the main program, `define`:

```
{ define -- simple string replacement macro processor }
procedure define;
#include "defcons.p"
#include "deftype.p"
#include "defvar.p"
    defn : string;
    token : string;
    toktype : sttype;    { type returned by lookup }
    defname : string;    { value is 'define' }
    null : string;       { value is '' }
#include "defproc.p"
begin
    null[1] := ENDSTR;
    initdef;
    install(defname, null, DEFTYPE);
    while (gettok(token, MAXTOK) <> ENDFILE) do
        if (not isletter(token[1])) then
            putstr(token, STDOUT)
        else if (not lookup(token, defn, toktype)) then
            putstr(token, STDOUT)    { undefined }
        else if (toktype = DEFTYPE) then begin  { defn }
            getdef(token, MAXTOK, defn, MAXDEF);
            install(token, defn, MACTYPE)
        end
        else
            pbstr(defn) { push replacement onto input }
end;
```

If the token returned by `gettok` is not a letter (as determined by `isletter`) it cannot be a defined symbol. We test for that right away, to avoid looking up every non-alphanumeric character. Here is one possible implementation of `isletter` for ASCII machines (but recall the discussion of character sets and `isupper` in Chapter 2):

```
{ isletter -- true if c is a letter of either case }
function isletter (c : character) : boolean;
begin
    isletter :=
        c in [ord('a')..ord('z')] + [ord('A')..ord('Z')]
end;
```

The token is looked up with lookup, which also returns the defining text and type if the token was found. If the token wasn't found by lookup, it has no special significance, and can be output immediately. If it was *define*, the name and replacement text are isolated with getdef and installed in the table by install. If the token was found and was not a *define*, the replacement text is pushed back onto the input. The type sttype is an enumeration of the possible symbol table entry types, which for define are just DEFTYPE for the built-in "define" and MACTYPE for a macro name:

```
type
    sttype = (DEFTYPE, MACTYPE);    { symbol table types }
```

install is used to place the keyword *define* in the table in the first place, along with a null string as its replacement and DEFTYPE as its type. This is better than entering it with a set of assignment statements, because the program doesn't need to know anything about the format of table entries. lookup returns the type DEFTYPE when it finds *define*, so we can quickly check whether a token is a *define*. Besides the elements of sttype, lookup and install are the only visible parts of the table-handling mechanism; they are the subject of the next section.

Here is getdef:

```
{ getdef -- get name and definition }
procedure getdef (var token : string; toksize : integer;
        var defn : string; defsize : integer);
var
    i, nlpar : integer;
    c : character;
begin
    token[1] := ENDSTR; { in case of bad input }
    defn[1] := ENDSTR;
    if (getpbc(c) <> LPAREN) then
        message('define: missing left paren')
    else if (not isletter(gettok(token, toksize))) then
        message('define: non-alphanumeric name')
    else if (getpbc(c) <> COMMA) then
        message('define: missing comma in define')
    else begin  { got '(name,' so far }
        while (getpbc(c) = BLANK) do
            ;    { skip leading blanks }
        putback(c); { went one too far }
        nlpar := 0;
        i := 1;
        while (nlpar >= 0) do begin
            if (i >= defsize) then
                error('define: definition too long')
            else if (getpbc(defn[i]) = ENDFILE) then
                error('define: missing right paren')
            else if (defn[i] = LPAREN) then
                nlpar := nlpar + 1
            else if (defn[i] = RPAREN) then
                nlpar := nlpar - 1;
            { else normal character in defn[i] }
            i := i + 1
        end;
        defn[i-1] := ENDSTR
    end
end;
```

Most of the task here is coping with balanced parentheses and invalid input. Where possible, getdef simply notes the error and continues, in an attempt to give the user as much information as possible per run.

For completeness, here is initdef; we will show inithash after we discuss table lookup in the next section.

```
{ initdef -- initialize variables for define }
procedure initdef;
begin
    { setstring(defname, 'define'); }
        defname[1] := ord('d');
        defname[2] := ord('e');
        defname[3] := ord('f');
        defname[4] := ord('i');
        defname[5] := ord('n');
        defname[6] := ord('e');
        defname[7] := ENDSTR;
    bp := 0;      { pushback buffer pointer }
    inithash
end;
```

Exercise 8-1. What happens if you say

```
define(d, define)
d(a, b)
a
```

What happens with

```
define(define, x)
define(a, b)
```

□

Exercise 8-2. What happens if you say

```
define(x, x)
```

or

```
define(x, y)
define(y, x)
```

and then ask for **x**? What would you like to have happen? □

Exercise 8-3. If you write

```
define(x, x x)
```

sooner or later the pushback buffer will overflow and `define` will exit. This is generally regarded as better behavior than causing an infinite loop. Can you devise a scheme for turning all potential infinite loops into stack overflows? □

Exercise 8-4. `getdef` deletes any blanks that might appear at the front of the replacement text. Why is this desirable? Would any harm result if they were retained? What happens to blanks around the macro name? □

Exercise 8-5. If a line contains nothing but a definition, any trailing blanks and the newline are copied to the output, even though it might seem more natural to eliminate them completely. Modify `getdef` or some other part of the program so no output is produced from a line containing only definitions. Is this an appropriate action if the output is fed to a compiler that uses line numbers for diagnostics? □

Exercise 8-6. As an alternate and more general solution to the previous problem, implement a built-in operation `dnl` (for "delete newline") which deletes all characters from its occurrence up to and including the next newline. Thus in the input

```
define(x, 1)dnl
```

the `dnl` deletes all text after the definition, and the line produces no output. □

8.2 Table Lookup

Let us now design `lookup` and `install`, the routines for handling tables of names and definitions. We have already made one important design decision — all information about table format, search strategy, and the like is private, known only by `lookup` and `install`. All other routines must access the table through them. Information hiding is critical to proper program design: routines that don't need to know about the internal representation of a data structure should not know about it. Not only does this ensure that data is not inadvertently changed, but more important, it breaks the program into independent pieces, where each can be changed without affecting the others. Each piece is a black box, presenting only a well-defined interface to the world. In our case, if we change some aspect of the table — to sort the names for binary search, for instance — we can do so with impunity, because no other routine knows what the tables look like. Of course the "need to know" has to be genuine. It's all too easy to design routines whose users "need" to know about the data, when with more care the structure could be concealed.

Inside the lookup code, the lookup strategy determines the table structures needed. The simplest table management is a linear table: add new entries to the end of a table as they arrive, and search the table from one end to the other each time a token must be looked up.

In the early stages of a program, fancy search techniques are not worth the extra complexity. Linear search is not always the best thing, but it is an excellent first choice. It is easy to implement and likely to work right the first time. If it later proves to be a bottleneck, it can be replaced with a faster algorithm without affecting the rest of the program. The expected time to find a token in the table (or determine that it is not present) is proportional to the length of the table, however, so the bottleneck can appear early.

The next step up in complexity is probably to sort the entries and use binary search to locate tokens. But if definitions arrive at unpredictable times rather than all at once, it is necessary to sort each time a definition arrives. The search time for such a table is proportional to the logarithm of the table size if the sorting time can be ignored, which is true so long as there are many more calls to `lookup` than to `install`. It runs faster, but it's more complicated.

A third solution, and in real life, usually the best, is to use a hash search. A token is "hashed" to create an index into a table of lists. Scanning the list at the hash index determines whether the token is present or not. If the hashing function does a good job, tokens are spread uniformly through the table and the search time is constant, that is, independent of the number of entries present, until the table becomes nearly full. Even then, the search time increases only linearly as more elements are added.

Clearly efficiency and simplicity are at conflict in the design of table searching strategies, but as it turns out, an efficient solution is not greatly more complicated than a simple one. The hash search is organized like this: One large table called `ndtable` contains the names and replacement texts, stored one after another as

   name ENDSTR *definition* ENDSTR *name* ENDSTR *defn* ENDSTR   . . .

This is the same idea that we used in `sort` in Chapter 4, except that since there is a name and a definition for each entry, we use a record to hold the `ndtable` indices. A second array, called `hashtab`, contains pointers to name-definition records. An element of `hashtab` points to the beginning of a linked list of records describing names that have that hash value; it is set to `nil` if no names have hashed to that value. (`nil` is a Pascal keyword. A pointer which does not point to an object should have the value `nil`.) Each record in the chain contains the `ndtable` indices of the name and definition, the type of the object (`DEFTYPE` or `MACTYPE`), and a pointer to the next name-definition record. This too is `nil` for the last record in the chain. A picture is worth about a thousand words:

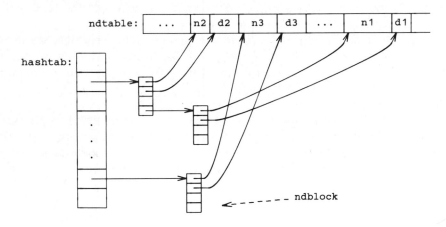

The declarations are as follows:

```
    { deftype -- type definitions for define }
    type
        charpos = 1..MAXCHARS;
        charbuf = array [1..MAXCHARS] of character;
        sttype = (DEFTYPE, MACTYPE);     { symbol table types }
        ndptr = ^ndblock;    { pointer to a name-defn block }
        ndblock =
            record        { name-defn block }
                name : charpos;
                defn : charpos;
                kind : sttype;
                nextptr : ndptr
            end;
```

The notation "ndptr = ^ndblock" is read as "ndptr is a pointer to an ndblock." Some character sets use an up-arrow '↑' instead of the circumflex '^'.

The corresponding variables are

```
    { defvar -- var declarations for define }
    var
        hashtab : array [1..HASHSIZE] of ndptr;
        ndtable : charbuf;
        nexttab : charpos;  { first free position in ndtable }
        buf : array [1..BUFSIZE] of character;  { for pushback }
        bp : 0..BUFSIZE;     { next available character; init=0 }
```

We have to put all these variables into global variables because lookup, install and any subordinates all have to know about them and there is no other way to pass the information.

nexttab is the next free position in ndtable; it must be initialized to 1 and all entries in hashtab made nil. This is done in inithash:

```
    { inithash -- initialize hash table to nil }
    procedure inithash;
    var
        i : 1..HASHSIZE;
    begin
        nexttab := 1;    { first free slot in table }
        for i := 1 to HASHSIZE do
            hashtab[i] := nil
    end;
```

lookup returns true and extracts the definition and type if the token was found; otherwise it returns false.

```
{ lookup -- locate name, get defn and type from table }
function lookup (var name, defn : string; var t : sttype)
       : boolean;
var
    p : ndptr;
begin
    p := hashfind(name);
    if (p = nil) then
        lookup := false
    else begin
        lookup := true;
        cscopy(ndtable, p^.defn, defn);
        t := p^.kind
    end
end;
```

A construct like p^.defn accesses the defn component of the record that p points to. cscopy is the string-copying procedure we wrote in Chapter 4 to copy a string from a big array of type charbuf to a string.

The real work of finding an occurrence of name is done by hashfind:

```
{ hashfind -- find name in hash table }
function hashfind (var name : string) : ndptr;
var
    p : ndptr;
    tempname : string;
    found : boolean;
begin
    found := false;
    p := hashtab[hash(name)];
    while (not found) and (p <> nil) do begin
        cscopy(ndtable, p^.name, tempname);
        if (equal(name, tempname)) then
            found := true
        else
            p := p^.nextptr
    end;
    hashfind := p
end;
```

The actual hashing done by hash. Ours is dead simple, though not especially good: it adds up the characters of the string, each time multiplying the previous sum by three, then takes the remainder modulo HASHSIZE. HASHSIZE ought to be prime to get a reasonably uniform distribution of hash values.

```
{ hash -- compute hash function of a name }
function hash (var name : string) : integer;
var
    i, h : integer;
begin
    h := 0;
    for i := 1 to length(name) do
        h := (3 * h + name[i]) mod HASHSIZE;
    hash := h + 1
end;
```

install adds a new name, definition and type to the head of the chain of
records which have that hash value; it is called when a *define* is encountered.
install does not check whether the name is already in the table, so names
may be redefined just by giving a new definition: since lookup scans the chain
from the front, the new definition supersedes the old.

Space for the pointer blocks is obtained by calling the Pascal storage
management function new. new(p) creates an object of the type that p points
to, then sets p to point to it. The contents of a dynamic object are accessed by
p^; if the object is actually a record, as it is here, then individual components
are selected with p^.*name*.

```
{ install -- add name, definition and type to table }
procedure install (var name, defn : string; t : sttype);
var
    h, dlen, nlen : integer;
    p : ndptr;
begin
    nlen := length(name) + 1;    { 1 for ENDSTR }
    dlen := length(defn) + 1;
    if (nexttab + nlen + dlen > MAXCHARS) then begin
        putstr(name, STDERR);
        error(': too many definitions')
    end
    else begin   { put it at front of chain }
        h := hash(name);
        new(p);
        p^.nextptr := hashtab[h];
        hashtab[h] := p;
        p^.name := nexttab;
        sccopy(name, ndtable, nexttab);
        nexttab := nexttab + nlen;
        p^.defn := nexttab;
        sccopy(defn, ndtable, nexttab);
        nexttab := nexttab + dlen;
        p^.kind := t
    end
end;
```

The constants and procedures needed by define are as follows:

```
{ defcons -- const declarations for define }
const
     BUFSIZE = 500;          { size of pushback buffer }
     MAXCHARS = 5000;        { size of name-defn table }
     MAXDEF = MAXSTR;        { max chars in a defn }
     MAXTOK = MAXSTR;        { max chars in a token }
     HASHSIZE = 53;          { size of hash table }


{ defproc -- procedures needed by define }
#include "cscopy.p"
#include "sccopy.p"
#include "putback.p"
#include "getpbc.p"
#include "pbstr.p"
#include "gettok.p"
#include "getdef.p"
#include "inithash.p"
#include "hash.p"
#include "hashfind.p"
#include "install.p"
#include "lookup.p"
#include "initdef.p"
```

PROGRAM
   define   expand string definitions
USAGE
   define
FUNCTION
   define reads its input, looking for macro definitions of the form
```
        define(ident, string)
```
and writes its output with each subsequent instance of the identifier ident replaced by the sequence of characters string. string must be balanced in parentheses. The text of each definition proper results in no output text. Each replacement string is rescanned for further possible replacements, permitting multi-level definitions.
EXAMPLE
```
        define
        define(ENDFILE, (-1))
        define(DONE, ENDFILE)
            if (getit(line) = DONE) then
                putit(sumline);
        <ENDFILE>


            if (getit(line) = (-1)) then
                putit(sumline);
```
BUGS
   A recursive definition such as define(x, x) will cause an infinite loop when x is invoked.

Exercise 8-7. Verify that getdef and install work correctly if the definition is empty, so that

```
define(nothing,)
```

defines a string with no replacement text. Why would you want to define such a thing? What is the effect of the macro call

```
nothing(this is a line of text)
```

□

Exercise 8-8. Redefining names without salvaging the old space is obviously profligate if done often. Modify `install` to make better use of the space in `ndtable`. □

Exercise 8-9. Add an `undefine` command

```
undefine(name)
```

that removes the most recent definition of *name*. What should happen if you `undefine` a name that wasn't defined? □

Exercise 8-10. Experiment with different hashing algorithms, to see how randomly they distribute the hash value between 1 and `HASHSIZE`, and what effect they have on `define`'s performance as a function of number of entries in the table. □

Exercise 8-11. Implement a version of `define` that does not use pushback in the sense that we have, but instead maintains a stack of current input sources, and switches those appropriately. Try another version that uses explicit recursion to select different inputs. Which version is easiest? Which version is fastest? □

Exercise 8-12. How does `define` deal with the comment conventions of common programming languages? Should `define` know about quoted strings? That is, should defined names appearing within quotes be replaced? □

Exercise 8-13. It is often useful to have at least a rudimentary conditional test. Suppose we say that a line like

```
ifdef(name, text)
```

means "if *name* is defined, put *text* in the input, otherwise skip over it." You could parameterize a program for different machines by writing definitions like

```
ifdef(pdp11, define(wordsize, 16) define(charsize, 8))
ifdef(pdp10, define(wordsize, 36) define(charsize, 7))
ifdef(ibm370, define(wordsize, 32) define(charsize, 8))
```

Then defining pdp11 with the (empty) definition

```
define(pdp11,)
```

sets parameters like `wordsize` correctly for the PDP-11 when the `ifdef` lines are encountered. Changing this single definition and reprocessing resets the program for some other machine. Implement this conditional facility. □

8.3 Some Measurements

We timed `define` by replacing all `const` symbols from the code for `edit` and its supporting routines with `define`'s and running it through `define`. Here are some data from one timing study, with `HASHSIZE` set to 53. Total time was 38 seconds on a DEC VAX 11/780.

	#calls	CPU time(%)
isalphanum	46997	21.2
putcf	36884	17.4
isletter	21830	14.8
getc	39917	10.2
gettok	21831	7.7
getpbc	47763	6.6
putstr	21182	4.3
cscopy	9915	3.1
hash	5890	2.5
hashfind	5781	2.4
define	1	2.1
equal	9375	1.6
length	6540	1.5
putback	7847	0.9
lookup	5781	0.7
getdef	108	0.1
install	109	0.1
pbstr	432	0.0

Our putstr calls putcf.

Before we consider the run time percentages, it's worth remarking that there is a lot of information in a measurement as simple as the number of times each procedure is called, especially if the program is carefully modularized so each routine does only one thing. For example, this data tells us that the input contains 39916 characters (one call of getc finds an ENDFILE), 36884 output characters, 108 defined tokens, 432 occurrences of defined tokens out of 5781 that were looked up (which means that most of the time lookup reports failure), and so on. Some of this data provides consistency checking on the operation of the program. For example, we expect one more install than getdef (installing the keyword define in the first place); if that is not so, something is badly amiss.

The CPU time data tells us checking the types of characters with isalphanum and isletter is surprisingly expensive, 36 percent, which suggests that a different implementation is called for. I/O time is next, somewhat over 27 percent. The table lookup mechanism is cheap; all of its components add up to only about 7 percent. The pushback mechanism is a modest cost on each character, well worth it for the clarity it brings to the program. Our decision to write pbstr in terms of putback is also vindicated.

We substituted range-test versions of isalphanum and isletter and repeated the test. Total time went down to 29 seconds; run-time percentages for isalphanum and isletter went to 8.6 and 4.3 respectively.

It is important to justify decisions made in the name of efficiency for one very good reason. Most of the time programmers have no real idea where time is being consumed by a program. Consequently nearly all the effort expended (and the clarity sacrificed) for "efficiency" is wasted. We have found that the best way to avoid too-early optimization is to make a regular practice of instrumenting code. Only from such first-hand experience can one learn a proper sense of priorities.

8.4 Macros with Arguments

Macros with arguments add to the power of the macro processor. For example, we said that `getc` and `putc` are equivalent to `getcf(c, STDIN)` and `putcf(c, STDOUT)` respectively. By defining `getc` and `putc` as macros that expand into references to `getcf` and `putcf`, we guarantee equivalence, and we eliminate a level of procedure call, which may improve efficiency. The replacement is not possible without an argument capability.

As another example with immediate relevance, we could replace `isalphanum` and `isletter` by macros. The entire body of `isletter` is just

```
isletter :=
    c in [ord('a')..ord('z')] + [ord('A')..ord('Z')]
```

and `isalphanum` is not much bigger. These are such short routines that they could readily be macros instead of functions, expanding into in-line code rather than calling another routine. We could define a macro

```
isletter(c)
```

that would expand into the lines above (or into appropriate range tests), with occurrences of the formal parameter c replaced by the actual argument used when the macro is invoked. For the user, there would be no difference.

The syntax for specifying macros with arguments is an extension of what we used before:

```
define(name, replacement text)
```

defines *name*. This time, however, any occurrence in the replacement text of $n, where n is between 1 and 9, will be replaced by the nth argument when the macro is actually called. Thus

```
define(isletter,
    ($1 in [ord('a')..ord('z')] + [ord('A')..ord('Z')]))
```

defines the `isletter` macro.

Specifying arguments with $n is not as pleasant as being able to use dummy names for the parameters, as in

```
define(isletter(c),
    (c in [ord('a')..ord('z')] + [ord('A')..ord('Z')]))
```

but it is easier to build. Write something clean and acceptable that works, then polish it later if necessary.

The restriction to nine arguments is another example of the same philosophy. It is silly to get sidetracked worrying about macros with lots of arguments until the rest of the processor is working. You will find that in practice there is rarely any call for more anyway. Hard cases can wait until the easy ones are well under control.

It's harder to write a macro processor that allows arguments than one that doesn't. Furthermore, we intend to add a small set of "built-in" operations in addition to *define*: a conditional statement, an arithmetic capability, and a couple of string functions, and we want these to go in without much effort. The main thing is to ensure that any operation — macro call, definition, other built-in — can occur in the middle of any other one. If this is possible, then in principle the macro processor is capable of doing any computation, although it may well be hard to express.

As long as no macro calls are encountered (or built-ins, since they are treated identically), the input is copied directly to the output. When a macro is called, however, its name, its definition, and its arguments (if any) are all collected. Once the argument collection is finished, the macro is evaluated as follows. If it is a built-in like *define,* an appropriate routine is called that does whatever it has to with the arguments. If the macro is not a built-in, the definition text is pushed back onto the input. As it is being pushed back, any $n's in it are replaced by the corresponding argument that was just collected.

The fun starts when one of the arguments includes a call of another macro or built-in. Although there are various ways to deal with this situation, one of the easiest is to interpret the arguments as they are being collected, then push them back onto the input.

When a macro invocation is seen, the name and definition are placed in an evaluation area organized as a stack. Any arguments that follow are copied into this area as well, except that when an argument contains another macro invocation (a nested one) a new stack frame is created, and that inner macro is evaluated *completely* and its translation pushed back onto the input before the stack is popped and we resume working on the outer macro. The outer macro never sees the inner one, just its translation. (Of course the inner macro may in turn call upon other macros; the process is recursive.)

The thing to keep firmly in mind at all times is that arguments are evaluated completely as they are being collected. This is different behavior from the string replacement process we showed earlier in the chapter, but for common uses like replacing symbolic parameters in programs, the two methods produce the same result. (We will also provide for deferred evaluation so we can have the benefits of the earlier method when we need them.) Here are some examples, before we start on the actual code.

Suppose we have

```
define(ENDSTR, 0)
```

When the define is seen, define and its replacement text (which is null) are put in the evaluation stack. Now we collect the arguments. ENDSTR at this point is nothing special, nor is 0, so they are put on the stack at positions 3 and 4 respectively. At the end of the define (when the definition is finished) we can evaluate, which in this case involves calling a routine to install the name and definition, which are the arguments at positions 3 and 4. Then the top four items on the stack are popped.

If we subsequently see ENDSTR in the input, it will be put on the stack with its definition, and no arguments. The definition 0 is pushed back onto the input and the stack popped.

More complicated, here is an example with arguments.

```
define(incr, $1:=$1+1)
```

defines incr to be a macro that generates code to increment its argument by 1. The input

```
incr(x)
```

causes incr and $1:=$1+1 to be copied onto the evaluation stack. x is collected as the argument; if it is not a defined name, we reach the end of the invocation of incr without incident. The definition is pushed back onto the input, with each occurrence of $1 replaced by x, to yield x:=x+1.

But imagine for a moment that x had earlier been defined to be something else, say a[i]. Then x is a macro call, so when it is encountered, a new stack frame is formed, and x and its definition are copied into that frame. Then the definition a[i] is pushed back onto the input, and the frame popped. When argument collection resumes for the previous level (incr), the input that used to be x has become a[i], and this becomes the actual argument to incr. As far as incr is concerned, it *was* called with a[i] as its argument, and the result is a[i]:=a[i]+1.

Exercise 8-14. Assuming that getc and putc have been defined in terms of getcf and putcf, go through the expansion process by hand for the input

```
putc(getc(c))
```

including the processing of values for STDIN and STDOUT. □

8.5 Implementation

The processing can now be spelled out in more detail.

```
while (gettok(token, maxtok) <> ENDFILE)
    if (type is letter)
        if (not lookup(token))
            copy token to current evaluation stack frame
                or directly to output
        else
            make new stack frame
            copy name and definition to current stack frame
    else if (stack empty)    { not saving arguments }
        copy directly to output
    else if (at end of an argument list)
        if (built-in)
            do appropriate function
        else
            push definition back onto input,
                replacing $n's by arguments
        pop stack frame
    else                        { saving arguments }
        copy token to current stack frame
```

Of course this skips over a few details like precisely how we know when we're at the end of an argument list, and what the stack looks like. We will get to them in due course.

First the evaluation stack. This is just a long array `evalstk`. The first free position in `evalstk` is kept in `ep`, which is initially 1. Whenever we are processing a macro or built-in, `evalstk` contains the strings for the name, definition and arguments. The array `argstk` contains the locations in `evalstk` where these strings begin: `argstk[i]` is the beginning of the `i`th string in `evalstk`. `ap` is the first free position in `argstk`; it is also initially 1.

Since macros and built-ins may be nested, the strings in `evalstk` that `argstk` points to are in general associated with different levels. The array `callstk` keeps track of each stack frame: `callstk[i]` points to the position in `argstk` that in turn points to the defining text of the `i`th macro. A parallel array `typestk` records the type of the corresponding macro or built-in. `cp` is the *current* call stack position. If `cp` is zero, we are not in any macro. Inside a single level of invocation, `cp` is one, and so on. Thus to find the first argument of the third level of invocation, we first set `i:=callstk[3]`. Then `argstk[i]` is the defining text of this macro, `argstk[i+1]` is the name, and `argstk[i+2]` is the first argument. Thus, `argstk` effectively becomes an array of variable length records, implemented of necessity as a less structured array of indices.

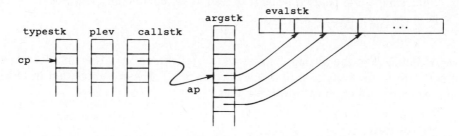

Argument collection requires keeping track of balanced parentheses independently for each level of macro, so we add another array `plev`, also parallel to
`callstk`, to count parentheses for the corresponding stack frame.

Several routines need to know about `cp` and the output buffer; `callstk`,
`typestk`, `argstk`, `ap`, and `plev` are used only in the main routine.

```
callstk : posbuf;     { call stack }
cp : pos;             { current call stack position }
typestk : array[1..CALLSIZE] of sttype; { type }
plev : array [1..CALLSIZE] of integer;  { paren level }
argstk : posbuf;      { argument stack for this call }
ap : pos;             { current argument position }
evalstk : charbuf;    { evaluation stack }
ep : charpos;         { first character unused in evalstk }
```

There is one last complication. Any macros encountered during argument
collection are expanded immediately. But there are times when we must defer
the evaluation until later. For example, consider this attempt to make a new
macro d synonymous with `define`:

```
define(d, define($1,$2))
```

On cursory inspection it should work, because the replacement text of d appears
to be `define($1,$2)`. But macros and built-ins are evaluated *as soon as they
are encountered*. The inner `define` is evaluated before the outer one. Because
a `define` has no replacement text, the net effect is to define d to be empty,
which is hardly what was wanted. To get around the problem of premature
evaluation, there must be a quoting convention, so input can be treated as
literal text when necessary. In our convention, any input surrounded by ` and
´ is left absolutely alone, except that one level of ` and ´ is stripped off. With
this facility we can write the macro d as

```
define(d, `define($1,$2)´)
```

The replacement text for d, protected by the quotes, is literally
`define($1,$2)`. Now when we say

```
d(a, bc)
```

everything works and a is defined to be bc.

Quotes must also be used when it is desired to redefine an identifier:

```
define(x,y)
define(x,z)
```

would define y in the second line, instead of redefining x. (The first definition is still active, however, so x ultimately becomes z.) If you do not want to redefine y, the operation must be expressed as

```
define(x,y)
define('x',z)
```

which will have the desired effect.

Because the right quote character ' means something in Pascal, sometimes it is a nuisance to have it pre-empted, so we will also add a built-in to permit the quote characters to be changed at will.

Putting all of these considerations together creates a long main program, but it is not really complicated. It follows the outline we gave earlier, except for the addition of quotes. It is a seven-way branch, with the code for each case in-line instead of in a separate routine. We have called it macro rather than define, because that better reflects what it does.

```
{ macro -- expand macros with arguments }
procedure macro;
#include "maccons.p"
#include "mactype.p"
#include "macvar.p"
    defn : string;
    token : string;
    toktype : sttype;
    t : character;
    nlpar : integer;
#include "macproc.p"
begin
    initmacro;
    install(defname, null, DEFTYPE);
    install(exprname, null, EXPRTYPE);
    install(subname, null, SUBTYPE);
    install(ifname, null, IFTYPE);
    install(lenname, null, LENTYPE);
    install(chqname, null, CHQTYPE);

    cp := 0;
    ap := 1;
    ep := 1;
    while (gettok(token, MAXTOK) <> ENDFILE) do
        if (isletter(token[1])) then begin
            if (not lookup(token, defn, toktype)) then
                puttok(token)
            else begin    { defined; put it in eval stack }
                cp := cp + 1;
                if (cp > CALLSIZE) then
                    error('macro: call stack overflow');
                callstk[cp] := ap;
                typestk[cp] := toktype;
                ap := push(ep, argstk, ap);
                puttok(defn);    { push definition }
                putchr(ENDSTR);
                ap := push(ep, argstk, ap);
                puttok(token);   { stack name }
                putchr(ENDSTR);
                ap := push(ep, argstk, ap);
                t := gettok(token, MAXTOK); { peek at next }
                pbstr(token);
                if (t <> LPAREN) then begin { add () }
                    putback(RPAREN);
                    putback(LPAREN)
                end;
                plev[cp] := 0
            end
        end
```

```
            else if (token[1] = lquote) then begin   { strip quotes }
                nlpar := 1;
                repeat
                    t := gettok(token, MAXTOK);
                    if (t = rquote) then
                        nlpar := nlpar - 1
                    else if (t = lquote) then
                        nlpar := nlpar + 1
                    else if (t = ENDFILE) then
                        error('macro: missing right quote');
                    if (nlpar > 0) then
                        puttok(token)
                until (nlpar = 0)
            end
            else if (cp = 0) then    { not in a macro at all }
                puttok(token)
            else if (token[1] = LPAREN) then begin
                if (plev[cp] > 0) then
                    puttok(token);
                plev[cp] := plev[cp] + 1
            end
            else if (token[1] = RPAREN) then begin
                plev[cp] := plev[cp] - 1;
                if (plev[cp] > 0) then
                    puttok(token)
                else begin   { end of argument list }
                    putchr(ENDSTR);
                    eval(argstk, typestk[cp], callstk[cp], ap-1);
                    ap := callstk[cp];   { pop eval stack }
                    ep := argstk[ap];
                    cp := cp - 1
                end
            end
            else if (token[1]=COMMA) and (plev[cp]=1) then begin
                putchr(ENDSTR); { new argument }
                ap := push(ep, argstk, ap)
            end
            else
                puttok(token);   { just stack it }
        if (cp <> 0) then
            error('macro: unexpected end of input')
    end;
```

We want to retain the property of define that a macro call without arguments (like ENDFILE or ENDSTR) does not require parentheses. Thus if a token is a defined name, and it is not followed immediately by a left parenthesis, we push back an empty set of balanced parentheses, so that macro calls without arguments are not a special case for the rest of the program. This is another example of altering some data representation in a minor way to avoid much greater complexity in the code.

You may have noticed that quotes are removed even outside macro definitions. Although this may look like unnecessary meddling on the part of the
macro processor, there are good reasons for doing it that way. As the simplest
example, if you really want a literal occurrence of the word define in your
text, you have to protect it with a layer of quotes or it will be interpreted as a
call to the built-in define. We will see some more substantial instances of this
shortly.

puttok and putchr put strings and characters respectively either into
evalstk (if we are in the middle of a macro), or directly onto the output with
putc (if we are not). The test for what destination to use occurs in a single
place in putchr, not scattered throughout the code.

```
{ puttok -- put token on output or evaluation stack }
procedure puttok (var s : string);
var
    i : integer;
begin
    i := 1;
    while (s[i] <> ENDSTR) do begin
        putchr(s[i]);
        i := i + 1
    end
end;

{ putchr -- put single char on output or evaluation stack }
procedure putchr (c : character);
begin
    if (cp <= 0) then
        putc(c)
    else begin
        if (ep > EVALSIZE) then
            error('macro: evaluation stack overflow');
        evalstk[ep] := c;
        ep := ep + 1
    end
end;
```

When a new argument is to be put into evalstk we have to record the
current value of the position ep and increment ap; this is done by push:

```
{ push -- push ep onto argstk, return new position ap }
function push (ep : integer; var argstk : posbuf;
        ap : integer) : integer;
begin
    if (ap > ARGSIZE) then
        error('macro: argument stack overflow');
    argstk[ap] := ep;
    push := ap + 1
end;
```

Once a macro has been identified and all its arguments collected in
evalstk (signaled by the parenthesis level becoming zero), eval is called to
process a built-in or to push back a definition with the appropriate arguments.

macro pushes the definition onto evalstk before the name, so when eval
is called, args[i] points to the defining text for the macro and args[i+1]
points to the name. args[i+2] through args[j] are the arguments, of
which there are j-i-1. This organization means that $0 is the name of the
macro itself. Although this will probably be little used, the regularity is nice to
have.

```
{ eval -- expand args i..j: do built-in or push back defn }
procedure eval (var argstk : posbuf; td : sttype;
        i, j : integer);
var
    argno, k, t : integer;
    temp : string;
begin
    t := argstk[i];
    if (td = DEFTYPE) then
        dodef(argstk, i, j)
    else begin
        k := t;
        while (evalstk[k] <> ENDSTR) do
            k := k + 1;
        k := k - 1; { last character of defn }
        while (k > t) do begin
            if (evalstk[k-1] <> ARGFLAG) then
                putback(evalstk[k])
            else begin
                argno := ord(evalstk[k]) - ord('0');
                if (argno >= 0) and (argno < j-i) then begin
                    cscopy(evalstk, argstk[i+argno+1], temp);
                    pbstr(temp)
                end;
                k := k - 1  { skip over $ }
            end;
            k := k - 1
        end;
        if (k = t) then       { do last character }
            putback(evalstk[k])
    end
end;
```

If the type is define, dodef is called; otherwise the definition is pushed back onto the input, with each $n replaced by the corresponding argument. The symbolic constant ARGFLAG is a $.

We haven't said what the macro processor should do when a macro definition asks for an argument that wasn't supplied. The most harmless thing is to ignore it — in effect to replace the $n by an empty string — and this is what eval does. This is true even if no arguments are present; that way if x is defined by

```
define(x, a$1b)
```

the inputs

```
x(+)
x(-,+)
x()
x
```

all produce something sensible: a+b, a-b, ab and ab respectively.
    dodef is easy: most of the work has already been done for it.

```
{ dodef -- install definition in table }
procedure dodef (var argstk : posbuf; i, j : integer);
var
    temp1, temp2 : string;
begin
    if (j - i > 2) then begin
        cscopy(evalstk, argstk[i+2], temp1);
        cscopy(evalstk, argstk[i+3], temp2);
        install(temp1, temp2, MACTYPE)
    end
end;
```

One of the first things to try with the macro processor is extending the syntax of our programming language. Suppose we try to use macros to create the
error primitive that we have been using throughout the book. If we say

```
define(error, `begin writeln($1); halt end')
```

then a "statement" like

```
error('argument stack overflow');
```

will be converted into

```
begin writeln('argument stack overflow'); halt end;
```

thus avoiding the problem of fixed-length strings.
    The halt statement is not standard Pascal either, by the way, though it is
widely available. If your Pascal has no such mechanism, you can go on to say

```
define(halt, goto 9999)
```

where 9999 is a label in the outermost block of your program, just after the call
of your main procedure.

Exercise 8-15. Modify the definition of error given above so that the error message
includes the name of the program being run. You might also arrange that output
appears on a different file than normal, so it does not disappear down a pipeline. Write
a macro for message as well. □

Exercise 8-16. The definition

```
define(sqr, $1 * $1)
```

defines a macro to square an expression. Or does it? What is sqr(x+1)? What can you do about it? How much should a macro processor know about the language(s) it is used with? □

Exercise 8-17. Invent a syntax that allows macros to have more than nine arguments. Make it compatible with the $n syntax if $n<10$. How difficult is it to implement? □

Exercise 8-18. Improve define to allow the parameters in a macro definition to be specified by dummy names instead of by $n. That is, if m is defined by

define(m(x,y), *replacement text containing tokens* x *and* y)

then the invocation m(a,b) should replace all occurrences of the tokens x and y in the replacement text by a and b respectively. How much existing machinery can you use? □

8.6 Conditionals, Arithmetic, and Other Built-ins

macro has been designed to make it easy to add new built-in functions as the need arises. The next step in the evolution is the addition of a conditional test, with a built-in function ifelse. The input

ifelse(*a,b,c,d*)

compares *a* and *b* as character strings. If they are the same, *c* is pushed back onto the input; if they differ, *d* is pushed back. As a rudimentary example,

define(compare, `ifelse($1,$2,yes,no)')

defines compare as a two-argument macro returning yes if its arguments are the same, and no if they're not. As usual, the quotes prevent the ifelse from being evaluated too soon.

While we are adding built-in functions, we will do four more.

expr (*expression*)

evaluates the string *expression* as an arithmetic expression and returns that as its replacement text (as a string of characters). *expression* had better be a valid expression, or the results may be undesirable. "Arithmetic expression" includes +, -, *, / (integer division only, like div), % for remainder (Pascal's mod), and parentheses.

Suppose that you need parameters such as

```
const
    SCREENWID = 80;
    MAXLINE = SCREENWID + 1;
```

But the second definition is illegal: a constant cannot be an expression, however appealing it might seem. The problem with writing two definitions, as in

```
    SCREENWID = 80;
    MAXLINE = 81;
```

is that you must remember to update both if one changes (and recognize that 81 is actually 80+1 in disguise). Clearly it is better to define one in terms of the other. With expr, the job is easy:

```
define(SCREENWID, 80)
define(MAXLINE, `expr(SCREENWID+1)')
```

`expr` has much more capability than this example would indicate; we'll show some more soon.

The next built-in is a function to take substrings of strings.

```
substr(s,m,n)
```

produces the substring of s which starts at position m (with origin one), of length n. If n is omitted or too big, the rest of the string is used, while if m is out of range the result is a null string.

```
substr(abc, 2, 1)
```

is b,

```
substr(abc, 2)
```

is bc, and

```
substr(abc, 4)
```

is empty.

The built-in `len` returns the length of its argument. Interestingly, `len` can be defined in terms of the other built-ins. What is the length of a string s? If s is empty, its length is zero. Otherwise it is one more than the length of the substring of s obtained by chopping off one character. This is a recursive definition, which is a natural form of expression if you happen to have a recursive language at hand — and we do. Let's say it with macros:

```
define(len,`ifelse($1,,0,`expr(1+len(substr($1,2)))')')
```

This is certainly a mouthful, but not hard to understand in the light of the recursive definition above. It is permissible, and often necessary, to define macros in terms of themselves. It works because conditional testing can be used to prevent an infinite loop. In this case the test is whether all the characters of the string have been chopped away.

The outer layer of quotes prevents all evaluation as the definition is being copied into the table. The inner layer prevents the `expr` construction from being done as the arguments of the `ifelse` are collected.

As you can imagine, computing a length this way is expensive, which is our main reason for including `len` as a built-in.

The final built-in is `changeq`, which permits the default quote characters `` ` `` and `'` to be set to something else. `changeq(xy)` sets the quotes to x and y; `changeq` without an argument resets them to the default.

The changes needed to add `ifelse`, `expr`, `substr`, `len` and `changeq` are minor. We modify `macro` to install the new keywords and their types (`IFTYPE`, `EXPRTYPE`, `SUBTYPE`, `LENTYPE`, `CHQTYPE`), and change `eval` to

look for them as well as for DEFTYPE. In eval we only have to add the extra
tests and procedure calls.

```
    ...
else if (td = EXPRTYPE) then
    doexpr(argstk, i, j)
else if (td = SUBTYPE) then
    dosub(argstk, i, j)
else if (td = IFTYPE) then
    doif(argstk, i, j)
else if (td = LENTYPE) then
    dolen(argstk, i, j)
else if (td = CHQTYPE) then
    dochq(argstk, i, j)
else begin
    { process normal macro as before }
    ...
```

doif compares the first two arguments, and pushes back the appropriate
one onto the input. If there is no else argument, a null string is returned.

```
{ doif -- select one of two arguments }
procedure doif (var argstk : posbuf; i, j : integer);
var
    temp1, temp2, temp3 : string;
begin
    if (j - i >= 4) then begin
        cscopy(evalstk, argstk[i+2], temp1);
        cscopy(evalstk, argstk[i+3], temp2);
        if (equal(temp1, temp2)) then
            cscopy(evalstk, argstk[i+4], temp3)
        else if (j - i >= 5) then
            cscopy(evalstk, argstk[i+5], temp3)
        else
            temp3[1] := ENDSTR;
        pbstr(temp3)
    end
end;
```

doexpr does the arithmetic, converts the number, and pushes the result
back as a character string with pbnum.

```
{ doexpr -- evaluate arithmetic expressions }
procedure doexpr (var argstk : posbuf; i, j : integer);
var
    temp : string;
    junk : integer;
begin
    cscopy(evalstk, argstk[i+2], temp);
    junk := 1;
    pbnum(expr(temp, junk))
end;

{ pbnum -- convert number to string, push back on input }
procedure pbnum (n : integer);
var
    temp : string;
    junk : integer;
begin
    junk := itoc(n, temp, 1);
    pbstr(temp)
end;
```

Most of the work in evaluating expressions is pushed off into expr, which uses recursive calls on several sub-functions to evaluate the components of the expression. The method is quite conventional: the grammar for an arithmetic expression can be written as

expr	: *term* + *term*
	¦ *term* - *term*
term	: *factor* * *factor*
	¦ *factor* / *factor*
	¦ *factor* % *factor*
factor	: *number*
	¦ (*expr*)

The recursion is in the process of finding the pieces. Each syntactic type (*expr*, *term*, *factor*) has a corresponding function. expr searches for a pair of *term*'s separated by + or -, term searches for *factor*'s, and factor looks for either a plain number or a parenthesized *expr*.

```
{ expr -- recursive expression evaluation }
function expr (var s : string; var i : integer) : integer;
var
    v : integer;
    t : character;
#include "gnbchar.p"
#include "term.p"
begin
    v := term(s, i);
    t := gnbchar(s, i);
    while (t in [PLUS, MINUS]) do begin
        i := i + 1;
        if (t = PLUS) then
            v := v + term(s, i)
        else
            v := v - term(s, i);
        t := gnbchar(s, i)
    end;
    expr := v
end;


{ term -- evaluate term of arithmetic expression }
function term (var s : string; var i : integer) : integer;
var
    v : integer;
    t : character;
#include "factor.p"
begin
    v := factor(s, i);
    t := gnbchar(s, i);
    while (t in [STAR, SLASH, PERCENT]) do begin
        i := i + 1;
        case t of
        STAR:
            v := v * factor(s, i);
        SLASH:
            v := v div factor(s, i);
        PERCENT:
            v := v mod factor(s, i)
        end;
        t := gnbchar(s, i)
    end;
    term := v
end;
```

```
{ factor -- evaluate factor of arithmetic expression }
function factor (var s : string; var i : integer)
            : integer;
begin
    if (gnbchar(s, i) = LPAREN) then begin
        i := i + 1;
        factor := expr(s, i);
        if (gnbchar(s, i) = RPAREN) then
            i := i + 1
        else
            message('macro: missing paren in expr')
    end
    else
        factor := ctoi(s, i)
end;
```

The function gnbchar finds the beginning of the next token; it differs from skipbl only in that it also skips newlines, and returns a character for testing.

```
{ gnbchar -- get next non-blank character }
function gnbchar (var s : string; var i : integer)
            : character;
begin
    while (s[i] in [BLANK, TAB, NEWLINE]) do
        i := i + 1;
    gnbchar := s[i]
end;
```

dolen is straightforward:

```
{ dolen -- return length of argument }
procedure dolen(var argstk : posbuf; i, j : integer);
var
    temp : string;
begin
    if (j - i > 1) then begin
        cscopy(evalstk, argstk[i+2], temp);
        pbnum(length(temp))
    end
    else
        pbnum(0)
end;
```

dosub does the substr function; it is entirely concerned with getting indices right, particularly in boundary cases where the substring requested is in some way outside the string. By calling expr instead of ctoi, dosub causes the second and third arguments to be evaluated as expressions without a surrounding call to expr.

```
    { dosub -- select substring }
    procedure dosub (var argstk : posbuf; i, j : integer);
    var
        ap, fc, k, nc : integer;
        temp1, temp2 : string;
    begin
        if (j - i >= 3) then begin
            if (j - i < 4) then
                nc := MAXTOK
            else begin
                cscopy(evalstk, argstk[i+4], temp1);
                k := 1;
                nc := expr(temp1, k)
            end;
            cscopy(evalstk, argstk[i+3], temp1);      { origin }
            ap := argstk[i+2];  { target string }
            k := 1;
            fc := ap + expr(temp1, k) - 1;   { first char }
            cscopy(evalstk, ap, temp2);
            if (fc >= ap) and (fc < ap+length(temp2)) then begin
                cscopy(evalstk, fc, temp1);
                for k := fc+min(nc,length(temp1))-1 downto fc do
                    putback(evalstk[k])
            end
        end
    end;
```

dochq is easy:

```
{ dochq -- change quote characters }
procedure dochq (var argstk : posbuf; i, j : integer);
var
    temp : string;
    n : integer;
begin
    cscopy(evalstk, argstk[i+2], temp);
    n := length(temp);
    if (n <= 0) then begin
        lquote := ord(GRAVE);
        rquote := ord(ACUTE)
    end
    else if (n = 1) then begin
        lquote := temp[1];
        rquote := lquote
    end
    else begin
        lquote := temp[1];
        rquote := temp[2]
    end
end;
```

Finally, here are the other components that make up the program:

```
{ mactype -- type declarations for macro }
type
    charpos = 1..MAXCHARS;
    charbuf = array [1..MAXCHARS] of character;
    posbuf = array [1..MAXPOS] of charpos;
    pos = 0..MAXPOS;
    sttype = (DEFTYPE, MACTYPE, IFTYPE, SUBTYPE,
        EXPRTYPE, LENTYPE, CHQTYPE); { symbol table types }
    ndptr = ^ndblock;
    ndblock =
        record
            name : charpos;
            defn : charpos;
            kind : sttype;
            nextptr : ndptr
        end;
```

```
    { maccons -- const declarations for macro }
    const
        BUFSIZE = 1000;      { size of pushback buffer }
        MAXCHARS = 5000;     { size of name-defn table }
        MAXPOS = 500;        { size of position arrays }
        CALLSIZE = MAXPOS;
        ARGSIZE = MAXPOS;
        EVALSIZE = MAXCHARS;
        MAXDEF = MAXSTR;     { max chars in a defn }
        MAXTOK = MAXSTR;     { max chars in a token }
        HASHSIZE = 53;       { size of hash table }
        ARGFLAG = DOLLAR;    { macro invocation character }

    { macvar -- var declarations for macro }
    var
        buf : array [1..BUFSIZE] of character;  { for pushback }
        bp : 0..BUFSIZE;     { next available character; init=0 }

        hashtab : array [1..HASHSIZE] of ndptr;
        ndtable : charbuf;
        nexttab : charpos;   { first free position in ndtable }

        callstk : posbuf;    { call stack }
        cp : pos;            { current call stack position }
        typestk : array[1..CALLSIZE] of sttype; { type }
        plev : array [1..CALLSIZE] of integer;  { paren level }
        argstk : posbuf;     { argument stack for this call }
        ap : pos;            { current argument position }
        evalstk : charbuf;   { evaluation stack }
        ep : charpos;        { first character unused in evalstk }

        { built-ins: }
        defname : string;    { value is 'define' }
        exprname : string;   { value is 'expr' }
        subname : string;    { value is 'substr' }
        ifname : string;     { value is 'ifelse' }
        lenname : string;    { value is 'len' }
        chqname : string;    { value is 'changeq' }

        null : string;       { value is '' }
        lquote : character;  { left quote character }
        rquote : character;  { right quote character }
```

```
{ initmacro -- initialize variables for macro }
procedure initmacro;
begin
    null[1] := ENDSTR;
    { setstring(defname, 'define'); }
        defname[1] := ord('d');
        defname[2] := ord('e');
        defname[3] := ord('f');
        defname[4] := ord('i');
        defname[5] := ord('n');
        defname[6] := ord('e');
        defname[7] := ENDSTR;
    { setstring(subname, 'substr'); }
        subname[1] := ord('s');
        subname[2] := ord('u');
        subname[3] := ord('b');
        subname[4] := ord('s');
        subname[5] := ord('t');
        subname[6] := ord('r');
        subname[7] := ENDSTR;
    { setstring(exprname, 'expr'); }
        exprname[1] := ord('e');
        exprname[2] := ord('x');
        exprname[3] := ord('p');
        exprname[4] := ord('r');
        exprname[5] := ENDSTR;
    { setstring(ifname, 'ifelse'); }
        ifname[1] := ord('i');
        ifname[2] := ord('f');
        ifname[3] := ord('e');
        ifname[4] := ord('l');
        ifname[5] := ord('s');
        ifname[6] := ord('e');
        ifname[7] := ENDSTR;
    { setstring(lenname, 'len'); }
        lenname[1] := ord('l');
        lenname[2] := ord('e');
        lenname[3] := ord('n');
        lenname[4] := ENDSTR;
    { setstring(chqname, 'changeq'); }
        chqname[1] := ord('c');
        chqname[2] := ord('h');
        chqname[3] := ord('a');
        chqname[4] := ord('n');
        chqname[5] := ord('g');
        chqname[6] := ord('e');
        chqname[7] := ord('q');
        chqname[8] := ENDSTR;
    bp := 0; { pushback buffer pointer }
    inithash;
    lquote := ord(GRAVE);
    rquote := ord(ACUTE)
end;
```

PROGRAM

    `macro`   expand string definitions, with arguments

USAGE

    `macro`

FUNCTION

`macro` reads its input, looking for macro definitions of the form

       `define(ident,string)`

and writes its output with each subsequent instance of the identifier `ident` replaced by the arbitrary sequence of characters `string`.

Within a replacement string, any dollar sign `$` followed by a digit is replaced by an argument corresponding to that digit. Arguments are written as a parenthesized list of strings following an instance of the identifier, e.g.,

    `ident(arg1,arg2,...)`

So `$1` is replaced in the replacement string by `arg1`, `$2` by `arg2`, and so on; `$0` is replaced by `ident`. Missing arguments are taken as null strings; extra arguments are ignored.

The replacement string in a definition is expanded before the definition occurs, except that any sequence of characters between a grave ` and a balancing apostrophe ' is taken literally, with the grave and apostrophe removed. Thus, it is possible to make an alias for define by writing

    `define(def,`define($1,$2)')`

Additional predefined built-ins are:

`ifelse(a,b,c,d)` is replaced by the string c if the string a exactly matches the string b; otherwise it is replaced by the string d.

`expr(expression)` is replaced by the decimal string representation of the numeric value of `expression`. For correct operation, the expression must consist of parentheses, integer operands written as decimal digit strings, and the operators +, -, *, / (integer division), and % (remainder). Multiplication and division bind tighter than addition and subtraction, but parentheses may be used to alter this order.

`substr(s,m,n)` is replaced by the substring of s starting at location m (counting from one) and continuing at most n characters. If n is omitted, it is taken as a very large number; if m is outside the string, the replacement string is null. m and n may be expressions suitable for `expr`.

`len(s)` is replaced by the string representing the length of its argument in characters.

`changeq(xy)` changes the quote characters to x and y. `changeq()` changes them back to ` and '.

Each replacement string is rescanned for further possible replacements, permitting multi-level definitions to be expanded to final form.

EXAMPLE

The macro `len` could be written in terms of the other built-ins as:

    `define(`len',`ifelse($1,,0,`expr(1+len(substr($1,2)))')')`

BUGS

A recursive definition of the form `define(x,x)` will cause an infinite loop.

Expression evaluation is fragile. There is no unary minus.

It is unwise to use parentheses as quote characters.

Exercise 8-19. (Frivolous) Define a macro `reverse` that will reverse a string. □

Exercise 8-20. The function `expr` is particularly vulnerable to syntactically invalid expressions. How would you make it more robust? Is it worth it? □

Exercise 8-21. Define an `assert` macro that will cause conditional compilation of assertions in a program: if assertions are turned on,

```
        assert(i < j)
```

should expand into something like

```
        if (not (i < j)) then
            error('false assertion: i < j')
```

Can you invent a way to include either the name of the procedure or the assertion number as part of the message? You will probably also want to define macros that turn assertion checking off and on at desired places. □

Exercise 8-22. Modify doexpr to do arbitrary precision arithmetic. Can you handle floating point operations? Add an exponentiation operator and a base 2 logarithm operation. Add relational operators. □

Exercise 8-23. Modify the storage management facilities in macro so that arrays are managed by calls to Pascal's new function. Add command-line arguments to permit the sizes of arrays to be specified when the program is run, with sensible defaults. □

Exercise 8-24. What changes would you make to macro to adapt it to providing a macro capability for the format program of Chapter 7? □

8.7 Applications

Let us write macros to handle the string declaration that we have been using in our programs. Suppose that

```
        setstring(name,'text')
```

is a shorthand for

```
        { setstring(name,'text'); }
            name[1] := ord('t');
            name[2] := ord('e');
            name[3] := ord('x');
            name[4] := ord('t');
            name[5] := ENDSTR;
```

The task is to convert the setstring declaration into this expanded form. The solution comes in three parts. First we replicate the call with braces:

```
        { setstring(name,'text'); }
```

Then we loop over the characters between quotes, producing lines of the form

```
        name[i] := ord('c');
```

where c is the ith character of text. Finally we end with

```
        name[n+1] := ENDSTR;
```

where n is the length of text.
    setstring itself is

```
changeq(<>)
define(setstring,<{ <setstring>($1,$2); }
str($1,substr($2,2),0)   $1[len(substr($2,2))] := ENDSTR;
>)
```

where we have changed the quote characters to < and > to avoid difficulties
with the ' used in Pascal. The call `len(substr($2,2))` computes the effective string length (excluding the quotes but including the ENDSTR). `str` creates
the intervening `ord` statements:

```
define(str,<ifelse($2,',,   $1[expr($3+1)] := ord('substr($2,1,1)');
<str($1,substr($2,2),expr($3+1))>)>)
```

It isolates one character, increments the index, generates the line, and calls itself
recursively until it sees the terminating quote.

This is obviously not the most transparent programming language in the
world. It takes some getting used to before you can think of looping in terms of
recursion, although with practice you get the hang of it. But beware of becoming too clever with macros. In principle, `macro` is capable of performing any
computing task, but it is all too easy to write incomprehensible macros.

It is also the case that complicated recursive macro operations like
`setstring` can be painfully slow. For example, here are some statistics for
processing two short strings, of three and nine characters in length:

	#calls	CPU time(%)
putchr	4114	18.8
putback	3010	12.9
gettok	1694	11.9
isalphanum	3278	9.9
getpbc	3278	6.9
macro	1	5.9
puttok	1357	5.9
cscopy	534	5.9
length	520	4.0
putc	366	4.0
isletter	1201	2.0
getc	268	1.0
eval	91	1.0
equal	168	1.0
pbstr	243	1.0
push	391	1.0

Total time was 1.6 seconds.

This is a lot of procedure calls for such a small input; if you did nothing but
process `setstring` macros, it would be intolerable. Fortunately the use of
`macro` as a front end for a language processor tends to involve primarily substituting one string for another, as in `define`. This is much less demanding, so
processing an occasional `setstring` is quite practical. The added complexity

of `macro` costs very little extra for this kind of application; `macro` takes about ten percent longer than `define` on the same input.

The measurements above do indicate where attention can be most profitably directed if it is necessary to speed `macro` up. One possibility is to observe that some of the calls to `gettok` could be replaced by calls to `getpbc`, since only a single character is involved (for example, while processing bracketed text). More generally, there are a number of rather small routines which we wrote to modularize the program properly. Part of the cost of `macro` is the overhead of the procedure calling mechanism, which can be very inefficient on some machines. We can avoid much of this by replacing procedure calls by in-line code in these places (although we would do it by defining macros to replace the procedure bodies, not by writing out the code!). Specifically, since virtually all of the calls to `putchr` originate in `puttok`, `putchr` can be moved into `puttok` with only minor rearrangements. If characters are small positive integers, `isalphanum` and `isletter` can be replaced by in-line references to an array which contains the type of the corresponding character; this will essentially eliminate the cost of finding character types. And if the variables for the pushback buffer are used more widely, `getpbc` and `putback` can also be made in-line operations.

Although care is necessary to keep the program relatively clean, the payoff can be substantial. The original version of `macro`, written in the language C, was speeded up by a factor of about four by such transformations. Similar results could be expected in Pascal on many machines. The process should be as we have described several times here, however: write a clean program that implements an appropriate algorithm; measure it to identify the hot spots; refine those as cleanly as possible. Starting from the other end is a sure way to an unworkable mess.

One thing that can be done to make macros faster and more comprehensible is to increase the set of built-ins, so computations don't have to be spelled out in excruciating detail. Here are some suggestions.

Exercise 8-25. Add a tracing facility to dump the name and definition of each macro as it is encountered. □

Exercise 8-26. Add a built-in analogous to the `index` function defined in Chapter 2: `index(s1,s2)` should return the position of the string `s2` in the string `s1`, or zero if `s2` does not occur in `s1`. Can you do `index` with the existing facilities? Should you? □

Exercise 8-27. Add a `translit` built-in that performs transliterations similar to the `translit` program of Chapter 2. Add a built-in `match(s,r)` which returns the position where the regular expression `r` begins in the string `s`, or zero if it doesn't. □

Exercise 8-28. Write a macro `rpt(s,n)` that evaluates `s(1)`, `s(2)`, ..., `s(n)`. Add a built-in that does the same job. □

Exercise 8-29. Add a built-in that will cause the contents of a file to be copied in at the point where it is encountered, as with the `include` processor of Chapter 3. Make sure that the included text is also scanned for macros! □

Exercise 8-30. Add a built-in `divert(f)` to cause the output of `macro` to be appended to file `f` instead of the standard output. Add another built-in `incl(f)` that will copy file `f` to the standard output without macro scanning. These two built-ins make it possible to do significant rearrangements of the input. For example in a Pascal program you can collect all `const`'s, all `type`'s, etc., in an arbitrary order and output them in the proper order. □

Bibliographic Notes

There is a lot more to macro processing than we have room for here. *An Introduction to Macros* by M. Campbell-Kelly (American-Elsevier, 1973) provides a brief discussion of several different forms of macro processors. *Macro Processors and Techniques for Portable Software* by P. J. Brown (Wiley, 1974) goes into more detail on the subtle aspects of macro processing.

The PL/I macro preprocessor is an attempt to make a macro language that is essentially the same as a compiler language. This is discussed in various PL/I texts and in reference manuals for particular implementations. For example, see *IBM System/360 PL/I Language Specification,* IBM Form Y33-6003, or *Student Text: An Introduction to the Compile-Time Facilities of PL/I,* IBM Form C20-1689.

Macros have been valuable in making "portable" software — programs that move from one machine to another with much less effort than complete rewriting. The program is written in terms of a modest number of macros; nothing but the macros must be written for a particular environment. Snobol is probably the best known example of a major language so implemented. See R. E. Griswold, J. F. Poage and I. P. Polonsky, *The Snobol4 Programming Language,* Prentice-Hall, 1969, or R. E. Griswold, *The Macro Implementation of Snobol4,* Freeman, 1972. The book by Brown discusses other work in this area.

Any number of books on data structures deal with the problems of maintaining tables of information. As usual, one standard reference is D. E. Knuth's *The Art of Computer Programming* (Addison-Wesley). Volume 1 (1968) is concerned with data structures; Volume 3 (1973) discusses searching techniques in great detail, including the selection of hashing functions.

It is possible to augment Pascal with a macro processor, even more than we have done, to overcome some of its drawbacks. For a description of one such effort, see "MAP: A Pascal macro preprocessor for large program development," by D. E. Comer, *Software Practice and Experience,* March, 1979.

The `macro` processor described in this chapter was originally designed and implemented in C by D. M. Ritchie; we are grateful to him for letting us steal it.

EPILOGUE

We have come a long way. Eight chapters stuffed with code is a lot to negotiate. If you didn't assimilate all of it the first time through, don't worry — you weren't really expected to. Even the best of code takes time to absorb, and you seldom grasp all the implications until you try to use and modify a program. Much of what you learn about programming comes only from working with code: reading, revising and rereading.

Reading and *revising* are the key words. No program comes out a perfect work of art on its first draft, regardless of the techniques you use to write it. We rewrote every routine in this book several times, yet we still would not claim that any one is flawless. Extensive revision may sound like a costly and time-consuming luxury, but when the programs are clean and the modules small, it is not. Moreover you will find that with practice in reading and revising, your first versions get better and better, since you soon learn what to use and what to avoid, what is good style and what is not. Even so, rewriting will always remain an important part of programming.

The purpose of most rewriting is to simplify a program, to make it easier to understand, to keep its complexity manageable. *Controlling complexity* is the essence of computer programming. We will always be limited by the sheer number of details that we can keep straight in our heads. Much of what we have tried to teach in this book is how to cope with complexity.

At the lowest level, we were careful in our choice of control structures and in how we used the ones we chose. We found no need for the `goto` statement, for instance, and, somewhat surprisingly, little for the `case`. `if`'s are seldom nested more than two levels deep, save in the restricted form of `else if`'s for multi-way decisions. Loops generally are tested at the top, before it's too late. Procedures and functions rarely spread over more than one page; most are much shorter. As a result the code is readable. It is easy to convince yourself that a module is probably correct, because it is broken up into pieces that you can grasp one at a time and read in sequence.

Each module is also *cohesive:* it has good reasons for being a separate entity. It is not a tangle of multiple functions lumped arbitrarily, nor is it a displaced fragment of some other module. This means that we can describe the function

311

of each routine in a line or two. Further, the routine is written to *meet* this specification, a discipline far superior to writing a procedure that might be useful, then describing how it does what it does.

Several programs in this book comprise five hundred to a thousand lines of source code, yet none is conceptually "big." Each can be understood a module at a time, a section at a time. This is because the hierarchy of procedures was designed so that no one module has to know about much of the total problem, nor deal with more than a handful of immediate neighbors. There is little fear that a change in one part of the hierarchy will cause unexpected repercussions in another part, because the modules are kept as uncoupled as possible, and the coupling that exists is kept visible.

We tried to make the programs easy to modify, by hiding design decisions and data structures so that routines that don't need to know about them don't. We built checks and firewalls into the code so that errors and inconsistencies are detected quickly. We expressed details of character set, parameters and flags in terms of symbolic constants so that only one change is needed to alter a value throughout a program. We were also careful to isolate as much as possible of the operating system interface in a small set of primitives, so the bulk of the code is independent of the local environment.

Finally, at the highest level, we wrote programs so they could work together, so complex tasks could be implemented by *combining* existing programs instead of by writing new ones. Each program so used is just a module, with a particularly simple interface to others.

This is "structured programming" in the best sense of the term. It is clear that the method works, and works well, for real programs. The rewards are great. We can write comprehensible, reliable, robust code and remain relatively unaffected by major changes in implementation strategies and even by changes from one computer to another. Proper structure, at all levels, is not just nice, it is vital to the successful control of a complex job.

Besides these considerations of structure, we tried to convey some helpful guidelines for attacking a programming task. Like all questions of judgment, they are subject to debate, but we have found that they work well.

Principle 1 is the most important: *keep it simple*. At all levels, be as clean as possible, and write the simplest, clearest thing that will do the job. You can't be utterly naive, of course; common sense is still needed. When you choose an algorithm, there has to be some hope that it will be economical. But if implementation details and strategies are concealed, an inadequate algorithm can be changed without affecting much else. Since you are building tools, you also have to remember the people who will use your program, and make *their* task lighter, even at the expense of complicating your own. Fortunately, a uniform and regular design is often reflected in a clean interface for users.

Principle 2 is related: *build it in stages*. Undertake a complex task only in manageable steps. Concentrate on the central, most important aspects first;

don't get sidetracked on frills. If your basic plan is good, later additions will fit in smoothly. In the meantime, people can use what you already have produced, and their advice and experience should help you decide what comes next. You may even find that the part already built is adequate by itself. Ninety percent of the right job done well and available today is a lot more valuable than ninety-nine percent promised for sometime next month.

Principle 3 is intuitively appealing: *let someone else do the hard part*. Build on what you or others have already done, instead of starting from scratch each time. If you write a routine for something, make it general enough that it can be used again for a related job. In a larger context, you can often get a great deal of leverage by interfacing a small program to a large one — putting a macro or file inclusion processor in front of Pascal is a good example. And of course, whenever you can, let the machine do the work, for that is the ultimate purpose of building tools.

One complication you probably have no control over is your local computing environment. But even if it's horrible, as many are, you don't have to suffer stoically. Even a modest improvement of frequently used parts, like your programming and job control languages, is well worth while, and there's no excuse for not trying to conceal the worst aspects.

Keep these thoughts in mind as you look back over the book. Although our suggestions were made during the development of specific programs, the lessons they contain are applicable in general. The design principles and guidelines summarized here are an effective way to produce tools that work properly, and that work well with people and with other programs. That should be your goal for every program you write.

APPENDIX: **IMPLEMENTATION OF PRIMITIVES**

To support the programs presented in this book, there must be implemented a special environment within whatever Pascal environment you currently have available. In this appendix, we will document the demands made on this special environment, so that you can appreciate the choices made in the implementation provided for your use, or so that you can make your own implementation. We will also show you the details of some versions that we have developed. Studying these implementations ought to suggest ways to make the primitives work on your system.

Most of the burden falls on the primitive functions and procedures that were introduced in earlier chapters. These are best documented with manual pages like those provided for each of the programs presented in this book. But there must also be a "wrapper" or standard context of some sort, which provides for the declaration of various constants and types, possibly some variables, and certainly the primitives and other useful routines. The wrapper must also include the definition of the program you are writing, perform any initializations required by the support routines, call your main routine, and perhaps even tidy up after that call.

Thus the wrapper must contain:

A program header. The program name is generally irrelevant, but the file parameters `input` and `output` must be named, to support standard input and output files. The error output file may have to be named as well.

Constant and type definitions. Constants may be provided by using macro definitions and preprocessing each Pascal program to expand them, or by declaring `const` identifiers, or by introducing the names as members of an enumerated type. One constellation of names that is amenable to any of these treatments includes: `IOERROR`, `STDIN`, `STDOUT`, `STDERR`, and `MAXOPEN`. There are presumably `MAXOPEN`-3 other members of this group, corresponding to the file descriptors that are handed out by calls on `open` or `create`. However implemented, these are the values that may be assumed by the type `filedesc`.

Similarly, the second argument to `open` or `close` is a creature of type `integer` called the *mode*, which may typically take on only the values `IOREAD`

315

and `IOWRITE`, but the door is left open for other file access modes if they should be needed.

Variables of type `character` must accept `integer` values equal to the ordinal positions of all the printable characters, plus blank and other common codes such as backspace, tab, and newline. In addition, there must be two distinct values accepted for end-of-file, `ENDFILE`, and end-of-string, `ENDSTR`.

A whole slew of names are provided for values of type `character` corresponding to various common keyboard characters. Our list includes a name for every ASCII graphic (for example, `DOLLAR`, `UNDERLINE`, etc.) and even a couple of synonyms; a complete list occurs later.

Finally, variables of type `string` are arrays of `character` with a subscript ranging from 1 to `MAXSTR`.

Primitives. These are the dozen or so functions and procedures that perform all interaction with the operating environment, and hence must be tailored to suit the circumstances. We're almost ready to discuss them.

Utilities. Certain functions and procedures are used so widely that we made no attempt to `include` them selectively in the tools as presented. Thus, they must be represented by adding `#include` lines in the tools themselves, or by adding `external` declarations in a Pascal implementation that supports separate compilation, or by including them all in the off chance that they may be called upon. For either of the latter two approaches, here is the list of utilities that must be declared: `addstr`, `equal`, `esc`, `index`, `isalphanum`, `isdigit`, `isletter`, `islower`, `isupper`, `itoc`, `length`, `max`, `min`, `scopy`, `ctoi`, `fcopy`, `mustcreate`, `mustopen`, and `putdec`. The order of presentation satisfies any mutual dependencies, if the utilities are declared in this order following the primitives. Descriptions of the individual routines may be found throughout the text with the aid of the Index of First Lines.

The target program. This must be `included` after all the other declarations so the entire standard environment is available to the program to be run. Note that most of the programs given here contain further `#include` lines for subprocedures.

Initialization. Before the target program can be invoked, any data structures needed by the standard environment must be initialized. For instance, the file descriptors `STDIN`, `STDOUT`, and `STDERR` must be associated with the proper files, and all other file descriptors must be made available for subsequent `open` or `create` calls. This operation may be nonexistent on a Pascal that supports static data initialization; it may be trivial on a system that lacks this extension but provides for file redirection at the command line level; or it may require prompting for a command line and doing all of the above as part of the system interface.

Invoking the target program. Since this involves merely calling a procedure with no arguments, it would appear to require little attention. We have given each program a different procedure name for the sake of clarity, so the standard wrapper must be modified for each compilation to call the proper routine, or each program must be modified to have a standard name. If you are already using the macro processor to elaborate definitions or procedures such as `error`, changing the name of the procedure invoked is a small additional complexity. Otherwise, circumstances may dictate editing the tools once and for all.

Wrapup. Frequently this involves no extra code, but there may be work to do if, say, files are not automatically closed and preserved in a satisfactory fashion upon program termination.

So much for the wrapper!

Here are the manual pages for the primitives that must accompany the declarations described above. Note that the pages differ from manual pages for programs in two significant ways: the USAGE section shows how the primitive is declared, not how it is invoked; and there is a new section, RETURNS, that documents the values returned by functions, or written in `var` parameters by functions or procedures. Any other side effects, such as altering the state of a file, are also spelled out in the FUNCTION section. We omit the EXAMPLE sections here, since the book is replete with usage of the primitives.

PRIMITIVE

    `close`   close a file descriptor

USAGE

    `procedure close (fd : filedesc);`

FUNCTION

    `close` releases the file descriptor and any associated resources for a file opened by `open` or `create`.

RETURNS

    Nothing.

PRIMITIVE

    `create`   make a new instance of a file available

USAGE

    `function create (name : string; mode : integer) : filedesc;`

FUNCTION

    `create` makes the file with external name `name` available for the type of access specified by `mode`, by placing it under control of a file descriptor. If the file already exists, it is truncated to zero length, otherwise it is introduced as a new zero length file. In general, the only sensible value of `mode` is `IOWRITE`, for write access.

    The file remains under control of the file descriptor returned until explicitly disconnected by a `close` call, or until the program terminates.

RETURNS

    `create` returns `IOERROR` if the file cannot be accessed as desired, for any reason; otherwise it returns a value of type `filedesc` suitable for use with subsequent calls to `close`, `putcf`, `putstr`, or `seek`.

PRIMITIVE
    error   print a message and exit
USAGE
    procedure error ('your message here');
FUNCTION
    error writes the literal string specified to a highly visible place, such as the user's terminal, then performs an abnormal exit.
RETURNS
    Nothing. Moreover, error never returns control to its caller.

PRIMITIVE
    getarg   get a command line argument
USAGE
    function getarg (n : integer; var str : string; maxsize : integer)
        : boolean;
FUNCTION
    getarg writes up to maxsize characters (including an ENDSTR) of the nth command line argument into the string str. The first argument on the command line is argument number one. No error is reported if the argument string is truncated.
RETURNS
    getarg returns true if the argument is present, otherwise false.

PRIMITIVE
    getc   get a character from standard input
USAGE
    function getc (var c : character) : character;
FUNCTION
    getc reads at most one character from the standard input STDIN. If there are no more characters available, getc returns ENDFILE; if the input is at end-of-line, it returns NEWLINE and advances to the beginning of the next line; otherwise it returns the next input character.
RETURNS
    getc returns the value of type character corresponding to the character read from the standard input, or one of the special values NEWLINE or ENDFILE as specified above. The return value is also written in the argument c.

PRIMITIVE

  `getcf`   get a character from a file

USAGE

  `function getcf (var c : character; fd : filedesc) : character;`

FUNCTION

  `getcf` reads at most one character from the file specified by the file descriptor `fd`. If there are no more characters available, `getcf` returns `ENDFILE`; if the input is at end-of-line, it returns `NEWLINE` and advances to the beginning of the next line; otherwise it returns the next input character and points past it in the file.

RETURNS

  `getcf` returns the value of type `character` corresponding to the character read from the file, or one of the special values `NEWLINE` or `ENDFILE` as specified above. The return value is also written in the argument `c`.

PRIMITIVE

  `getline`   get a line of text from a file

USAGE

  `function getline (var str : string; fd : filedesc;`
    `maxsize : integer) : boolean;`

FUNCTION

  `getline` reads at most one line of text from the file specified by file descriptor `fd`. The characters are written into `str` up to and including the terminating `NEWLINE`; an `ENDSTR` is then appended to the input text. No more than `maxsize-1` characters are returned, so a line of length `maxsize-1` that does not end with `NEWLINE` has been truncated.

RETURNS

  `getline` returns `true` if a line is successfully obtained; `false` implies end of file.

PRIMITIVE

  `message`   print a message and continue

USAGE

  `procedure message ('your message here');`

FUNCTION

  `message` writes the literal string specified to a highly visible place, such as the user's terminal, then continues execution.

RETURNS

  Nothing.

PRIMITIVE

  `nargs`   get number of command line arguments

USAGE

  `function nargs : integer;`

FUNCTION

  `nargs` determines the number of arguments used on the command line that invoked the program, suitable for copying by `getarg`.

RETURNS

  `nargs` returns the number of arguments found on the command line, i.e., a number greater than or equal to zero.

PRIMITIVE
    open   make a file available for input or output
USAGE
```
function open (name : string; mode : integer) : filedesc;
```
FUNCTION
    open makes the file with external name name available for the type of access specified by mode. Legitimate values of mode are IOREAD for read access and IOWRITE for write access. No other values are currently defined. In either case, the file is not modified by the open call, and access commences with the first character of the file.
    The file remains associated with the file descriptor returned until explicitly disconnected by a close call, or until the program terminates.
RETURNS
    open returns IOERROR if the file cannot be accessed as desired, for any reason; otherwise it returns a value of type filedesc suitable for use with subsequent calls to close, getcf, getline, putcf, putstr, or seek.

PRIMITIVE
    putc   put a character on standard output
USAGE
```
procedure putc (c : character);
```
FUNCTION
    putc writes the character c to the standard output STDOUT; if the value of the argument c is NEWLINE, an appropriate end-of-line condition is generated.
RETURNS
    Nothing.

PRIMITIVE
    putcf   put a character in a file
USAGE
```
procedure putcf (c : character; fd : filedesc);
```
FUNCTION
    putcf writes the character c to the file specified by file descriptor fd; if the value of c is NEWLINE, an appropriate end-of-line condition is generated.
RETURNS
    Nothing.

PRIMITIVE
    putstr   put string in a file
USAGE
```
procedure putstr (var str : string; fd : filedesc);
```
FUNCTION
    putstr writes the characters in str, up to but not including the terminating ENDSTR, to the file specified by file descriptor fd. An unsuccessful write may or may not cause a warning message or early termination of the program.
RETURNS
    Nothing.

PRIMITIVE

   `remove`   remove a file

USAGE

   `procedure remove (name : string);`

FUNCTION

   `remove` causes the file with external name `name` to be discarded, i.e., a subsequent call to open with the same name will fail and a subsequent `create` will be obliged to make a new instance of the file. In general, the file to be removed should not be connected to any file descriptor at the time of the `remove` call.

RETURNS

   Nothing.

PRIMITIVE

   `seek`   position file access pointer

USAGE

   `procedure seek (recno : integer; fd : filedesc);`

FUNCTION

   `seek` positions the file controlled by `fd` so that a subsequent `read` or `write` call will access the record whose ordinal number is `recno`. Records are presumed to be of type `string`; the first record is number one.

RETURNS

   Nothing.

BUGS

   Our version of this primitive is far from general, having been written just to satisfy the needs of one form of the program `edit`. It assumes a system that can support simultaneous read and write access to the same file.

Note that `error` and `message` may have to be implemented as macros, since they each take an argument that is a variable length string and since `error` is obliged to terminate execution early; neither of these operations is easily encapsulated in a standard Pascal procedure.

The UC Berkeley Interpreter Primitives

Here are the environment and primitives we developed for the Pascal interpreter written at the University of California at Berkeley ("UCB") by Bill Joy and Charles Haley. These run on Unix, the system on which we did the original development of the programs.

We wrote these primitives in Pascal, which makes them relatively easy to understand, but it does mean that sometimes they are not especially efficient. A knowledgeable and serious user can generally make a substantial improvement in performance by speeding up the I/O primitives by fair means or foul. Furthermore, the interpreter does not make all Unix capabilities accessible, so some of the primitives are incomplete, notably in their handling of error returns.

Although they are far from fast, we used the `getc` and `putc` shown at the beginning of Chapter 1, because they are easy to explain, and because they really are independent of any particular Pascal system.

```
{ getc (UCB) -- get one character from standard input }
function getc (var c : character) : character;
var
     ch : char;
begin
     if eof then
          c := ENDFILE
     else if eoln then begin
          readln;
          c := NEWLINE
     end
     else begin
          read(ch);
          c := ord(ch)
     end;
     getc := c
end;


{ putc (UCB) -- put one character on standard output }
procedure putc (c : character);
begin
     if c = NEWLINE then
          writeln
     else
          write(chr(c))
end;
```

Once we get into more complicated situations, we must discuss the outer block that forms the surrounding context for all of the programs we presented. Each program was wrapped in an envelope that looks like this:

```
program outer (input, output);
#define error(s) begin message(s); halt end
#include "globdefs.p"
#include "prims.p"
#include "utility.p"
#include "program.p"
begin
     initio;
     program
end.
```

A few words of explanation are in order. *program* is the name of the outermost procedure of the program being run, for example, macro or archive. The *program* field is actually filled in by the command interpreter, but the details are not germane here. #include does file inclusion as described in Chapter 3; #define handles macro definitions as described in Chapter 8, though with a slightly different syntax. The procedure message is identical to writeln except that its output is guaranteed to appear on a user's terminal, so it is exactly our message primitive. halt causes a clean process termination. The file prims.p contains #include's for all primitives.

```
{ prims -- primitive functions and procedures for UCB }
#include "initio.p"
#include "open.p"
#include "create.p"
#include "getc.p"
#include "getcf.p"
#include "getline.p"
#include "putc.p"
#include "putcf.p"
#include "putstr.p"
#include "close.p"
#include "remove.p"
#include "getarg.p"
#include "nargs.p"
```

Similarly, utility.p contains #include lines for routines like scopy that may be freely used by any program.

```
{ utility -- generally useful functions and procedures }
#include "addstr.p"
#include "equal.p"
#include "esc.p"
#include "index.p"
#include "isalphanum.p"
#include "isdigit.p"
#include "isletter.p"
#include "islower.p"
#include "isupper.p"
#include "itoc.p"
#include "length.p"
#include "max.p"
#include "min.p"
#include "scopy.p"
#include "ctoi.p"
#include "fcopy.p"
#include "mustcreate.p"
#include "mustopen.p"
#include "putdec.p"
```

The file globdefs.p contains all const and type declarations and some variables for the I/O system:

```
{ globdefs (UCB) -- global constants, types and variables }

const

{ standard file descriptors. subscripts in open, etc. }
    STDIN = 1;        { these are not to be changed }
    STDOUT = 2;
    STDERR = 3;

{ other io-related stuff }
    IOERROR = 0;      { status values for open files }
    IOAVAIL = 1;
    IOREAD = 2;
    IOWRITE = 3;
    MAXOPEN = 10;     { maximum number of open files }

{ universal manifest constants }
    ENDFILE = -1;
    ENDSTR = 0;       { null-terminated strings }
    MAXSTR = 100;     { longest possible string }

{ ascii character set in decimal }
    BACKSPACE = 8;
    TAB = 9;
    NEWLINE = 10;
    BLANK = 32;
    EXCLAM = 33;      { ! }
    DQUOTE = 34;      { " }
    SHARP = 35;       { # }
    DOLLAR = 36;      { $ }
    PERCENT = 37;     { % }
    AMPER = 38;       { & }
    SQUOTE = 39;      { ' }
    ACUTE = SQUOTE;
    LPAREN = 40;      { ( }
    RPAREN = 41;      { ) }
    STAR = 42;        { * }
    PLUS = 43;        { + }
    COMMA = 44;       { , }
    MINUS = 45;       { - }
    DASH = MINUS;
    PERIOD = 46;      { . }
    SLASH = 47;       { / }
    COLON = 58;       { : }
    SEMICOL = 59;     { ; }
    LESS = 60;        { < }
    EQUALS = 61;      { = }
    GREATER = 62;     { > }
    QUESTION = 63;    { ? }
```

```
    ATSIGN = 64;      { @ }
    ESCAPE = ATSIGN;
    LBRACK = 91;      { [ }
    BACKSLASH = 92;   { \ }
    RBRACK = 93;      { ] }
    CARET = 94;       { ^ }
    UNDERLINE = 95;   { _ }
    GRAVE = 96;       { ` }
    LETA = 97;        { lower case ... }
    LETB = 98;
    LETC = 99;
    LETD = 100;
    LETE = 101;
    LETF = 102;
    LETG = 103;
    LETH = 104;
    LETI = 105;
    LETJ = 106;
    LETK = 107;
    LETL = 108;
    LETM = 109;
    LETN = 110;
    LETO = 111;
    LETP = 112;
    LETQ = 113;
    LETR = 114;
    LETS = 115;
    LETT = 116;
    LETU = 117;
    LETV = 118;
    LETW = 119;
    LETX = 120;
    LETY = 121;
    LETZ = 122;
    LBRACE = 123;     { left brace }
    BAR = 124;        { ¦ }
    RBRACE = 125;     { right brace }
    TILDE = 126;      { ~ }

type
    character = -1..127;  { byte-sized. ascii + other stuff }
    string = array [1..MAXSTR] of character;
    filedesc = IOERROR..MAXOPEN;
    ioblock = record     { to keep track of open files }
        filevar : text;
        mode : IOERROR..IOWRITE;
    end;

var
    openlist : array [1..MAXOPEN] of ioblock; { open files }
```

This file is actually pretty machine-independent. Our version uses the ASCII character set and other conventions suitable for a Unix environment.

Each open file has a record that contains the `file` variable and the mode. These records are contained in the array `openlist`, indexed by file descriptor. The procedure `initio` sets up the open file environment by initializing `openlist`. The only magic is arranging for `STDERR` to be connected to the user's terminal.

```
{ initio (UCB) -- initialize open file list }
procedure initio;
var
    i : filedesc;
begin
    openlist[STDIN].mode := IOREAD;
    openlist[STDOUT].mode := IOWRITE;
    openlist[STDERR].mode := IOWRITE;

    { connect STDERR to user's terminal ... }
    rewrite(openlist[STDERR].filevar, '/dev/tty ');

    for i := STDERR+1 to MAXOPEN do
        openlist[i].mode := IOAVAIL;
end;
```

With initialization out of the way, we can look at `open` and `create`. Both rely on non-standard forms of `reset` and `rewrite` that permit a filename argument to be given. Regrettably, there is no way to regain control if the file access fails, so these routines never actually return `IOERROR` after failure — in fact they never return at all. Access failures are handled by the run-time environment before `open` or `create` get a chance.

```pascal
{ open (UCB) -- open a file for reading or writing }
{    non-portable -- uses the Berkeley interface to Unix }
{    no status can be returned, unfortunately }
function open (var name : string; mode : integer) : filedesc;
var
    i : integer;
    intname : array [1..MAXSTR] of char;
    found : boolean;
begin
    i := 1;
    while (name[i] <> ENDSTR) do begin
        intname[i] := chr(name[i]);
        i := i + 1
    end;
    for i := i to MAXSTR do
        intname[i] := ' ';   { pad name with blanks }
    { find a free slot in openlist }
    open := IOERROR;
    found := false;
    i := 1;
    while (i <= MAXOPEN) and (not found) do begin
        if (openlist[i].mode = IOAVAIL) then begin
            openlist[i].mode := mode;
            if (mode = IOREAD) then
                reset(openlist[i].filevar, intname)
            else
                rewrite(openlist[i].filevar, intname);
            open := i;
            found := true
        end;
        i := i + 1
    end
end;
```

```
{ create (UCB) -- create a file }
{    non-portable -- uses the Berkeley interface to Unix }
{    no status can be returned, unfortunately }
function create (var name : string; mode : integer) : filedesc;
var
    i : integer;
    intname : array [1..MAXSTR] of char;
    found : boolean;
begin
    i := 1;
    while (name[i] <> ENDSTR) do begin
        intname[i] := chr(name[i]);
        i := i + 1
    end;
    for i := i to MAXSTR do
        intname[i] := ' ';   { pad name with blanks }
    { find a free slot in openlist }
    create := IOERROR;
    found := false;
    i := 1;
    while (i <= MAXOPEN) and (not found) do begin
        if (openlist[i].mode = IOAVAIL) then begin
            openlist[i].mode := mode;
            rewrite(openlist[i].filevar, intname);
            if (mode = IOREAD) then
                reset(openlist[i].filevar, intname);
            create := i;
            found := true
        end;
        i := i + 1
    end
end;
```

close calls the UCB procedure flush to force out any remaining buffered output, then marks the file descriptor available.

```
{ close (UCB) -- release file descriptor slot for open file }
procedure close (fd : filedesc);
begin
    if (fd > STDERR) and (fd <= MAXOPEN) then begin
        flush(openlist[fd].filevar);    { in case buffered }
        openlist[fd].mode := IOAVAIL
    end
end;
```

Our version of remove does nothing but print a message, since we found it helpful for debugging to leave the temporary files in place. This would obviously need fixing in a production implementation.

```
{ remove (UCB) -- remove file s from file system }
{   this version just prints a message }
procedure remove (var s : string);
begin
    message('If we had remove, we would be removing ');
    putcf(TAB, STDERR);
    putstr(s, STDERR);
    putcf(NEWLINE, STDERR);
    flush(openlist[STDERR].filevar)
end;
```

getline and putstr are straightforward loops that call getcf and putcf.

```
{ getline (UCB) -- get a line from file }
function getline (var s : string; fd : filedesc;
        maxsize : integer) : boolean;
var
    i : integer;
    c : character;
begin
    i := 1;
    repeat
        s[i] := getcf(c, fd);
        i := i + 1
    until (c = ENDFILE) or (c = NEWLINE) or (i >= maxsize);
    if (c = ENDFILE) then   { went one too far }
        i := i - 1;
    s[i] := ENDSTR;
    getline := (c <> ENDFILE)
end;


{ putstr (UCB) -- put out string on file }
procedure putstr (var s : string; f : filedesc);
var
    i : integer;
begin
    i := 1;
    while (s[i] <> ENDSTR) do begin
        putcf(s[i], f);
        i := i + 1
    end
end;
```

getcf and putcf are essentially the same as getc and putc.

```
{ getcf (UCB) -- get one character from file }
function getcf (var c: character; fd : filedesc) : character;
var
    ch : char;
begin
    if (fd = STDIN) then
        getcf := getc(c)
    else if eof(openlist[fd].filevar) then
        c := ENDFILE
    else if eoln(openlist[fd].filevar) then begin
        read(openlist[fd].filevar, ch);
        c := NEWLINE
    end
    else begin
        read(openlist[fd].filevar, ch);
        c := ord(ch)
    end;
    getcf := c
end;


{ putcf (UCB) -- put a single character on file fd }
procedure putcf (c : character; fd : filedesc);
begin
    if (fd = STDOUT) then
        putc(c)
    else if c = NEWLINE then
        writeln(openlist[fd].filevar)
    else
        write(openlist[fd].filevar, chr(c))
end;
```

Next we come to getarg and nargs. The UCB system provides a function called argv(n,s) that returns the nth argument as a packed array of char in s, and a function argc that returns the number of arguments. Both argv and argc include the command that invoked the program as argument 0. argv can do nothing sensible about trailing blanks, so neither does getarg.

```
{ nargs (UCB) -- return number of arguments }
{   non-portable.  uses Berkeley conventions }
function nargs : integer;
begin
    nargs := argc - 1
end;
```

```
{ getarg (UCB) -- copy n-th command line argument into s }
{   uses the Berkeley function argv(i,s), }
{   which returns the 0th to argc-1th argument in s. }
function getarg (n : integer; var s : string;
        maxs : integer) : boolean;
var
    arg : array [1..MAXSTR] of char;
    i, lnb : integer;
begin
    lnb := 0;
    if (n >= 0) and (n < argc) then begin    { in the list }
        argv(n, arg);    { get the argument }
        for i := 1 to MAXSTR-1 do begin
            s[i] := ord(arg[i]);
            if arg[i] <> ' ' then
                lnb := i
        end;
        getarg := true
    end
    else
        getarg := false;
    s[lnb+1] := ENDSTR
end;
```

Our version of seek is just barely adequate to make edit work; it is in no way a general implementation. It is grossly inefficient for backwards seeks.

```
{ seek (UCB) -- special version of primitive for edit }
procedure seek (recno : integer; var fd : filedesc);
var
    junk : boolean;
    temp : string;
begin
    flush(openlist[scrout].filevar);  { necessary for UCB }
    if (recno < recin) then begin
        close(fd);
        { cheat: open scratch file by name }
        fd := mustopen(edittemp, IOREAD);
        recin := 1;
    end;
    while (recin < recno) do begin
        junk := getline(temp, fd, MAXSTR);
        recin := recin + 1
    end
end;
```

The Whitesmiths Primitives

The Pascal compiler developed by Whitesmiths, Ltd., uses many of the techniques described in this book to obtain a high degree of portability. All interaction with a host operating system is performed through about a dozen primitive functions; all input/output is translated to the same uniform internal form as is used here; all system interfaces support command line file redirection; and a preprocessor for file inclusion and macro definition is part of the standard language package. Consequently, most of the work of providing an interface to the tools in this book is caused by slight differences in naming conventions and argument types.

The primitives for the interpreter and compiler from the Free University of Amsterdam (developed by Andy Tanenbaum and Johan Stevenson) and for the UCB compiler for the DEC VAX are quite similar to the Whitesmiths primitives because these systems all support external procedures.

The Whitesmiths implementation of Pascal is currently available for the PDP-11 (Unix, Idris, RSX-11, RT-11, IAS), Intel 8080 and Zilog Z/80 (CP/M and CDOS), VAX-11 (Unix and VMS), and for the Motorola MC68000 (VERSAdos).*

A program is assembled by the define/include preprocessor, from three sources: a standard header that defines the environment, the procedure to be run, and a simple program body that calls the procedure. Since this implementation of Pascal permits separate compilation, most of the environment consists of `external` function declarations. Thus, the wrapper is:

---

*Idris is a trademark of Whitesmiths, Ltd. RSX-11, RT-11, and IAS are trademarks of Digital Equipment Corporation. CP/M is a trademark of Digital Research. VERSAdos is a trademark of Motorola, Inc.

```
{ prims -- external declarations for Whitesmiths primitives }
program xxx (input, output, errout);
#include <tools.h>

{ Environment supplied primitives ... }
procedure close (fd : filedesc);
    external;
procedure exit (status : boolean);
    external;
function getarg (n : integer; var str : string;
        maxsize : integer) : boolean;
    external;
function nargs : integer;
    external;
procedure remove (name : string);
    external;

{ Externally supplied primitive interfaces ... }
function getc (var c : character) : character;
    external;
function getcf (var c : character; fd : filedesc)
        : character;
    external;
function getline (var str : string; fd : filedesc) : boolean;
    external;
function pcreate (var name : string; mode : integer)
        : filedesc;
    external;
function popen (var name : string; mode : integer) : filedesc;
    external;
procedure pputstr (var str : string; fd : filedesc);
    external;
procedure putc (c : character);
    external;
procedure putcf (c : character; fd : filedesc);
    external;

{ Externally supplied utilities ... }
function addstr (c : character; var outset : string;
        var j : integer; maxset : integer) : boolean;
    external;
function ctoi (var s : string; var i : integer) : integer;
    external;
function equal (var str1, str2 : string) : boolean;
    external;
function esc (var s : string; var i : integer) : character;
    external;
procedure fcopy (fin, fout : filedesc);
    external;
```

```
function index (var s : string; c : character) : integer;
    external;
function isalphanum (c : character) : boolean;
    external;
function isletter (c : character) : boolean;
    external;
function islower (c : character) : boolean;
    external;
function isupper (c : character) : boolean;
    external;
function itoc (n : integer; var str : string; i : integer)
        : integer;
    external;
function length (var s : string) : integer;
    external;
function max (x, y : integer) : integer;
    external;
function min (x, y : integer) : integer;
    external;
procedure putdec (n, w : integer);
    external;
procedure scopy (var src : string; i : integer;
        var dest : string; j : integer);
    external;

{ Internally supplied primitives ... }
function create (var name : string; mode : integer)
        : filedesc;
begin
    create := pcreate(name, mode)
end;

function open (var name : string; mode : integer) : filedesc;
begin
    open := popen(name, mode)
end;

procedure putstr (var str : string; fd : filedesc);
begin
    pputstr(str, fd)
end;

#include <mustcreate.p>
#include <mustopen.p>

{ The body in question ... }
    { procedure included here }
begin
    { procedure called here }
end.
```

Various constants and type declarations are off-loaded to a separate header file `tools.h`; the angle brackets in "`#include <tools.h>`" signal the preprocessor to obtain the header from a standard place in the file system. We chose to `#define` most constants, to ease the burden on the Pascal translator, which may have to operate in restricted memory; for the most part, the values are identical to those shown above for the UCB system, so we show only part of the file.

```
{ tools.h -- definitions and types for WS primitives }
...
#define IOERROR -1
#define STDIN   0
#define STDOUT  1
#define STDERR  2
#define MAXOPEN 8

#define IOREAD  0
#define IOWRITE 1

#define MAXSTR   100

type
    character = -128..127;
    filedesc = integer;
    string = array [1..MAXSTR] of character;

#define message(str)    writeln(errout, str)
#define error(str)  begin message(str); exit(false) end
#define isdigit(c)  ((ord('0') <= c) and (c <= ord('9')))
```

Characters are stored as one-byte integers; `message`, `error`, and `isdigit` have been implemented as macros.

The primitives `close`, `getarg`, `nargs`, and `remove` are implemented by direct calls to the standard system interface routines provided with this Pascal. Others require some adaptation, and are provided as a library of separately compiled modules. Still others, such as `create`, `open`, `putstr`, `mustcreate`, and `mustopen` are provided directly in the header file, to avoid publishing external names that would collide with standard routines having slightly different meaning in this environment.

Our primitive `create`, for instance, ends up calling an externally defined function `pcreate`, which in turn calls the underlying operating system routine, whose name is also `create`.

```
{ pcreate (WS) -- Pascal create primitive }
function create (var name : string; mode, rsize : integer)
       : filedesc;
    external;

function pcreate (var name : string; mode : integer)
       : filedesc;
var
    fd : filedesc;
begin
    fd := create(name, mode, 0);
    if (fd < 0) then
        fd := IOERROR;
    pcreate := fd
end;
```

popen, used by open, is very similar, since it has to deal with the same kind of name conflict.

```
{ popen (WS) -- Pascal open primitive }
function open (var name : string; mode, rsize : integer)
       : filedesc;
    external;

function popen (var name : string; mode : integer)
       : filedesc;
var
    fd : filedesc;
begin
    fd := open(name, mode, 0);
    if (fd < 0) then
        fd := IOERROR;
    popen := fd
end;
```

The current implementation of getc and getcf is to read one character at a time. This is inefficient under Unix, where read is a system call; other implementations buffer input more effectively.

```
{ getc and getcf (WS) -- get one character of input }
function read (fd : filedesc; var c : character;
      size : integer) : boolean;
   external;

function getc (var c : character) : character;
begin
   if (not read(STDIN, c, 1)) then
      c := ENDFILE;
   getc := c
end;

function getcf(var c : character; fd : filedesc) : character;
begin
   if (not read(fd, c, 1)) then
      c := ENDFILE;
   getcf := c
end;
```

getline is a bit more elaborate, but uses the same approach:

```
{ getline (WS) -- get a line from file }
function read (fd : filedesc; var c : character;
      size : integer) : boolean;
   external;

function getline (var s : string; fd : filedesc;
      maxsize : integer) : boolean;
var
   i : integer;
   c : character;
   done : boolean;
begin
   i := 1;
   done := false;
   repeat
      if (read(fd, c, 1)) then
         s[i] := c
      else
         done := true;
      i := i + 1
   until (done) or (c = NEWLINE) or (i >= maxsize);
   if (done) then   { went one too far }
      i := i - 1;
   s[i] := ENDSTR;
   getline := (not done)
end;
```

putc, putcf and putstr are even simpler than the input routines:

```
{ putc and putcf (WS) -- put one character of output }
procedure write (fd : filedesc; var c : character;
        size : integer);
    external;

procedure putc (c : character);
begin
    write(STDOUT, c, 1)
end;

procedure putcf(c : character; fd : filedesc);
begin
    write(fd, c, 1)
end;

{ pputstr (WS) -- Pascal putstr primitive }
procedure write (fd : filedesc; var c : string;
        size : integer);
    external;

procedure pputstr (var str : string; fd : filedesc);
var
    i : integer;
begin
    i := 1;
    while (str[i] <> ENDSTR) do
        i := i + 1;
    if (i > 1) then
        write(fd, str, i-1)
end;
```

Finally, seek is specialized to edit:

```
{ seek (WS) -- special version of primitive for edit }
procedure lseek (fd : filedesc; off, hioff, mode : integer);
    external;    { PDP-11 long format only }

procedure seek (recno : integer; fd : filedesc);
begin
    lseek(scrout, 0, MAXSTR * recno, 0)
end;
```

The UCSD Primitives

The University of California at San Diego has developed a stand-alone system, under the direction of Ken Bowles, for entering and interpretively executing Pascal on microcomputers. Now distributed by Softech Microsystems, Inc., UCSD Pascal is available for a variety of configurations using: the Zilog Z/80, the Intel 8080 and 8085, Signetics 6502, Motorola 6800 and 6809, Texas

Instruments 9900, and the DEC LSI-11.†

This implementation is substantially more difficult than the others, because the UCSD system has no provision for command line entry, much less file redirection; even the editing of typed input lines is left to the discretion of each program. And files must be closed properly upon program termination, lest newly created files be discarded.

We assembled the pieces of each program on a larger computer, using an existing define/include processor as before, then wrote them to diskettes for operation under the UCSD system. The same operation can, of course, be performed entirely under UCSD, provided the #defines are changed to the format expected by macro. Here is the wrapper we used:

```
{ prims -- external declarations for UCSD primitives }
program xxx (input, output);
{ Copyright (c) 1981 by Bell Telephone Laboratories, Inc.
  and Whitesmiths, Ltd. }

#include <chars.h>
#define error(str)  begin message(str); exit(program) end
#define isdigit(c)  ((ord('0') <= c) and (c <= ord('9')))
#define message(str)    writeln(str)

const
    IOERROR = 0;    { filedesc constants }
    STDIN = 1;
    STDOUT = 2;
    STDERR = 3;
    MAXOPEN = 7;

    IOREAD = 0;     { mode constants }
    IOWRITE = 1;

    MAXCMD = 20;    { limits }
    MAXSTR = 100;
type
    character = -128..127;
    filedesc = IOERROR..MAXOPEN;
    xstring = array [1..MAXSTR] of character;
    filtyp = (CLOSED, STDIO, FIL1, FIL2, FIL3, FIL4);
```

---

† UCSD Pascal is a trademark of the Regents of the University of California. LSI-11 is a trademark of Digital Equipment Corporation.

```
var
    cmdargs : 0..MAXCMD;
    cmdidx : array [1..MAXCMD] of 1..MAXSTR;
    cmdlin : xstring;
    cmdfil : array [STDIN..MAXOPEN] of filtyp;
    cmdopen : array [filtyp] of boolean;
    file1, file2, file3, file4 : text;
    kbdline : xstring;
    kbdn : integer;
    kbdnext : integer;

procedure scopy (var src : xstring; i : integer;
        var dest : xstring; j : integer);
begin
    while (src[i] <> ENDSTR) do begin
        dest[j] := src[i];
        i := i + 1;
        j := j + 1
    end;
    dest[j] := ENDSTR
end;

{ the primitives }
#include <getkbd.p>
#include <getc.p>
#include <getline.p>
#include <putc.p>
#include <getarg.p>
#include <nargs.p>
#include <close.p>
#include <open.p>
#include <remove.p>

{ alias names that collide }
#define close    xclose
#define string   xstring

{ utilities }
#include <addstr.p>
#include <equal.p>
#include <esc.p>
#include <index.p>
#include <isalphanum.p>
#include <isletter.p>
#include <islower.p>
#include <isupper.p>
#include <itoc.p>
#include <length.p>
#include <max.p>
```

```
#include <min.p>
#include <ctoi.p>
#include <fcopy.p>
#include <mustcreate.p>
#include <mustopen.p>
#include <putdec.p>

{ command line input and file redirection }
#include <initcmd.p>

    { procedure included here }
begin
    initcmd;
    { procedure called here }
    endcmd
end.
```

The header file chars.h has the same character constant definitions as the previously discussed tools.h and globdefs.p files. Other types are also much the same, except that string must be changed to xstring to avoid collision with the special UCSD type needed to represent file names. Note that close is similarly redefined, for all files other than those holding the primitives.

At program startup, the interface prompts for a command line by writing '$ ' to the terminal, then accepts a line of input. This is parsed into command arguments, which are stored in the buffer cmdlin and pointed at by indices in the array cmdidx. File redirection of the form <infile or >outfile causes the array cmdfil to be altered to indicate the opened or created files.

Normally, the elements cmdfil[STDIN], cmdfil[STDOUT], and cmdfil[STDERR] contain the code STDIO (the rest are CLOSED); but they can take on the values FIL1 through FIL4 to indicate that they control one of the four text variables file1 through file4. All this machinery is required because UCSD Pascal doesn't support arrays of files, or pointers to files, or records containing files. It is administered primarily by the functions packaged in open.p:

```
{ ftalloc -- allocate a file }
function ftalloc : filtyp;
var
    done : boolean;
    ft : filtyp;
begin
    ft := FIL1;
    repeat
        done := (not cmdopen[ft] or (ft = FIL4));
        if (not done) then
            ft := succ(ft)
    until (done);
    if (cmdopen[ft]) then
        ftalloc := CLOSED
    else
        ftalloc := ft
end;


{ fdalloc -- allocate a file descriptor }
function fdalloc : filedesc;
var
    done : boolean;
    fd : filedesc;
begin
    fd := STDIN;
    done := false;
    while (not done) do
        if ((cmdfil[fd] = CLOSED) or (fd = MAXOPEN)) then
            done := true
        else
            fd := succ(fd);
    if (cmdfil[fd] <> CLOSED) then
        fdalloc := IOERROR
    else begin
        cmdfil[fd] := ftalloc;
        if (cmdfil[fd] = CLOSED) then
            fdalloc := IOERROR
        else begin
            cmdopen[cmdfil[fd]] := true;
            fdalloc := fd
        end
    end
end;
```

```
    { strname -- map to native string filename }
    procedure strname (var str : string; var xstr : xstring);
    var
        i : integer;
    begin
        str := '.text';
        i := 1;
        while (xstr[i] <> ENDSTR) do begin
            insert('x', str, i);
            str[i] := chr(xstr[i]);
            i := i + 1
        end
    end;

{ create (UCSD) -- create a file }
(*$I-*)
function create (var name : xstring; mode : integer) : filedesc;
var
    fd : filedesc;
    snm : string;
begin
    fd := fdalloc;
    if (fd <> IOERROR) then begin
        strname(snm, name);
        case (cmdfil[fd]) of
        FIL1:
            rewrite(file1, snm);
        FIL2:
            rewrite(file2, snm);
        FIL3:
            rewrite(file3, snm);
        FIL4:
            rewrite(file4, snm)
        end;
        if (ioresult <> 0) then begin
            xclose(fd);
            fd := IOERROR
        end
    end;
    create := fd
end;
(*$I+*)
```

```
{ open (UCSD) -- open a file for reading or writing }
(*$I-*)
function open (var name : xstring; mode : integer) : filedesc;
var
     fd : filedesc;
     snm : string;
begin
     fd := fdalloc;
     if (fd <> IOERROR) then begin
         strname(snm, name);
         case (cmdfil[fd]) of
         FIL1:
             reset(file1, snm);
         FIL2:
             reset(file2, snm);
         FIL3:
             reset(file3, snm);
         FIL4:
             reset(file4, snm)
         end;
         if (ioresult <> 0) then begin
             xclose(fd);
             fd := IOERROR
         end
     end;
     open := fd
end;
(*$I+*)
```

UCSD Pascal provides for opening files by name with the nonstandard functions reset(file, name) and rewrite(file, name). Here, name is of the special built-in type string, which is not the same as ours, so the procedure strname is required to translate between forms. Note that we elected to make all file names end in .text, so they are compatible with the compiler and editor with a minimum of fuss.

The peculiar comments (*$I-*) and (*$I+*) serve to disable automatic error checking after a reset or rewrite. Thus, the primitives are able to retain control after a failure, and can detect the failure by calling the nonstandard function ioresult.

The last of the variables declared in the wrapper are used to keep track of input lines typed at the terminal keyboard. A whole line must be input before any of it can be read, to permit deletion of erroneous input by backspacing over it. Input lines are read and edited by getkbd:

```
{ getkbd -- read character from keyboard }
function getkbd (var c : character) : character;
var
    done : boolean;
    ch : char;
begin
    if (kbdn <= 0) then begin
        kbdnext := 1;
        done := false;
        if (kbdn = -2) then begin
            readln;
            kbdn := 0
        end
        else if (kbdn < 0) then
            done := true;
        while (not done) do begin
            kbdn := kbdn + 1;
            done := true;
            if (eof) then
                kbdn := -1
            else if (eoln) then begin
                kbdn := kbdn - 1;
                kbdline[kbdn] := NEWLINE
            end
            else if (MAXSTR-1 <= kbdn) then begin
                writeln('line too long');
                kbdline[kbdn] := NEWLINE
            end
            else begin
                read(ch);
                kbdline[kbdn] := ord(ch);
                if (kbdline[kbdn] <> BACKSPACE) then
                    { do nothing }
                else if (1 < kbdn) then
                    kbdn := kbdn - 2
                else
                    kbdn := kbdn - 1;
                done := false
            end
        end
    end;
    if (kbdn <= 0) then
        c := ENDFILE
    else begin
        c := kbdline[kbdnext];
        kbdnext := kbdnext + 1;
        if (c = NEWLINE) then
            kbdn := -2
        else
```

```
                    kbdn := kbdn - 1
            end;
            getkbd := c;
        end;
```

getkbd is called as needed by getcf, which maps a file descriptor into
either a keyboard read request or a file read:

```
{ fgetcf -- get character from file }
function fgetcf (var fil : text) : character;
var
    ch : char;
begin
    if (eof(fil)) then
        fgetcf := ENDFILE
    else if (eoln(fil)) then begin
        readln(fil);
        fgetcf := NEWLINE
    end
    else begin
        read(fil, ch);
        fgetcf := ord(ch)
    end;
end;


{ getcf (UCSD) -- get one character from file }
function getcf (var c : character; fd : filedesc)
        : character;
begin
    case (cmdfil[fd]) of
    STDIO:
        c := getkbd(c);
    FIL1:
        c := fgetcf(file1);
    FIL2:
        c := fgetcf(file2);
    FIL3:
        c := fgetcf(file3);
    FIL4:
        c := fgetcf(file4)
    end;
    getcf := c
end;


{ getc (UCSD) -- get one character from standard input }
function getc (var c : character) : character;
begin
    getc := getcf(c, STDIN)
end;
```

getline is implemented in terms of getcf, which causes a noticeable loss of efficiency, but makes for more readable code:

```
{ getline (UCSD) -- get a line from file }
function getline (var str : xstring; fd : filedesc;
        size : integer) : boolean;
var
    i : integer;
    done : boolean;
    ch : character;
begin
    i := 0;
    repeat
        done := true;
        ch := getcf(ch, fd);
        if (ch = ENDFILE) then
            i := 0
        else if (ch = NEWLINE) then begin
            i := i + 1;
            str[i] := NEWLINE
        end
        else if (size-2 <= i) then begin
            message('line too long');
            i := i + 1;
            str[i] := NEWLINE
        end
        else begin
            done := false;
            i := i + 1;
            str[i] := ch
        end
    until (done);
    str[i + 1] := ENDSTR;
    getline := (0 < i)
end;
```

The constellation of output routines is quite similar to those for input, but much simpler:

```
{ fputcf -- put a character to file }
procedure fputcf (c : character; var fil : text);
begin
    if (c = NEWLINE) then
        writeln(fil)
    else
        write(fil, chr(c))
end;
```

```
{ putcf (UCSD) -- put a single character on fd }
procedure putcf (c : character; fd : filedesc);
begin
    case (cmdfil[fd]) of
    STDIO:
        fputcf(c, output);
    FIL1:
        fputcf(c, file1);
    FIL2:
        fputcf(c, file2);
    FIL3:
        fputcf(c, file3);
    FIL4:
        fputcf(c, file4)
    end
end;

{ putc (UCSD) -- put one character on standard output }
procedure putc (c : character);
begin
    putcf(c, STDOUT)
end;

{ putstr (UCSD) -- put out string on file }
procedure putstr (str : xstring; fd : filedesc);
var
    i : integer;
begin
    i := 1;
    while (str[i] <> ENDSTR) do begin
        putcf(str[i], fd);
        i := i + 1
    end
end;
```

Before the target program is called, initcmd is called to initialize the various input/output variables and to read the command line. All of this work can be done in fairly conventional Pascal, given the other primitives:

```
{ initcmd (UCSD) -- read command line and redirect files }
procedure initcmd;
var
    fd : filedesc;
    fname : xstring;
    ft : filtyp;
    idx : 1 .. MAXSTR;
    junk : boolean;
begin
    cmdfil[STDIN] := STDIO;
    cmdfil[STDOUT] := STDIO;
    cmdfil[STDERR] := STDIO;
    for fd := succ(STDERR) to MAXOPEN do
        cmdfil[fd] := CLOSED;
    write('$ ');
    for ft := FIL1 to FIL4 do
        cmdopen[ft] := false;
    kbdn := 0;
    if (not getline(cmdlin, STDIN, MAXSTR)) then
        exit(program);
    cmdargs := 0;
    idx := 1;
    while ((cmdlin[idx] <> ENDSTR)
      and (cmdlin[idx] <> NEWLINE)) do begin
        while (cmdlin[idx] = BLANK) do
            idx := idx + 1;
        if (cmdlin[idx] <> NEWLINE) then begin
            cmdargs := cmdargs + 1;
            cmdidx[cmdargs] := idx;
            while ((cmdlin[idx] <> NEWLINE)
              and (cmdlin[idx] <> BLANK)) do
                idx := idx + 1;
            cmdlin[idx] := ENDSTR;
            idx := idx + 1;
            if (cmdlin[cmdidx[cmdargs]] = LESS) then begin
                xclose(STDIN);
                cmdidx[cmdargs] := cmdidx[cmdargs] + 1;
                junk := getarg(cmdargs, fname, MAXSTR);
                fd := mustopen(fname, IOREAD);
                cmdargs := cmdargs - 1;
            end
            else if (cmdlin[cmdidx[cmdargs]] = GREATER) then begin
                xclose(STDOUT);
                cmdidx[cmdargs] := cmdidx[cmdargs] + 1;
                junk := getarg(cmdargs, fname, MAXSTR);
                fd := mustcreate(fname, IOWRITE);
                cmdargs := cmdargs - 1;
            end
        end
```

```
        end
    end;
```

The wrapup procedure endcmd is called after the main program has executed; it ensures that all files are closed and preserved by repeated calls to close.

```
{ endcmd (UCSD) -- close all files on exit }
procedure endcmd;
var
    fd : filedesc;
begin
    for fd := STDIN to MAXOPEN do
        xclose(fd)
end;

{ xclose (UCSD) -- interface to file close }
procedure xclose (fd : filedesc);
begin
    case (cmdfil[fd]) of
    CLOSED, STDIO:
        ;    { do nothing }
    FIL1:
        close(file1, LOCK);
    FIL2:
        close(file2, LOCK);
    FIL3:
        close(file3, LOCK);
    FIL4:
        close(file4, LOCK)
    end;
    cmdopen[cmdfil[fd]] := false;
    cmdfil[fd] := CLOSED
end;
```

With the command line parsed into strings by initcmd, the primitives getarg and nargs are straightforward:

```
{ getarg (UCSD) -- get n-th command line argument into s }
function getarg (n : integer; var s : xstring;
        maxsize : integer) : boolean;
begin
    if ((n < 1) or (cmdargs < n)) then
        getarg := false
    else begin
        scopy(cmdlin, cmdidx[n], s, 1);
        getarg := true
    end
end;
```

```
{ nargs (UCSD) -- return number of arguments }
function nargs : integer;
begin
    nargs := cmdargs
end;
```

The final primitive of note is remove, which must operate by opening the file in question, then closing it in a special way:

```
{ remove -- remove a file }
procedure remove (name : xstring);
var
    fd : filedesc;
begin
    fd := open(name, IOREAD);
    if (fd = IOERROR) then
        message('can''t remove file')
    else begin
        case (cmdfil[fd]) of
        FIL1:
            close(file1, PURGE);
        FIL2:
            close(file2, PURGE);
        FIL3:
            close(file3, PURGE);
        FIL4:
            close(file4, PURGE)
        end
    end;
    cmdfil[fd] := CLOSED
end;
```

Despite the quantity of code needed to implement the standard tools environment, the cost in compilation time and program size is not unreasonable. On a 4MHz Z/80 running UCSD Pascal, the simplest programs in this book took just over a minute to compile and produced code files of nine disk blocks (512 bytes per block). Equally important, less than a quarter of the compiler work area, on a full memory system, is consumed by including all of the utilities and primitives on each compile.

INDEX OF FIRST LINES

INDEX